Centre for Research
on Canadian-Russian Relations
at Carleton University

Slavic Research Group
at the University of Ottawa

CANADA/RUSSIA SERIES

Volume 2

General Editors
J.L. Black
Andrew Donskov

ГОСУДАРСТВЕННЫЙ СОВѢТЪ,

въ

СОЕДИНЕННЫХЪ ДЕПАРТАМЕНТАХЪ

ЗАКОНОВЪ

и

ГОСУДАРСТВЕННОЙ ЭКОНОМІИ.

9 Октября 1899 года.

№ 100.

Министерство Иностранныхъ Дѣлъ.

Объ учрежденіи должности консула въ Канадѣ.

Представленіе по сему дѣлу разослано Членамъ Государственнаго Совѣта въ печатныхъ экземплярахъ.

Соединенные Департаменты Законовъ и Государственной Экономіи, разсмотрѣвъ настоящее представленіе въ присутствіи Товарища Министра Финансовъ—Тайнаго Совѣтника Романова и Товарища Государственнаго Контролера, а также при участіи Государственнаго Секретаря, и соглашаясь съ заключеніемъ Гофмейстера Высочайшаго Двора Графа Муравьева, *полагаютъ*:

I. Дѣйствующіе штаты заграничныхъ установленій Министерства Иностранныхъ Дѣлъ дополнить учрежденіемъ должности консула въ Канадѣ.

II. Означенной должности (отд. I) присвоить VI классъ по чинопроизводству, VI разрядъ по шитью на мундирѣ и годовой окладъ содержанія въ *десять тысячъ пятьсотъ* рублей, а на канцелярскіе расходы назначить *тысячу пятьсотъ* рублей въ годъ.

III. Вызываемый вышеуказанною мѣрою ежегодный расходъ въ количествѣ *девьнадцати тысячъ* рублей принять, начиная съ 1 Января 1900 г., на счетъ государственнаго казначейства.

Подлинный подписали:

П. Семеновъ.
Баронъ Менгденъ.
Н. Герардъ.
А. Сабуровъ.
Графъ А. Игнатьевъ.

Н. Чихачовъ.
Н. Шидловскій.
В. Череванскій.
Вл. Верховскій.

А. Иващенковъ.
Графъ В. Ламздорфъ.
Н. Романовъ.

Скрѣпилъ: Статсъ-Секретарь *Г. Шамшинъ.*

Russian Ministry of Foreign Affairs
"On Establishing the Duties of the Consul in Canada"

The Peasant Kingdom:
Canada in the 19th-Century Russian Imagination

J.L. Black

With Translations
by
Yana Kuzmin, Marina Sabanadze,
George Bolotenko, and Larry Black

A CRUISE THROUGH OLD RUSSIAN BOOKS
AND ARCHIVES

PENUMBRA PRESS

This is a first edition published by Penumbra Press. Printed and bound in Canada.

NATIONAL LIBRARY OF CANADA CATALOGUING IN PUBLICATION DATA

Black, J.L. (Joseph Laurence), 1937-
The peasant kingdom: Canada in the 19th-century Russian imagination: a cruise through old Russian books and archives

(Canada/Russia series; v. 2)
Includes bibliographical references and index.
Includes translations from Russian of 6 articles written 1803-1917.
ISBN 1-894131-23-1

1. Canada–Relations–Russia–Sources. 2. Russia–Relations–Canada–Sources. 3. Government publications–Russia–Translations into English. 4. Travelers' writings, Russian–Translation into English. 5. Canada–Description and travel. 6. Canada–In literature. 7. Canada–History–19th century. 8. Russia–History–19th century. I. Kuzmin, Yana II. Title. III. Series.

FC251R8B58 2001   971.03   C2001-902958-6
F1029.5.RB58 2001

The publisher gratefully acknowledges the Canada Council for the Arts and the Ontario Arts Council for supporting Penumbra Press's publishing programme.

All pictures are nineteenth century depictions of Canada; original captions were in Russian.

Authors and Translators

J.L. (Larry) Black, Mount Allison, Boston University, McGill University (Ph.D), is Professor Emeritus at Carleton University, History Department, and Director of the Centre for Research on Canadian-Russian Relations (CRCR). He is the author, editor or co-editor of some 30 books on Russian and Soviet history, education and foreign policy, and founding editor of *Russia and Eurasia Documents Annual*, published in Florida since 1988 and now in its 24th volume.

George Bolotenko, University of Western Ontario, University of Toronto (Ph.D.), is with the National Archives of Canada (NAC), and is in charge of overseas archival acquisitions at the CRCR. He has conducted a great many research trips in Russian and Ukrainian archival collections for both the NAC and the CRCR, and has published accounts of his discoveries in professional journals.

Yana Kuzmin currently is employed by Carleton University as the Administrator of the Institute of European and Russian Studies and Project Manager for the Centre for European Studies. She holds two MAs, one in Linguistics (Dagestan State University), the other in Central/East European and Russian Area Studies (Carleton). Her company, Yana Kuzmin and Associates, provides a range of translation, interpretation and consulting services, as well as Russian language instruction. She also is pursuing a Ph.D. with Carleton's Department of Sociology and Anthropology.

Marina Sabanadze has a doctorate in General Linguistics from the State University of St. Petersburg (Leningrad), Russia, and was the director of the Russian Department, Interlangues Language School and Foreign Service Language Institute, Department of Foreign Affairs and International Trade. She served as an official translator during the visit of M.S. Gorbachev to Canada in 1990 and has been an award-winning teacher of Russian at Carleton University since 1988.

The Calendar and Old Spelling

Unless otherwise stated, dates in Russian archival sources are old style, i.e., from the Julian calendar, which ran 12 days behind the Western (Gregorian) calendar in the 19th century and 13 days behind in the 20th century.

All titles of books, reports and journals are transliterated as they were in the original, so spelling will sometimes seem at variance with later, post-1917 Russian spelling. Except for commonly Anglicized names, e.g., the tsars Nicholas (instead of Nikolai) and Alexander (instead of Aleksandr), and the great authors Tolstoy and Dostoevsky, standard transliteration of names from the Russian has been followed.

Measurements

1 mile = 1.5 versts
1 acre = .37 desyatins or 1 desyatin = 2.7 acres
1 Cdn dollar (1897) = 1 ruble, 94 kopeks

Acknowledgements

Special thanks go to the Donner Canadian Foundation for generous financial support, making the CRCR's search for and acquisition of Russian documents related to Canada possible. Archival materials used in the text for this study were located, for the most part, in Moscow and St. Petersburg by Dr. George Bolotenko of the National Archives of Canada, and by Dr. Sergei Danilov of the Institute for the USA and Canada (ISKRAN) in Moscow.

Thanks as well go to the T.R. Meighen Foundation, St. Andrews, New Brunswick, whose grant in 1998 facilitated the search, by a graduate student, for materials related to Nova Scotian and British Columbian fishing schooners seized by the Russian navy in the 1890s.

The author is indebted to Joseph L. Black, Assistant Professor of English at the University of Tennesee, Knoxville, for thoroughly reading the manuscript and offering many useful suggestions. R.C. Elwood, Professor, and Vadim Koukouchkine, Ph.D. candidate at Carleton University's History Department, and Andrew Donskov, Professor of Russian Language and Literature, University of Ottawa, also were kind enough to read this work in manuscript form.

To Joe & Lisa; Jen & Ron;
Laura & Michael

Бобры.

"Beavers"

ARCHIVAL REFERENCE CODE   10

FOREWORD   11

Introduction
Snapshots of 19th-Century Imperial Russia   17

Chapter 1
The Peasant Kingdom: Canada as Role Model in Russia   29

Chapter 2
The "Canada Card" in Russian Diplomacy and War   65

Chapter 3
Canada as a Place to Live: Haven and Economic Model   109

Conclusion
Russian Consuls in Canada During Imperial Russia's
Final Decades   147

TRANSLATIONS

A. Nikolai Karamzin
"An Englishman's Letter from Quebec" (1803)   161
"A Letter of a Young Frenchman From Montreal" (1803)   163

B. Pavel Svinin
"Fishing On the Grand Banks of New [Found] Land" (1811)   165

C. Aleksandr Borisovich
Lakier's Travels through Central Canada (1857)   169

D. N.A. Kriukov
Canada. Agricultural Economy in Canada . . . . (1897)   214

E. N. Struve
"A Sketch of Canada," Report to Russian Ministry of Foreign Affairs
(1900)   220

F. Emiliia Kirillovna Pimenova
The Land of Grain Growers (1917)   236

INDEX   243

Archival Reference Code

GARF	State Archives of the Russian Federation, Moscow
RGAE	Russian State Archives of the Economy, Moscow
TsKhSD	Centre for the Preservation of Contemporary Documentation, Moscow
MID/ AVPRI	Ministry of External Affairs of the RF/ Foreign Affairs Archives of the Russian Empire, Moscow
RGIA	Russian State Historical Archives, St. Petersburg (formerly, Central State Historical Archives of the USSR — TsGIA)
RGAVMF	Russian State Archives of the Naval Fleet, St. Petersburg
AAN- StP	Russian Academy of Sciences, St. Petersburg Filial
LI-RA-MA	Russian Consular Collection, National Archives of Canada, 1900-1921, Ottawa
JMP	James Mavor Papers. Thomas Fisher Rare Books Library at the University of Toronto

Published Documentary Sources

VPR	Vneshnaia politika Rossii XIX i nachala XX veka
Martens, ed.	Sobranie Traktatov i Konventsii Zakliuchennykh Rossieiu s Inostrannymi Derzhavami
DCER	Documents on Canadian External Relations

Foreword

This book highlights a selection of the archival documents and Imperial Russian published sources located in Russian collections, photocopied and placed in the Centre for Research on Canadian-Russian Relations (CRCR), Carleton University, Ottawa. The CRCR has been gathering Russian published and documentary materials on Canada since 1990, continuing a project started at the old Institute of Soviet and East European Studies, Carleton University, in 1984. The archival documentation has been gathered most energetically since 1997, when the Donner Canadian Foundation generously allocated funds to the project. With few exceptions every reference to an archival source, a Russian book, or a report is to a source now available to researchers at the CRCR, some of it in translation. The materials discussed here represent a small fraction of the documents now at the CRCR. But they exemplify the richness of the still growing collection, revealing its potential as a wellspring for much more detailed study of Russia's perception of and relations with Canada during the 19th century.

* * *

Early in the 20th century an intriguing series of essays about the history, population, politics, and economy of Canada appeared in one of Russia's leading journals of education. This coverage was not an unusual phenomenon, for Canada had been a topic of some interest throughout the 19th century and, with the emigration of Russian Doukhobors to Canada in 1899, was more prominently in the news than usual. What made these new pieces unusual was that they so caught the fancy of readers that they were gathered together and published as a book in 1905 and reissued in a second edition the following year. More importantly, they mirrored a prominent cross current of unrest in Russia itself. In this connection, the author of *Krest'ianskoe Tsarstvo* (*The Peasant Kingdom*) glorified the order and stability ensured in Canada by constitutional monarchy and celebrated the accomplishments of a free people in a just society. Because this particular version of Canada had a long history in Russia, *The Peasant Kingdom* has been chosen as a title for this book

In light of the fact that Canada had little or no autonomous presence in the international arena during the 19th century, the extent to which the government of Imperial Russia, Russia's writers, and its rigorously censored social commentators monitored real and imagined events in this country may at first sight seem remarkable.

On closer examination it is obvious why Canada's vast size, its geographical location, the nature of its government, industry and trade, and its relationships with both London and Washington attracted notice in the Russian Empire. As the century unfolded, Canada became an economic model for, and competitor with, various departments of the government in St. Petersburg. We were each other's rivals for international markets in agricultural products and lumber. Because Canada was much more successful in such marketing ventures than Russia, we were studied by Russian bureaucrats as a model for economic advancement. Canada was held up in Siberia as an example of how best to settle and develop vast steppe lands — with railroads and free farmers.

Canada's propagandists for immigration gave it a presence of a different sort in Russia and Central Europe, whence tens of thousands of individuals and families emigrated to this country. Large groups, such as Mennonites and Doukhobors, sought refuge here, as did thousands of labourers seeking temporary employment and individuals looking for land to till.

While the first Russian Consul General did not arrive in Canada into 1900 and full diplomatic relations between Canada and Russia (then the USSR) were not established until 1942, Canada was far from invisible to St. Petersburg's court circles. In the diplomatic sphere, the territory of Canada served as a huge arena in which the 'Great Game' between Russia, Britain and the United States could be played out. From the competition between the Hudson's Bay Company and the Russian American Company, which began in the last year of the 18th century, the War of 1812, rebellions in Upper and Lower Canada during the late 1830s, and the tsar's stamp of approval on a Russian consulate here in 1899, the intricacies of Canada's proximity to the USA and its status as part of the British Empire excited notice in St. Petersburg.

There were other considerations as well. As a wellspring of practical guidance for the rapidly developing Russian economy, a whimsical sounding board for social and political ideals, and as a haven for oppressed and poor people, Canada ranked very high in the Russian imagination.

To avoid censorship, Russia writers regularly looked for ways to present otherwise forbidden messages to readers. An Aesopian vision of Canada as a paradise filled with hard-working, cheerful hewers of wood and drawers of water, living in a disciplined but free society was one such means. The case for a stable and progressive constitutional monarchy in Russia, for example, was made by comparing Canada favourably to the more violent and greedy world that was said to have evolved in revolutionary, republican America.

One should not assume from the purposely narrow focus of this book, however, that Canada was uppermost among Russia's foreign policy considerations. Of course it was not: Britain, France, Austro-Hungary, Germany and Turkey were always primary concerns for Imperial Russian policy formulators. In the latter third of the 19th century Japan and China rose in Russia's peripheral vision. In North America, the United States was written about and considered as ally, enemy or trade partner more often than Canada was. Yet Canada was always on the horizon. In addition to the obvious geostrategic reality of Canada's land mass and sea ports linking Russia, Britain, the United States and Japan, Canada and Russia shared a number of political, social, economic, technoloigcal, even linguistic concerns. These common causes are the stuff of this book, which traces patterns in 19th-century Russian visions of Canada. Complementing the discussion is a never-before translated travel account by Aleksandr Borisovich Lakier, a prominent Russian jurist who toured Central Canada in 1857 taking notes for the edification of Russians, plus briefer accounts by five other writers, two of whom never visited Canada.

* * *

This story winds down at 1914, though there are further projections into later years, rather than at the usual early dividing lines in modern Russian history, that is, 1905, 1917 or 1921. Canadian-Russian relations during the war years and the Russian revolutionary era, 1914-1921, have, in fact, been written about, though not yet fully.[1] Moreover, the relationships between our two countries changed so dramatically in 1914 that a quite different tale than the one that is offered here would have to be told. The relationship had changed already in the spring of 1900 when the Russian Consulate finally opened in Montreal. Traditional government to government and ministry to ministry discourse slowly came into play and questions of trade, immigration, and international diplomacy replaced the more personal visions that had been prominent in earlier decades. Thus, the 17-year period after the turn of the century is examined in a purposely sweeping manner, seeking closure to earlier patterns.

Canada is the common focal point of all the writings and points of view discussed here, and Canadianists should be interested in what individuals and bureaucrats in our largest neighbour thought of their country and its peoples, and how the Canadian image — and Canada's 'know-how' — contributed to development in the vast expanse of Tsarist Russia. On the other hand, readers should bear in mind that this story is also about Russia. Endeavours to resolve problems endemic to Imperial Russia yet perceived to have been resolved elsewhere, above all in a country analogous to it, are among the volume's central themes.

The text is prepared in a chronological format, though in each chapter Canada is viewed through the lens of a different theme. The purpose of the brief introduction is to provide a picture of continuity and change in 19th-century Russian history, giving readers a context for each of the subsequent thematic chapters. In the first chapter, Russian literary perceptions of Canada, often intended as vehicles for circumventing censorship, are described. Political essays, travel narratives, book reviews, and newspapers are the main sources of information. Canada's place in the "Great Game" of international diplomacy, at least from St. Petersburg's perspective, is the central theme of Chapter two, the main sources for which are diplomatic correspondence. The myth and reality of Canadian economic and social development as they were presented to Russians; emigration to Canada from Russia; and the way Russian state planners looked to Canada for modernization techniques, are all featured in the final chapter. More travel accounts, government reports, emigration files, and official memoranda come into play here. The conclusion covers the period after 1899 and the opening of Russia's first consulates in Canada. Thus, reports from the Consuls themselves are central to the final section. There will be some minor overlap between the chapters, but a unique portrait of Canada in the 19th century will emerge; and our knowledge of attempts in Russia either to modernize or to retain the status quo will be expanded.

---

1 For general information and further reading on this, see David Davies, "The Pre-1917 Roots of Canadian-Soviet Relations," *Canadian Historical Review*, 70: 2 (1989), pp. 180-205, and J.L. Black, *Canada in the Soviet Mirror. Ideology and Perception in Soviet Foreign Policy, 1917-1991* (Ottawa: Carleton UP, 1998), distributed by McGill-Queen's UP, Chapter 1. A recent Russian book, G.I. Luzianin, *Rossiia i Kanada v 1893-1927* [Russia and Canada, 1893-1927] (Moscow: MGPI, 1997), covers the years when diplomatic (consular) connections were first proposed in 1893 to 1927, when Canada unilaterally withdrew its still limited diplomatic relations with the USSR.

Окруженное палисадами убѣжище поселенцевъ въ Канадѣ.

"Palisades Providing Protection to Settlers in Canada"

Nikolai Karamzin

Portrait by Varnek, 1819

Introduction

Snapshots of 19th-Century Imperial Russia

IF IT HAD NOT PROVIDED such an ill-omened and prophetic inauguration to Imperial Russia's final full century, there would be little reason for more than passing mention here of the short reign of Paul I, 1796-1801. His capricious, sometimes malevolent, and often injudicious behaviour set a pattern for governance in Russia that many came to believe only revolution could break. In the economic sphere, Paul shattered the gentry's monopoly on serf holding and restored to merchants their previous right to own serfs as factory workers. In so doing, he pitted two classes against each other in competition for an economic foothold in their country. The dilemma of serfdom, the nature of life in the village, and the availability of factory workers became the central social and economic questions in Russia for the remainder the century.

In international affairs, Paul was nothing if not erratic. After he allied with England, Austria and Turkey in 1797 for war against France, his most famous general, Alexander Suvorov, won victory after victory. But in 1800, Paul switched sides and joined the French to battle the British, illustrating by his own conduct the predominance of caprice in tsarist foreign policy-making. This change in allegiance did not mean that Paul supported the principles espoused by Napoleon in France. Indeed, he forbade entry into Russia of books and forms of dress from Europe generally, and from France particularly, fearing that they might convey revolutionary ideas. Paul's unpredictable antics cost him his life. He was murdered in March, 1801, by Guards officers led by the military governor of St. Petersburg and a former foreign minister.

For the next quarter century Russia was governed by Paul's son, Alexander I, whose first decade in office was marked by an extraordinary outburst of 'liberal' practices: political amnesties, open intellectual debate, easing of censorship, lively and diverse publishing activity, and doors re-opened widely to traverse with foreigners.

Previously taboo subjects, such as constitutional government and the abolition of serfdom, were discussed openly, if cautiously. An Unofficial Committee of enlightened friends, with whom the tsar met regularly, made dramatic change appear possible to its proponents and threatening to its opponents. For a wide variety of reasons, not the least being the hardening of Alexander's own attitude towards change and a religious fatalism that overtook him in his later years, the early grand schemes came to naught. Herein lay the quandary of Russia.

As the century progressed, the huge country was continuously caught between the Scylla and Charybdis of tradition and modernization. Intense, almost frantic efforts to modernize inevitably were followed by equally zealous reversions to tradition. Short periods of openness and thriving intellectual activity were preceded by longer stretches of stagnation and mindless censorship. Throughout the century, great constitutional reformers, and/or proponents of modern economic development, such as M. M. Speranskii (constitutional adviser to Alexander I), Count S. Yu. Witte (Minister of Finance, 1892-1903), or Count P. A. Stolypin (Prime Minister, 1906-1911), were to have their efforts undone or thwarted by reactionary mandarins, such as Count A.A. Arakcheev (Speranskii's successor as advisor to Alexander I), Count S. S. Uvarov (Nicholas I's Minister of Education), or Konstantin Pobedonostsev (adviser to Alexander III and Nicholas II, and Ober-Procurator of the Holy Synod, 1881-1905). Or was it the other way round? Abetting and shaping these dizzying transformations was the autocracy, that is, a system of governance in which the tsar was above all law and could overrule or initiate any policy if whimsy prompted it.

At the turn of the 19th century, the population of Russia stood at 36 million. Nearly 95 percent of these were peasants divided almost equally between state peasants and those whose status was personal bondage to members of the gentry; that is, they were serfs before emancipation in the 1860s. Only about four percent of the population lived in an urban setting as the century opened. At that time, Russia could boast of an industrial labour force of only about 200,000, fully half of whom were serfs performing labour service (*barshchina*). Judged in terms of the industrial revolution which drove society in Britain, Germany and elsewhere, Russia was a backward, agrarian country, in which a huge number of people lived in the firm and debilitating grip of serfdom. What little industry there was suffered from very low levels of technology and production.

In the international sphere, the previous century had been one of almost constant warfare — successful in so far as battles won and territory gained, but very costly to Russia's economy and in the lives of its subjects. Turkey was defeated and Russia became a Black Sea Power. Poland was sliced up and shared out with Prussia and Austria, and the Russian Empire moved westward. By 1801, its territory was immense, though the central government's hold on large tracts of it was still tenuous at best. Russia did not conquer Georgia, in the Southern Caucasus, until 1813 and that was accomplished only after a long war with Persia. The process of full subjugation took another fifty years. Other parts of the Caucasus were not wrested from Turkey until the 1870s. Finland was taken from Sweden in 1809, but the vast lands of Central Asia, the Muslim lands east of the Caspian Sea and south of Siberia were not won until the end of the 1880s, making Russia a neighbour of Persia and Afghanistan — and a direct competitor with Britain for influence in both. From the 1850s to the 1870s, Russia expanded and consolidated its borders in the Far East and on the Pacific, at the expense of China and in competition with Japan, Britain and the United States.[1]

Siberia, a territory larger than Canada, had been explored already in the late 17th century. The nature and scale of its resources and peoples were realized after the great Bering expeditions during the first half of the 18th century. Yet Siberia's immense resources remained virtually untapped and its vast spaces unsettled by Russians until late in the 19th century.

The Russian Empire of the late 19th century was very different both in territorial size and in the make-up of its population from what it had been in 1801. In many other respects, however, Russia had evolved very little. The harsh indictments in Marquis de Custine's 1839 report on Russia may be a little one-sided to use as evidence of the true nature of that state, but its basic themes have merit. They typified and helped shape how Russia was seen both by outsiders and by many of its own thinking population. For example, the Parisian visitor's account of Nicholas I calling constitutional government "a government of lies, fraud, and corruption" is undoubtedly what the tsar believed. Custine was appalled at the absolute power of the tsar over even the greatest of noble families, over their actions, their thoughts and their words. Secrecy governs everything in Russia, he wrote, and imitation of things Western was mere subterfuge to hide a naturally barbaric state. The impression left by Custine was that little progress had been made in Russia since Peter the Great recast the autocracy in the early 18th century.[2] Similar conclusions about the Russian world as unchanging, isolated and backward were drawn later by Baron August von Haxthausen who compiled detailed studies of peasant life in Russia during the 1840s. Hoping that he would provide an antidote to Custine's withering criticism, Nicholas encouraged the German to travel freely and write about what he saw. Unusually generous though he was in his description of Russian village life — his main interest — even Haxthausen called serfdom an "unnatural relationship" and argued for its abolition.[3]

The accession of Alexander II in 1855 initiated yet another flush of enthusiasm for change and valiant attempts to drag Russia into modern times. Halting the crippling and embarrassing Crimean War, Alexander launched a series of reforms so fundamental that only the innovations of Peter the Great could be called their equal. By far the best known of the "Great Reforms" accomplished in the 1860s was the emancipation of serfs in 1861. Lesser-known by-products of that remarkable event included the creation of limited forms of local self-government for the countryside, known as *zemstvo* boards (1864), and a sweeping judicial reform (1864), separating courts from direct control by the administration, granting judges tenure of position, and introducing very limited trial by jury. Censorship was reduced, the education system was overhauled, and progressive measures were instituted in the financial structure of the empire. Even constitutional proposals were being considered by the tsar in 1881. Paradoxically these and other major changes from the top were accompanied by an exponential increase in radical revolutionary movements. For his pains, in fact, Alexander II was assassinated by a revolutionary terrorist in 1881.

Not surprisingly, the reformer's successor, Alexander III (Tsar 1881-1894) came to office determined to curb revolution and dissent, and to shield the Autocracy from advocates of change. Ending all talk of constitutions, he instituted a period of counter-reform, promoted reactionaries, watered down the authority of *zemstvo* and other newly semi-autonomous organs of governance, and approved "Temporary Regulations" allowing officials broad freedom of action in dealing with suspected revolutionaries. Out of this atmosphere sprang the *Okhrana* (Protection), a special secret political police whose members were trained to infiltrate and gather intelligence on all anti-government activities and groups.

Change came anyway, of course, but for certain elements of continuity one need only to turn to Imperial Russia's first and final inclusive census, taken in 1897 and printed in two volumes in 1905. The census still provides us with a rare social map of Russian society at the turn of the 20th century and unwittingly exposes by its very structure the volatile mix of old and new habits that characterized the

Russian Empire. On the face of it, Russia had mutated dramatically since the opening of the 19th century and significantly since the introduction of "Great Reforms." As a consequence of those reforms, which Alexander II's successors could not fully undo, a small professional middle class, an industrial proletariat and even a prosperous peasant class, slowly began to take shape, growing relatively rapidly in size by the late 1890s. Radical as such changes may have been in comparison with Russia itself a century earlier, they couldn't conceal the fact that in almost all categories of modernization (mass education, industrialization, governing institutions), the huge country was behind — and falling further behind — Western Europe's major powers. And the census still categorized citizens according to the old social estates.

The accuracy of the census may be challenged from several points of view, yet its overall numbers remain useful as a source of insight into the Russian world at the end of the 19th century. It tells us that the hereditary noblemen and their dependents numbered some 1.2 million people. For the most part, they held government and military posts, ranging from senior positions in officialdom to very minor, even poverty ridden, ranks. We owe much of our understanding of that class to the vivid characterizations left by N.V. Gogol in *Revizor* (The Inspector-General) and *Mertvye dushi* (Dead Souls), as well as by I.A. Goncharov in *Oblomov* (Apathy).

The census counted nearly 127 million people, a huge increase over the early part of the century. About 350,000 were "Ecclesiastics" of all religions, about 70 percent of them Orthodox. Town dwellers fell into three categories, each defined by their tax returns: Honoured Citizens (340,000), Merchants (280,000), and a broader grouping, known as *meshchane*, of slightly over 13 million small shopkeepers, tradesmen, white collar workers, self-employed artisans, and urban workers.[4] There were as well 3 million Cossacks; 800,000 "aliens," that is "uncivilized" aboriginal peoples; and 600,000 "foreigners."

The peasantry made up the rest — a whopping 97 million.

Resting heavily on top of this huge hierarchical edifice was the Autocracy. The tsar combined in himself, or in his office, the authority vested in all branches of government. Moreover, the Russian Orthodox Church attributed divine origins to the tsar's autocratic authority. Even after Nicholas II granted Russia a representative legislature (Duma) by the October Manifesto of 1905, he retained power of veto over legislation and most of the budget. The executive branch of government (the ministries and their officials), remained responsible only to the tsar.

Author of the Manifesto, Count Witte, survived as Russia's first constitutional premier for only a matter of months. As finance

minister over the previous decade, he had pushed for rapid modernization, concentrating on heavy industry and on creating large,
densely packed work forces in Russia's urban centres. Because Witte
assumed that private investment and capital were too slow and cautious to get the job done, he introduced state capitalism on a grand
scale, providing clear precedents for Soviet economic policies. To
accomplish these changes, Witte secured huge foreign loans, mostly
from France, put Russia on the gold standard, raised tariff barriers,
and built railroads. But his haste caused horrendous waste.

Witte's industrialization project was paid for by disproportionate
taxation of the peasantry and low-status townspeople. Furthermore,
food remained the cheapest in Europe and, because of high protec-
tionist tariffs, manufactured goods were the most expensive in
Europe. Peasants earned too little from their production to become
consumers of goods their compatriots were manufacturing in towns
and cities. The only viable consumer was the government, competition was forestalled, and employers had little incentive to provide
safe working conditions or even to worry much about the quality of
their goods. As villagers flocked to the cities to earn enough to pay off
both the debt to the *mir* (village council) before 1905 or to sustain rel-
atives left behind, urban working families moved from flats, to rooms
in flats, and finally to corners of rooms. Crowded living conditions
bred disease and discontent.

The key to understanding the explosive nature of the urban work-
place is twofold: 1) well developed revolutionary ideologies in their
myriad forms reached Russia almost simultaneously with a sudden
emergence of the worst working conditions in Europe; 2) there was a
direct connection between industrial owners and the government, the
latter providing much of the financing and almost the entire market,
not to mention the arm of the law in times of labour unrest.

Revolutionary sub-currents were constant in the 19th century. They
had their first major manifestation with the famous Decembrist insurrection in 1825, when socially conscious members of the upper strata,
mostly officer corps and members of various secret societies,
attempted to force the Senate to call a constituent assembly rather
than swear an oath to the new emperor, Nicholas I. They failed miserably. Later movements sprang from among the *littérateurs* of the
1840s. Confronted on one side by arbitrary and reactionary government and church, and on the other by the mass of illiterate peasantry,
they took up the monumental task of bearing the enlightened Western
word, as they saw it, to Russia.[5] Later movements included a cross-
section of populist organizations, whose members focussed on the

plight of the peasantry, which they saw as naturally socialist and revolutionary. Some populist groups advocated terrorism, others a more moderately activist course. Their ambitions had been epitomized forever in N.G. Chernyshevskii's novel *What is to be Done?* (1862), whose idealistic characters, "new men and women," served as models for a generation of dedicated revolutionaries. Populist fervour was unsettling to the state and was responsible for a number of acts of terror and assassination, but did not become truly threatening until late in the century when their remnants came together as Socialist Revolutionaries committed to overthrowing the entire existing state system.

Marxism was a latecomer to Russia, attracting advocates in small numbers only by the 1880s. Its popularity grew in part to fill the vacuum left by failed populism and because its basic tenets had greater resonance among large pockets of urban workers living in horrendous conditions. Revolutionary Marxists, the eventual 'winners' in the revolutionary sweepstake, were mainly a phenomenon of post-1900 Russia. They and populists were bitter rivals in the struggle for adherents, yet both groups were themselves divided into competing hostile factions. In the long run, Marxists benefitted from the apparent futility of populism and eventually were able to instill enough order and discipline in their ranks to earn success.

The country was beset as well by extreme right-wing movements, the best known of which were the Black Hundreds, and left-wing nihilist revolutionaries whose philosophy was best expressed in a "Catechism of the Revolutionary" (1868). Prepared by the famous M.A. Bakunin and S.G. Nechaev (the inspiration for Dostoevsky's anti-revolution *The Possessed*, 1871), the Catechism insisted that all means to revolution are justified and that true revolutionaries must be prepared to sacrifice everything, including their lives, for the cause ("A revolutionary is a doomed man," Para. 1).

The ideas and practices of Russian revolutionaries appeared to have fertile soil in which to incubate. In the villages, illiteracy and superstition reigned supreme (although literacy rates rose rapidly after the 1890s), making the labour pool a universally unskilled one. Foreign visitors to Russia around 1900 were almost unanimously amazed by the humbleness of the peasantry in the face of authority. They described daily life in the villages as one of grinding poverty, violence, disease, fires and famine. Diverse contemporary sources, such as the accounts by scholars Sir John Maynard, who first visited Russia in the 1890s, and Geroid Tanquary Robinson, who spent much time in Russia in the mid-1920s, the populist revolutionary and assassin Sergei Kravchinskii (Stepniak), as well as memoirist émigrés like Nina Berberova, who told of her privileged position as a child of the landed gentry, all leave readers with the same impression. Village life was marked by constant hardship. Agricultural methods were so backward in most regions that government reports of 1901 described farm implements as "unimproved" from previous centuries.[6] The horrendous famines that swept through Russia in 1891-1892, and again in 1911, threw these conditions into stark relief, revealing at the same time the inability of government institutions to handle crises on a national scale.[7]

Compounding the difficulty of circumstances in Russia was the fact that for a twenty-five year period the religious and educational scene was dominated by a man much better suited to an earlier era. The lay head of the Holy Synod of the Orthodox Church and adviser to the last two tsars, Konstantin Pobedonostsev left an imprint on Russian society at least the equal to, if not greater than, Witte's. Like the autocrats, Pobedonostsev viewed reform as a corruption of traditional Russian values. His standpoint was summarized best in his own exposition, *Reflections of a Russian Statesman* (1896), in which he demonstrated contempt for the principle of the sovereignty of the people, terming it "the great falsehood of our time." Electoral democracy was a system of manipulation and sloganizing, he wrote, adding that the press was sensationalist and lying and that public opinion was uninformed ("the mass, always and everywhere, is *vulgus*, and its conceptions of necessity are vulgar").[8]

Pobedonostsev's opinions exemplified the belief system embodied in Nicholas I's reign a half century earlier. He encouraged the persecution of religious and other minorities and called for an advanced education system for the upper classes only. Pobedonostsev's ideal for Russia was the society mirrored in the census of 1897: all citizens should know and hold to their place and the Church and Tsar were to be constantly revered. His policy of Russification in practice meant enforcing the use of the Russian language and culture, and Orthodoxy, as instruments of homogenization. These were by no means new policies for Russia: all remnants of Polish autonomy within Russia disappeared after a second rebellion, in 1863, and Ukrainian nationalist sentiment had been ruthlessly repressed. Under Pobedonostsev such practices were raised to a new level. Russification was turned into an official doctrine and was directed even against normally loyal Baltic Germans, Finns and Armenians. Official anti-semitism rose exponentially from the early 1880s. New "Temporary Rules" restricting Jews to towns and large villages and forcing them into business and selected professions prevailed during his entire tenure in office. Pogroms became increasingly common. It is little wonder that emigration and rebellion became the two greatest forms of mass release for citizens of Russia.

Pobedonostsev would not have had such success, of course, if his philosophy of life had not mirrored that of his rulers so closely. Russia's last tsar, Nicholas II (1894-1917), his tsarina Alexandra, and the people closest to them and chosen by them to govern upheld the Romanov's title to Autocracy by divine right, as did government agencies, schools and churches. Two examples will suffice to confirm the prevalence of such thinking among those in position of great power. In August 1915, after Russian armies were smashed at Tannenburg and symptoms of political and social unrest were already affecting Russia's urban centres, Chairman of the Council of Minister I.L. Goremykin told his colleagues that

> In my mind, His Majesty the Emperor is the Anointed of God, the hereditary Bearer of Supreme Power. He personifies Russia ... Loyal subjects must submit, no matter the consequence. And then there is only the Will of God. So I think, and in this knowledge I will die.

The tsarina was both more direct and more out of touch with her subjects, writing her husband at the front as late as December 1916,

> It's all getting calmer & better [in Petrograd], only one wants to feel Your hand — how long, years, people have told me the same — "Russia loves to feel whips" — it's their nature — tender love & then the iron hand to punish & guide . . . [and the next day] We have been placed on the throne & we must keep it firm & give it over to our Son untouched.[9]

Custine would not have been surprised at any of this. The nature of the state was such that, before 1906, all political parties or movements, ranging across the entire spectrum from left to right, functioned outside the legal domain. Notwithstanding that some of them were quite open about their existence, and most clandestine groups were well known to the authorities, they had no constituted institutions in which to express their political, social or economic opinions. There was no Parliament, no Diet, no Reichstag. With the exception of scattered *zemstvo* boards there were no elected political bodies. Thus, the practice of political debate in open forums was alien even to proponents of constitutional monarchy.

Despite the archaism of its political and economic structure, Imperial Russia still had an important international role to play. Caught up in Europe's enthusiasm for territory, St. Petersburg was constantly conducting wars of conquest or pacification in Central Asia and the Caucasus. Russia was obsessed with settling the affairs of, and benefiting from, the regularly projected demise of the Ottoman Empire, the so-called "sick man of Europe." Russia and Britain confronted each other in the Caucasus, in Afghanistan and, to a lesser extent, on the North Pacific, at least before Russia was soundly thrashed by Japan in 1904-05. After that, Russia and Britain slowly moved together, coming to terms over Afghanistan and jointly opposing the ambitions of Germany in Europe and on the sea.

At the turn of the 20th century, everyone in Russia was still expected to be a soldier and the Russian Empire was governed by military outposts. The country needed desperately to strengthen its frontiers by settlement, harness and exploit its apparently limitless natural resources, and modernize its industrial and agricultural sectors. It also needed a citizenry that was loyal and educated. After the general strike and rebellion of 1905 it had neither.

Where does Canada fit into this scenario? That is what the rest of this book is all about.

---

[1]   A fascinating contemporary reflection of this latter competition is Albert J. Beveridge, *The Russian Advance* (New York: Harper & Brothers, 1904).

[2]   See Astolphe Louis Léonor, Marquis de Custine, *La Russie en 1839* (Paris, 1843), and George F. Kennan's commentary on it: *The Marquis de Custine and His Russia in 1839* (London: Hutchinson, 1972). *La Russie* was translated into English as *Empire of the Czars: A Journey Through Eternal Russia* (London: Longman, 1843).

[3]   Haxthausen, *Etudes sur la situation intérieure, la vie nationale et les institutions rurales* (Hanovre: Hahn, 1847), Vol. 1, pp. 97-99. Von Haxthausen's original *Studien über die innern Zustände, das Volksleben und insbesondere die landlichen Einrightungen Russlands* (Hannover und Berlin, 1847-52), appeared in three volumes, and was translated immediately into French and English. The most recent English-language edition is Frederick Starr, ed. *Studies on the Interior of Russia* (Chicago: University of Chicago Press, 1972).

4   In Soviet parlance *meshchane* meant "petty bourgeois," but in the 19th century the term referred to a very broad category of "small burghers" who were neither capitalists nor artisans in guilds. An earlier term for them was the *possadskie*.

5   On this see Isaiah Berlin, "A Marvellous Decade," a series of essays that run over four issues of *Encounter*, 1955-1956.

6   Sir John Maynard, *Russia in Flux* (London: Viktor Golanz, 1941), p. 90. G.T. Robinson, *Rural Russia under the Old Regime* (Berkeley: University of California Press, 1967), original in 1932; Nina Berberova, *The Italics are Mine* (New York: Harcourt & Brace, 1969).

7   On the earlier famine, see Richard G. Robbins, Jr., *Famine in Russia, 1891-1892* (New York: Columbia UP, 1975).

8   The first English translation was *Reflections of a Russian Statesman* (London: Grant Richard, 1898). There are a number of later English-language editions. In addition to the original Russian, it was translated into German, French and Italian and widely read in Europe and North America.

9   *The Letters of the Tsaritsa to the Tsar, 1914-1916* (Stanford, CA: Hoover Institution Press, 1973), pp. 454-456. Reprint of 1923 edition. For the Goremykin remarks, see minutes of the Council of Ministers meetings, 1915, in *Prologue to Revolution*. Edited by Michael Cherniavsky (Englewood Cliff, NJ: Prentice-Hall, 1967).

Вождь ирокезовъ (снимокъ съ картины).

"Iroquois Chief"

1

The Peasant Kingdom:
Canada as Role Model in Russia

THE TERRITORY NOW KNOWN AS CANADA was drawn to the attention of Russian writers and officials early in the eighteenth century. At that time great expeditions were organized in St. Petersburg with such varied purposes as searching for a northeastern passage to India, charting the waters between the Far East of the Russian Empire, North America and Japan, and establishing trade relations with the North American continent. Peter the Great (Tsar, 1682-1725) entertained proposals on charting the North Pacific from European and Russian scientists and explorers.[1] Russia's north and its waters everywhere were closed to foreigners, so no exploration could take place without sponsorship from the tsar.

The best known West European advocate of large scale expeditions to unravel the still mysterious connection between Asia and North America was the German academician Gottfried Leibnitz, who on several occasions urged Peter to seek answers to the question. The cause was espoused by Russians too, one of the earliest of whom was Fedor Saltykov, a Russian naval expert serving as Peter's purchasing agent in London between 1712 and 1715, ordering ships for his country's nascent fleet. He advised sending an expedition by boat to see if it was possible to reach the Pacific via an Arctic route.[2] Peter took this and other recommendations seriously and ordered preliminary studies on the viability of a northeast passage. Finding routes to North America and Japan so as to establish trade with their inhabitants and explore the geographic connection between Russia and North America were the primary motives of expeditions from St. Petersburg to Kamchatka led by Vitus J. Bering, 1725-1730, 1733-1741. As a result of these large scale explorations, the Aleutian and Alaskan waters and coasts were investigated and claimed for the Russian Empire. The first Russian settlers arrived on Kodiak Island in the 1780s and, in 1799, Paul I approved the creation of the Russian American Company to manage all trade and settlement in Russian North America. Russian attention was not yet focussed on Canada, but a Far Eastern watch tower had been set in place.

The first known writings devoted specifically to political and economic conditions in Canada did not appear until early the next century. They were prepared by the prominent Russian man-of-letters and historian, Nikolai Karamzin, whose stories appeared in his famous journal, *Vestnik Evropy* (Messenger of Europe), in 1803. They featured native people in their habitat — Abenaki and Mohawks — extolling their many virtues in the classic manner of Rousseau. Karamzin mentioned cruelties as well, including a tradition of killing male prisoners. In Upper Canada, the land is rich, the settlers are "hardworking and skilful," and towns are constructed as if overnight by free labour, he proclaimed. Quite a scene to set before readers in serf-ridden autocratic Russia! Moreover, Karamzin's tales appeared at precisely the time when the Russian America Company was struggling to maintain a foothold on the Pacific coast of North America in competition with the Hudson's Bay Company for whom many of the characters in his short narratives laboured.[3]

Karamzin's items on Canada are interesting not so much because of their substance as for their author's own great reputation. The decade of the 1790s is usually termed the "Karamzin Period" in Russian literature. In addition to an epoch-forming contribution to the literary world, Karamzin served after 1803 as the imperial court historiographer and wrote political essays. His most lasting accomplishment in this regard was the twelve-volume *Istoriia gosudarstva Rossiiskogo* (History of the Russian State), the most widely-read history in 19th-century Russia.[4] The history and his essays served later as a wellspring of ideas for the most prominent conservative and patriotic political thinkers in Imperial Russia. Karamzin's perspective on Canada was limited, but survived him because it was a particularly useful one. He drew on an impression of Canada to extoll the virtues of hard work, cleanliness, order, and paternalistic (in this case, monarchical) government, and as a contrast to the anarchy, greed and violence he attributed to the republican United States.[5]

The fact that Karamzin never visited North America himself did not deter him, or later Russian writers, from turning to new world images — real or imagined — as offering lessons for readers in their strictly censored country. The *Vestnik Evropy* reflected renewed Russian curiosity about the cultural cross-currents of European Enlightenment and Aufklärung after the stifling policies of Paul I were eased by Alexander I. The journal was an important part of the literary response to one of the several exciting and short lived eras in Russian history marked by a promise of sweeping change in the country's political and culture life. Alexander I's outlook seemed to be opposite to that of his unpredictable and tyrannical father. A new generation of Russian westernizers emerged. Ardent Russian nationalists and confident in their own country's worth, they were more selective in their genuflections to western intellectual trends than their predecessors had been. Many sought intellectual leadership from Karamzin, who in the 1790s had described foreign values, customs, literature, ideas and art in his *Pis'ma russkogo puteshestvennika* (Letters of a Russian Traveller). Admiring much of what he saw in Europe, Karamzin used his experiences to convey lessons about the folly of revolution and encourage pride in ideas that he thought were more natural to Russia.

The literateur-turned-historian's lessons were of two types. The first was political. Karamzin's message was simply that no one country's practices could serve as a model for another's political system, although much could be learned from practices elsewhere. Even the English system, which he admired, "would be bad in another country."[6] Because of its size, only autocracy was suitable for Russia. The second general lesson was that the Enlightenment, or rule of reason, was the ultimate cure for all the ills of humankind. By Enlightenment Karamzin meant education in citizenship — the subject must learn how and why to obey, the monarch must learn to rule firmly and wisely. The pedagogic potential of literature, indeed, was its most important characteristic.

Karamzin used a wide variety of topics to serve as object lessons, among them life in Canada and the United States. Because the United States had won its freedom by means of violence, he believed that violence would remain forever part of its heritage. On the other hand, his vision of Canada recalled the 18th century opinion that mankind was better off away from urban decadence and the rot of political life. "*The spirit of trade* is the main characteristic of America, where everyone strives for acquisitions," Karamzin wrote.[7] His point seems to have been that an urge for riches crowded out all other interests in the United States. The antithesis to the sharp division between wealth and poverty (and slavery), said to be an attribute of the United States, could be found in Canada, which had the advantages of a "benign government," few taxes, and evenly distributed wealth. Elsewhere, Karamzin wrote that American industry and agriculture relied almost entirely on its eight million slaves.[8]

During the early years of Alexander I's reign in Russia things American became popular at court, and Karamzin hoped to counter that trend. In an 1802 issue of *Vestnik Evropy*, Karamzin wrote that the "[French] revolution clarified our ideas: we saw that civil order is sacred ... that its authority is not a tyranny for the people, but is a defence from tyranny; ... even the Turkish government is better than the anarchy which always will be the result of state upheavals."[9] He was both speaking for and nurturing a persistent political assumption in Russia: Russia is large and unusually diverse, it needs authority and centralized government in order to be strong and survive.

Writing to advise was itself an act of patriotism for Karamzin, whose essay "On Love for the Fatherland and National Pride" was one of the most significant appeals to Russian national self-consciousness in the 19th century. A central purpose of literature, he believed, was to inspire pride in Russians, to teach them "to respect what is their own."[10] This worthy goal was not easy to achieve in Russia and literary device often had to be resorted to. The image of Canada as antithesis to America was one convenient tool with which Karamzin could illustrate his point. The comparative approach, in fact, came to be used by Russian political thinkers throughout the century, particularly after it again became dangerous to offer uninvited and unwanted political advice to Russia's autocrats.

The Canada model served as a vehicle for an additional and important message, for which the United States could not serve. In Karamzin's own time a writer more radical than he wrote about Canada to camouflage an attack on the institution of serfdom in Russia. Members of the Free Society of Lovers of Literature, Science and Arts, one of several "enlightened" movements to emerge during the first decade of Alexander's reign, published pieces in which slavery generally, and more particularly American slavery, was condemned. Open criticisms of serfdom in Russia would have led to jail sentences, so one member of the Free Society, A.E. Izmailov, printed "A Sonnet of an Iroquois. Written in His Native Language" describing severe circumstances faced by Indians in "Canada." Although it was recognized by readers as a hostile analogy to serfdom, the censors let the poem pass.[11]

There were casual references to Canada in nineteenth-century Russian travelogues, newspapers (both radical and official), and government reports. The artist Pavel Svinin remarked briefly on Canada in his recollection of years spent in the United States, 1811-1813, where he was a member of Russia's first diplomatic mission. His travels in North America were exclusively in the United States, yet they included detailed and glowing descriptions of the Canadian side of Niagara Falls, and a painting (the book was in part a collection of paintings) of his ship stopped so that sailors could fish cod on Newfoundland's Grand Banks. Svinin described this event ("200 fish in three hours," some of which were up to 45 pounds) with obvious relish and suggested that the heavy fogs of the area were good for consumptives because of the high level of oxygen in it. In light of the present day circumstances on the Grand Banks, Svinin's statement that "fishermen coming here always have luck and return with a sure catch," and his description of whales ("huge tsars of the sea") swarming around his ship are depressing evidence of what has been lost.

Still earlier visits to Halifax by Russian naval officers seconded to the British navy were noted in a travelogue published by Yu.F. Lisianskii in 1812, but they said little about Canada beyond describing its port facilities.[12] Observations by Lisianskii himself though held implications for Canada's west coast. He travelled around the world during the first decade of the 19th century as second-in-command in a naval expedition led by I.F. Kruzenshtern, who also had been seconded to the British navy in the 1790s. Their experience taught them the importance of the navy for expanding a country's trade throughout the world. Lisianskii and Kruzenshtern became zealous promoters of Russian domination in the North Pacific, for which a naval presence at Kamchatka (Petropavlovsk) and Sitka Island (Novo Archangel'sk) would have to be expanded. Inevitably, Russia's ambitions in that region raised Canada's profile on the Russian Far Eastern horizon.

In the early 1830s, as Russian writers began debating the Slavophile-Westernizer approaches to understanding their own country and Nicholas I closed the door to open discourse with Europe, very little was written about Canada as a country. Its native peoples, pristine wilderness, and the fur trade continued to attract some notice.[13] Similar pieces appeared on America, but that country also bore the brunt of both the Slavophile and Westernizer distrust of materialism and was perceived by many Russians as a land with no deep rooted spiritual values.[14]

A prominent scholar, journalist and government ideologist, Osip Senkovskii, used the example of Canada to explain the righteousness of imperial expansionism and the ease with which a metropolitan government could rule distant cities and even kingdoms "with a regiment and a representative." In this instance, Senkovskii was glorifying Karamzin, who had given Russia an historical consciousness and provided its citizens with a literature that explained and justified the actions of their ancient slavic forebears. In his own journal *Biblioteka dlia Chteniia* (The Reader's Library), the most popular in

Russia by that time, Senkovskii concentrated mostly on literature, but political commentary of the Karamzin type crept in regularly. Among other things, the journal carried scathing criticisms of "freedom" as it had evolved in both France and the United States, accepting fully the view that large states could only afford "freedom" if it was accompanied by strong central government.[15] Apparently peaceful and prosperous conditions in the British territories of North America were grounds for this presumption, just as they had been for Karamzin thirty years earlier. Senkovskii and others were disabused of their idyll when rebellions broke out in Upper and Lower Canada just a few years later in the 1830s.

As readers will see in Chapter Two, the government in St. Petersburg took a keen interest in the tumultuous events in the Canadas during the late 1830s. The uprisings were watched by a small public audience in Russia as well, and by commercial groups associated with the Russian American Company. Strict censorship ensured that Russian newspapers normally would not write accounts in support of rebellion, but restrained versions of events in Canada were reported in the official Russian press, *Sankt-Peterburgskie vedomosti* (St. Petersburg News), *Moskovskiia vedomosti* (Moscow News), and in the conservative-nationalist journals *Severnaia pchela* (Northern Bee) and *Syn Otechestva* (Son of the Fatherland). Most of the official news was drawn from the British press, and came from French sources, such as the *Journal des Débats*, whose version of events did not coincide with the British perspective. Reaction to news of Canada as it was filtered through the censoring apparatus underscored some strange contradictions in Russia's world of ideas. In the first place, the nature of Russian press commentary was such that it corroborated the view that the extremely conservative Russian court was for a time prepared to act on behalf of rebels in Canada. Secondly, the idea that rebellion and resentment were common in the British Empire shocked moderate political thinkers in Russia who had offered British governance as a model. Finally, though the reports were riddled with errors of fact, they brought to a small Russian readership the first detailed information about the history, population, resources, and political and economic character of Canada — a country like theirs geographically, but vastly different in most other respects.

In contrast to trends in most West European countries, government censorship was still developing in Russia, where publication had been a government monopoly to the end of the eighteenth century. Censorship committees had existed in Russia since the 1790s and an official censorship code was introduced in 1804. Revised again in

1826, shortly after the Decembrist uprising, the code was turned over to the ministries of internal affairs and education expressly for the purpose of "directing public opinion in keeping with ... the views of the government." The code was moderated a few years later, but its central goal, to prevent the circulation of any ideas that might be seen as harmful to Orthodoxy, monarchy, or morality, remained in place until 1905. Censorship was especially strict during the reign of Nicholas I, which saw such famous writers as Pushkin banished by the tsar himself and, in 1836, Piotr Chaadaev declared insane because of his criticism of the nature of Russia and its mission in history.[16]

One can take it for granted then that legally printed Russian words were carefully chosen, either to conform with an official prescription or to have the appearance of conforming. The bi-weekly *Moskovskiia vedomosti* carried regular information about events in Canada in its "Foreign News" section, where parliamentary debates in London, and items from American, British and Canadian newspapers were summarized. A wide cross-section of viewpoints was synthesized without any apparent editorializing. The fact that there were supporters of the "insurgents" in the British parliament was made known, the rebels were mentioned by name, and the potential for an American-British conflict was highlighted. On 3 March 1838, as the violence in Canada diminished, the Russian paper quoted some "welcome news" from the American press that the United States "wishes to promote the interests of Great Britain and preserve friendship between the two states."[17] That this cheerful public pronouncement did not necessarily represent the opinions dominant in the governing circles of Washington or St. Petersburg will be demonstrated in the next chapter.

In a monthly section called "Chronology of Events," *Syn otechestva*, included regular and surprisingly thorough updates on events in Canada throughout 1838, especially after Lord Durham was despatched to the scene.[18] His mission to settle the "disastrous uprising in Canada" was noted in the January issue and the "decisive measures" taken against the "rebels" were extolled. Durham's actions were reported in every subsequent "Chronology" during the year. His proclamation of 27 May in Quebec was published verbatim and an unusually detailed description was given later of his proposal for a new government in British North America, in which five existing provinces would have considerable autonomy. It was regularly said that although most Canadians opposed the uprisings, they also hoped to have a number of grievances redressed. Statements such as these must have intrigued, even baffled, Russians who were themselves living in an extremely restrictive society and would not have dared engage in public discussion of such issues at home.[19]

In September, the paper reported optimistically that "Official views from Canada consistently contain the belief that the insurrection is calmed, the rebels are dispersed, there is a general trust in Lord Durham, and friendly relations are re-established with the United States." In the very next month, however, *Syn otechestva* announced that new outbreaks had occurred, men were arming along the American border and Durham was returned to London. This "Chronology," an extraordinary dozen pages, included quotations from British, Canadian, and American papers that offered a wide variety of opinions on the uprisings that again were spreading across the country. From the very beginning of the accounts, rebel aims and their names were made known to Russian readers, as were their punishments (execution and exile), along with the debates in London for and against various policies instituted by the British parliament.

Growing American popular support for the Canadian rebels was announced repeatedly in the Russian press during the fall of 1838. There were eye catching tales in June of a rebel group "under the leadership of someone named William Johnson, who is extremely daring. He attacked the English steamship, *Sir Robert Peel*, pillaged and burned it ... he calls himself a defender of Canadian independence and an enemy of England; he plunders and murders Englishmen and their allies; there is a large reward on his head." In July it was noted that Johnson had been captured on Lake Erie and that he had taken on a larger than life image. "For want of news," *Syn otechestva* told its readers, "journals now regale about Johnson, describing him as some kind of a secret corsair, in the style of a [James Fenimore] Cooper hero. They write that no one knew where he lived and from whence he suddenly appeared; that he always walked and slept with pistols; that he was very tall and handsome; that he had a beautiful daughter, 18 years-old, a fearless amazon who sailed about alone on the lakes and rivers, and so on, and so on."[20] Episodes of rebellion in Canada were becoming an adventure story in Russia, and it is obvious from the details provided that Russian officials provided editors with information from such radical journals as the *Mackenzie's Gazette*.[21] Perhaps they expected, or suspected, that their government would intervene in Canada's affairs.

Even magazines that normally limited their content to literary matters introduced material on Canada. In an extract from the diary of a well-known Russian writer living in Europe, for example, *Sovremennik* (The Contemporary) noted in February 1838 that A.I.

Turgenev kept finding himself in conversations about what was transpiring in Canada while visiting Paris.[22] The outburst of interest in the Canadian political situation prompted the publication of other informative pieces. One journal carried an account in 1839 of steamship traffic on the Great Lakes. In another there was a detailed history of the fur trade in North America. It demonstrated the remarkable significance of the evolution and importance of the fur trade to the development of both North America and Siberia.[23] With only slight stretches of the imagination, the role of *coureurs-de-bois* in Canada, which the essay detailed, could be likened to that of Cossacks who opened up Siberia to Russians in the 16th and 17th centuries; the battles between the Hudson's Bay Company and the North West Company resembled struggles between various Russian merchant families in Siberia such as the Stroganovs and their rivals; charters given to the Hudson's Bay Company were similar to the terms of reference granted to the Russian American Company. To Russian readers who had shown a fascination for tales about Siberia and its peoples since the middle of the eighteenth century,[24] stories about Canada, its flora and fauna, native peoples, and untapped riches, all rang true. They corroborated the image carried in popular works about America by James Fenimore Cooper, whose *The Last of the Mohicans* (1826) was translated into Russian in the 1830s. François de Chateaubriand's descriptions of the new world as a wild paradise untainted by decadent European civilization had been translated as well, though most Russian intellectuals could read them in the original French.[25]

The relative wealth of information about events in Canada turned out to be one of the last occasions during Nicholas I's reign when public discussion of constitutional issues and varied political systems could take place. As revolution swept over Europe once again in 1848, censorship was tightened up in Russia and foreign travel was banned for anything but official business. The infamous Third Section, or secret police, founded in the aftermath of the Decembrist uprising, now became a dominant force in society.[26] Among other things, it ensured that no political debate took place in any open Russian forum. Only after the debacle of the Crimean War and the accession of Alexander II in 1855 could competing viewpoints on European and North American social, economic and political issues once again be found in Russian bookstalls and periodical literature.

In the late 1850s, in fact, just as Russia was recovering from the Crimean War and moving into a period of dramatic reform, a young Russian scholar and bureaucrat toured North America. At that time, the United States of America were embroiled in the internal strife that would soon carry them to the brink of Civil War, and various parts of British North America were moving towards economic and political union.

Russia suffered a crushing defeat at the hands of Britain and France during the Crimean conflict. The ramrod Nicholas I had died before war's end, leaving his son, Alexander II, to pick up the pieces. The new tsar disliked the terms of the Treaty of Paris (1856), which greatly limited Russia's field of action on the Black Sea, recognizing at the same time that a radical overhaul of Russian society and its institutions was necessary before anything could be done about it. As it happened, Aleksandr Borisovich Lakier's wanderings through North America would make a small, but illuminating contribution to the nationwide deliberations that were soon to get underway.

Lakier's voyage to North America had a purpose beyond a mere desire to learn. Knowing that Russia needed to change, he sought lessons from the "great experience of the Americas." His vehicle for conveying those lessons was a remarkable two-volume travelogue, filled with detailed description and few judgements, for the latter mode of expression still carried risks if the analysis proved too discomforting to Russian authorities.[27]

Only thirty-two when he visited the United States, Canada, and Cuba in 1857, Lakier already was reasonably well-known in Russia as an historian. He held a position with the Russian Ministry of Justice until 1856, then journeyed around western Europe, North America and Palestine before settling into a position with the Ministry of Internal Affairs in 1858. One of his tasks with the Ministry was to serve as secretary to the Editing Commission which eventually submitted the plan by which serfs were emancipated in Russia, 19 March (os) 1861.

Although Lakier's tour and the books were primarily in and about the United States, he included an entire chapter on Canada. His first contact with Canadians came as he crossed Lake Champlain from Whitehall, New York, on a steamboat, on which "quite unexpectedly there was a predominance of French-speaking passengers." He proceeded through the Province of Canada (created from Upper and Lower Canada by the Act of Union in 1841), touring and remarking upon the main cities and towns, the rivers (above all the St. Lawrence and Ottawa), trade, politics, legal system, and French-English relations. Commentary about parts of Canada he did not visit, among them Nova Scotia, was added. The books attracted considerable notice in Russia because they represented a special form of political and social commentary at a time when the autocracy was again sponsoring a major reconstruction programme from above. Public discussion of hitherto taboo topics, such as freeing the serfs, reforming the legal system, building railroads, and other types of political reform and economic change, were allowed and even encouraged for the first time in many decades and to a greater extent than in the days when Karamzin wrote about Canada. Among the most active participants in this discourse was Prince P.A. Viazemskii, who quoted Karamzin as the source of his vision of a monarchical Russia, governed by enlightened principles.

Lakier's portrayal of the United States and Canada was to add substance to this viewpoint. It is clear from the text that he was familiar with the writing of Chateubriand and with Alexis de Tocqueville's study on democracy in America. His many references to the special kind of freedoms that thrived in North America and his praise for the relatively open border between Canada and the United States were symptomatic of the desire of many Russians to end their own country's economic isolation. "Thanks to this freedom," Lakier wrote, "American well-being grows and huge cities rise suddenly in places where man seems to have come only recently." In contrast to the reigning European (and Karamzin's) assumption that America was a land of violence, where guns and fists provided final recourse to all disputes, Lakier insisted that the "American understanding of freedom is: do as you please, help yourself, but do not disturb your neighbour, and do not violate his interests!"[28] This particular remark was his summary of responses by Canadians to his questions about the danger of American domination, and even potential take-over of Canada. Apparently French and English-speaking Canadians were united in their rejection of any such possibility.[29]

A thorough evaluation of American constitutionalism was probably Lakier's greatest contribution to the debate in Russia. But his contempt for slavery, a "hateful ulcer" which he found in the United States and not in Canada, was more closely tied to Lakier's opinion on what should be changed in Russia. The analogy with Canada was therefore central to his message. Russian readers would understand his objection to slavery on both moral and economic grounds as reflections upon Russia's own institution of serfdom. His descriptions of the school systems in Canada, its immensely successful free farming, legal institutions, trial by jury and penal systems all had resonance for Russians actively seeking change in their own land.

Other Lakier observations on Canada fit well into the great debate at home. He commended the foresight of the Canadian government in building railways, hailed as "the first bearers of civilization" to uninhabited areas. More to the point, railroads attracted settlement to areas rich in natural resources, timber, and farmland. In Russia, large-scale railroad building was a relatively recent phenomenon and even by the late 1850s, still not without considerable opposition.[30] Admiration, even astonishment at the great success of municipal governments in generating a flourishing economy independently of any central authority, were other features of lakier;s picture of Canada. He witnessed a jury-run trial in Quebec, proclaiming it an unusually just system; enthused over the proliferation of political parties; and extolled the "local press, organs of publicity" that enabled everyone to know what was happening throughout their country.[31] In this way, both the real and imagined merits of Canada and the United States were used as models for discussion by Russians.

Acknowledging that Canadians had had their difficulties, Lakier said that the English government learned its lesson when it lost America and so now allowed, and even helped, Canada to evolve on its own. The English learned another lesson when their "obstinacy and lack of foresight" in an undescribed "event" of 1837 compelled them to extend municipal rights and provide "equalization" to both nationalities in Canada. Able to take advantage of their own natural thrift and industriousness, all Canadians — English, French and native peoples — seemed "happier" than Americans. They were "polite and attentive. Their faces did not express the eternal thoughts of Americans about dollars and cents."[32] This last trait is what struck Lakier most forcefully in Canada. It was the clearest message in connection with Canada that his book presented to Russian readers, and where his opinions coincided most closely with Karamzin's.

In addition to its practical accounting of urban and village institutions, infrastructure, and communications, Lakier's work was permated with lingering traits of the romantic age of travel literature: wild and glorious nature, heroic but fading native peoples. Naturally much attention was given to Niagara Falls, a natural phenomenon already well known to, but not often seen by, Europeans.[33] Along with flowery portrayals of Niagara's grandeur, Lakier added much about the engineering and even private marketing "genius" making it a tourist attraction, something virtually unheard of in Russia.

The enthusiastic image conveyed by Lakier was influenced by the fact that the mid-1850s was a time of great prosperity for Canada. The Crimean War (1854-56) raised Britain's need for Canadian timbers and ship building, and a railway construction frenzy was underway. A Reciprocity Treaty signed with the United States in 1854 also contributed to the boom in Canada. Although the good times were beginning to fade in 1857, that could not have been noticeable to Lakier. Images carried in his two volumes were also spread through Russia by reviews written for it's most prestigious journals by some of the country's best known writers and critics. Most contemporary editors hoped to participate in one way or another in the changes promised for Russia and did so vicariously in their book review sections, criticism being the genre best suited to conveying political and social lessons subtly and with less chance of affronting authority. Though these focussed on Lakier's portrayal of the United States, a sometime discordant impression of Canada bore through in the reviews.

Because the *Sovremennik* was dominated in the late 1850s by the famous radical Chernyshevskii, Lakier could be assured that its critique of his volumes was at least noted by Russia's entire intelligentsia. Little was said about Canada in the 25-page essay, other than to complain that Lakier should have said more about it. Citing his description of North America's legal systems, the "anonymous" reviewer demonstrated by innuendo that societies that were decentralized politically and provided protection in law for individual rights, could thrive. "But for us these debates [about democracy] are completely alien," he added, as if Russians really were not interested in such matters. The reviewer, who was in fact N.A. Dobrolyubov, assumed that readers would understand him to mean the opposite of what he wrote.[34] The famous radical literary critic charged that Lakier neither understood nor conveyed the democratic quality of life in the United States and accused him, wrongly, of practically ignoring the issue of slavery. In this way, Dobrolyubov made clear his own opinions about the iniquities of Russian society.

Long reviews appeared as well in the *Severnaia pchela* and *Otechestvennye zapiski* (Notes of the Fatherland). The *Severnaia* pchela was edited by zealous patriot F. Bulgarin, flamboyant publicist, novelist and, it seems, sometime informant to the secret police. The *Otechestvennye zapiski*, whose outstanding contributor in the 1840s had been the illustrious critic V.G. Belinskii, had a distinctive "westernizer" leaning. These journals had long histories as each other's main competition for readers. Both were closely watched by Nicholas I's Third Section until that tsar's death in 1855, and then had considerably more leeway for opinion-shaping as the reform movement dominated the public conversation. Lakier's travelogue became part of the discourse. Reviewers lauded him for bringing such a wealth of useful detail about America to Russia. As others had done much earlier, they concentrated on the anomaly of slavery in a society where the merits of freedom were preached so self-righteously and they emphasized the materialistic orientation of American society. The conservative *Severnaia pchela* allocated nearly half an issue to an analysis of Lakier's work, observing that, "while [the author's] diligence in describing the order and fairness [in the American education system] was good . . . as is the dissemination of useful knowledge to children, it is worth noting that it has one purpose — to make money!" For Americans, the reviewer went on to say, "the ring of dollars is much more pleasant than any symphony by Beethoven ...." There was an echo of Karamzin here.

Neither Canada nor Cuba were featured prominently in these two magazines, although *Otechestvennye zapiski* took care to cite Lakier's opinion that the English government treated Canada very well, not wanting to risk losing it. No direct reference was made to the rebellions of 1837-38; rather it was suggested that even though there were some people in Canada "devoted" to the United States, most Canadians, including the French, were now satisfied with their lot in life. Reviewers were inclined to highlight the fact that the institutions they admired most in North America had originated in Britain and hint that constitutional monarchy was the best starting point for progress and modernization. Where Lakier's accounts of the United States and Canada indicated different examples to follow in Russia, the Canadian way, real or fictional, was the way of choice.[35]

Lakier's volumes and the reviews they generated tended to confirm long-standing stereotypes of the United States held in most of Europe and Russia, and often encouraged by American pulp literature. It was a country where individual liberties thrived, but at the same time was a society overwhelmed by its commercial orientation, tainted by slavery — seen even by Russian democrats as a greater evil than serfdom — and caught in the trap of eternal political and social anarchy.[36] Readers of Lakier's volumes could find no such characteristics in his description of Canada, which may have been the reason why Dobrolyubov regretted that Canada had not received more attention.

Dobrolyubov's concern notwithstanding, a contemporary body of literature about Canada did trickle out to Russian readers during this crucial period in tsarist history. Lakier's work was preceded in print by a travel memoir edited for publication in 1855 by F. Studitskii, who relayed the observations of an unnamed sea captain (and his children) who visited ports on the eastern seaboard of Canada and the United States in his frigate *Semiramid*. More than half of the slim volume included descriptive accounts of Canada as the vessel sailed from Labrador through the Hudson's Straits to Hudson Bay and then back to the St. Lawrence, which he followed up to Kingston, taking long stops at Quebec City and Montreal along the way. The book was very anthropological in character, describing the people, native and European, their manner of dress, customs, habitat and religions.[37]

Native peoples, whom Studitskii's raconteur usually called "Indians" in contrast to Lakier who generally translated the French "sauvages" into the Russian words for "savages" or "wild people," came in for special attention, as did the country's flora and fauna. Canada's forests were discussed in great detail and an entire section was allocated to the beaver, both to the animal itself and to the historical and current importance of its pelt for Canadian trade and settlement.[38] Echoing the impressions left a half-century earlier by Karamzin, Studitskii praised the hardworking "peasants of Canada" for their "frankness, honour and integrity."[39]

A slightly later contribution came from one D. Romanov, who in 1862 reported on a visit to Montreal.[40] He too sailed up Lake Champlain from Whitehall and remarked on the easy passage through customs officialdom and the prevalence of French spoken on the railroad, which he rode in Canada. One French speaker told him loudly, while complaining about some discomfort in the American rail service, that the "Yankees everywhere put money above all else, even honour and virtue." Romanov was perplexed that everything shut down on Sundays in Montreal and wondered how such a trade oriented and practical people could be so religious. He came away with a view on French-English relations that was jarringly different from Lakier's: "[French] farmers and bourgeois nurture a hatred of the English, but the English language is still widely used." The "Yankees" are disliked as much as the English, he wrote, claiming that there was widespread support for Napoleon [III] in Montreal and Quebec City. For this reason, he could not agree with a widely held belief that sooner or later Canada and the United States would be united. The French in Canada want an independent state of their own, Romanov mused, going on to project that such independence would be fatal, for it would bring almost immediate annexation by the United States. Turning to the example of Louisiana, he pronounced that only cooperation within Canada would make it possible for the French to sustain their language and culture.

Romanov made much of the way Canada's vast lands were connected along the St. Lawrence and then all the way to the east coast and Halifax by canals, huge bridges and inexpensive rail. Like Lakier, he was an advocate of railroad construction for Russia and so stressed

the great value of rail to the success of trade and settlement in
Canada. If one considers that Russia's own railroad building programme was underway only in the mid-1840s when the future
Alexander II was placed at the head of a committee to supervise the
construction of a line between St. Petersburg and Moscow, then it is
easy to imagine how taken Russians were with rail traffic in the new
world. Real investment in rail traffic began only in the late 1850s and
it was not until the 1880s that Russia could boast of some 16,000 kilo-
metres of rail, about one-quarter of which was owned by the
government. Expansion of these lines to Siberia became a matter of
great debate, in which proponents regularly would hold up Canada
as an example to emulate. Romanov was clearly one of these a full
quarter century before Russian planners were fully persuaded by the
famous Canadian Pacific Railway.

Russian travellers continued to criss-cross Canada, though they did
not all leave detailed memoirs. One such tourist was the Grand Duke
Aleksei Mikhailovich, who came to Canada incognito (though not
very) in 1872 and left an unpublished, handwritten account of recep-
tions, people and the geography of Ottawa, Toronto and Niagara
Falls. It was rumoured that he went on Buffalo hunts and remembered Canada mostly for the good time he had.[41] Less than two years
later, the Grand Duke's elder brother, Tsar Alexander II, visited
England, where his daughter was married to the Duke of Edinburgh.
The tsar was greeted there as "Liberator of the Serfs" and contributed
to his own popularity by donating a large sum of money to poor relief
in London. The harsh image of Russia as enemy was therefore temporarily ameliorated in the British Empire.

The most consistent observers of Canada were navy people, whose
accounts were usually intended for the Admiralty and not published.
Captain I.A. Shestakov, for example, left very detailed impressions of
a tour over much the same ground covered by Lakier, that is, along
the St. Lawrence, through Quebec City and Montreal to Niagara Falls.
In fact he sailed into Canadian ports only a few months later than
Lakier and, like him, reported on the geography (scenery), cities, people, and native people of the areas he passed through. For the navy's
purposes, he provided information on fishing practices and the role of
the British fleet in protecting Canadian and Newfoundland fishing
grounds, recommending that such methods be adapted to Russian
ocean fishing regions, for example, on the White Sea.

Shestakov was sent to the United States in 1856 to purchase ships
and observe their construction. As an adjutant to Grand Prince
Konstantin, another brother of the tsar, he was very well connected

in Russia. As a representative of the Russian Admiralty and captain of the naval vessel *Empress Maria*, he was invited to commemorative events, including the celebration in New York of the laying of cable between North America and Europe. In connection with that occasion, he contrasted what he believed to be American and Canadian behaviour, remarking on American "vanity and brazenness" and cautioning that they would use "tricks to increase the value of their shares."[42] The contents of these navy despatches were shaped by the ongoing tensions between St. Petersburg and London: the information their authors selected often had strategic or economic implications for Russia. Shestakov's missives were no exception. Indeed, he warned his superiors that the Welland Canal, additions to which were completed during his stay in America. The canal allowed ships to sail from Lake Erie to Lake Ontario, bypassing Niagara River and Falls, and from there to the St. Lawrence and directly to England: "The voyage was so successful that the route promises to become permanent and, indeed, at present there is direct traffic between North America and Europe, which harms our wheat trade." Here was an early warning that advantages to Russia based on geographic proximity to the lucrative European market would diminish rapidly as the United States and Canada modernized their transportation systems.

The Russian public imagination was not piqued by events in Canada much between the 1860s and 1880s, although the American Civil War, the sale of Alaska, Canadian confederation, and the increasing participation of both North American countries in international trade were all watched with interest, and sometimes concern, by Russia's foreign ministry. It was not until another round of rebellion, this time led by Louis Riel, that the Russian reading public was again titillated by stories about Canada. One monthly magazine printed an entire series of essays on what it called the Métis-Indian rebellion, referring to Louis Riel as "the Garibaldi of the New World" and turning the entire episode into a romantic adventure story. The participation of Charles Dicken' son as a Canadian police inspector was highlighted in one of the essays. In another Canada was described as the "Achilles heel of England," an "unruly daughter now beginning to agitate and attempt to throw off the hated yoke, like its neighbour Uncle Sam."[43]

The popular *Journal de St. Petersbourg* carried almost daily reports on events in Canada during March-May, 1885, and followed them up throughout the summer. Some of these accounts were particularly detailed. One was a full reprint from a French-Canadian paper published in France, *Paris-Canada*, in which all the grievances of the

Métis and of French-Canadians were clearly laid out. French and Belgian papers, such as Le Temps and L'Indépendance Belge, tending to support the Métis cause, were cited, as were English-language Canadian papers. Extracts from Montreal papers (e.g., La Minerve), always in quotation marks so that the Russian editors could not be censored easily, consistently provided Riel's side of the story. His manifesto listing Métis demands and their vow to fight to the death rather than surrender was printed in St. Petersburg in mid-April. These provided Russian readers with a reportorial balance to which they were still unaccustomed, in part of course because at that very moment Russia and Britain were threatening each other with real war in the Balkans and in Afghanistan.

Other, more sensationalistic stories also included lurid accounts of Indian "massacres" in Manitoba, tales of the torture of priests by "savages," day-to-day notices about battles, the advance and success of the Canadian militia led by F.D. Middleton and, eventually, the capture of Riel, his lieutenant Gabriel Dumont, and various Indian chiefs.[44]

As it happened, the Riel rebellion occurred while Russia was in the throes of one of its most reactionary periods. The assassination in March 1881 of Alexander II, Russia's greatest reformer of the 19th century, ushered in a long period of harsh political repression. Increased censorship and police terror were conducted by the newly formed Okhrana, whose job it was to crush revolutionary movements. Russia's cultural and political milieu was dominated after 1881 by Konstantin P. Pobedonostsev, whose very conservative social and political world view was noted in the introduction to this volume. In addition to his scorn for the notion of sovereignty of the people, he called parliamentarianism rule by "narrow fanaticism" and characterized democracy as the "most burdensome system of government recorded in the history of mankind." His opinion that the "mass, always and everywhere, is vulgus, and its conceptions of necessity are vulgar" was already noted in the introduction, but warrants repetition as a reminder that the Russian state was reverting to kind in the 1880s. Under Pobedonostsev's leadership, the written word again became the object of rigid and consuming censorship, university autonomy and access were curtailed sharply (especially for women), and schools once again were expected to be little more than incubators of loyal citizens for the tsar. Rebellion anywhere, therefore, was not a matter to be written about casually.

Why then the relatively balanced reporting on the Riel rebellion? As we shall see in the next chapter, there were reasons of state for highlighting flaws within the British Empire. On the point of war with

Britain in both Afghanistan and Bulgaria, in fierce competition for fishing and sealing rights in the North Pacific, and fearful of revolution at home, examples of weakness elsewhere were useful. And the rebels were, after all, caught and punished.

Until the end of the century the Russian image of Canada remained a creation of travelogues, wildlife stories and political essays, with a limited audience in a country where the majority of people were illiterate. There was one exciting moment when six Canadian sealing ships were seized by the Russian navy on the Bering Sea in 1892. Because this event was part of an international dispute involving Russia, Britain, the United States, Japan and Canada, the Russian press dealt with it at length, and its diplomatic manifestations for Canada and Russia will be left here to the next chapter. The Russian public was handed a very limited version of the saga. St. Petersburg papers *Svet* (World) and *Vedomosti* (News) printed angry refutations of Canadian charges that the Russian fleet had breached international law. They accused the British Columbian and Nova Scotian captains of the ships and the Canadian press of lying, saying that the Canadians were well-treated in spite of their very bad behaviour. In the Russian account, the captains and crews were taken first to Petropavlovsk, where they "drank, created disturbances, and assaulted the inhabitants."[45] Few other details were offered Russian readers.

In point of fact, Lakier's long chapter and a half represented the last substantial Russian piece on Canada until close to the turn of the 20th century. Only then did monographs dedicated solely to Canada begin to proliferate. Studies of Canada's railroad building, agricultural development, and even its political system became near commonplace. Even at that, the nature of Imperial Russia, whose government still relied on censorship to shelter its subjects from "wrong" or dangerous ideas, ensured that the authors' perspective on Canadian political matters was couched in carefully constructed terminology. In some instances, when Canadian social or political situations were being described, it was obvious that the Russian writer hoped to convey a subversive lesson to his or her audience. On other occasions, Canada was a welcomed model in economic and development matters for government planners in Russia who took up the investigation of practices in Canada. Though that too is a matter for another chapter, it is worth mentioning here that the image of a vibrant Canada doing much better than a Siberia believed to be wealthier in resources was an analogy often heard in St. Petersburg official circles.

The notion that Canada and Siberia had much in common was the central theme of an essay that appeared in 1882 in a journal edited by

N.M. Yadrintsev, a longtime proponent of Siberian autonomy. Yadrintsev invited the essay from D.I. Zavalishin, who had been sentenced to exile in Siberia in 1825 for his association with Decembrists. When he and other Decembrists were granted amnesties in the 1850s, Zavalishin decided to stay on and became a prolific polemicist against the central government's administration of Siberia. His essay "Siberia and Canada" was a clarion call not for revolution but for efficiency and development. The great economic and political strides forward that he imagined to be taking place in Canada could be duplicated in Siberia, Zavalishin proclaimed, only if the Russian government relinquished its centralist policies.[46]

Noting the "remarkable similarity in the external events," which saw the French, British and Russians conquer their respective territories in North America and Eurasia, Zavalishin found "significant differences in their internal development which led to an immense difference in the conditions of these countries at the present time."[47] In Canada, "free industry" and "voluntary settlement" developed, whereas Siberia was a land of "exile and forced labour." In Canada a number of industries evolved and a "healthy population" led to a natural increase of both people and wealth. In Siberia the heavy hand of the central government and the constant influx of criminals and "vicious exiles" prevented natural growth. "Bad local administration" became a chronic disease in Siberia while in Canada a constantly improving government administration — introduced by Britain primarily "to prevent Canada from uniting with the USA" — created a thriving community. This notion had been heard before, in Lakier's treatise. The Siberiak noted that whereas Canada and Siberia had approximately the same population, Canada already was criss-crossed with railroads and telegraph lines. Siberia had no railroads and barely any telegraph lines.

Zavalishin's comparisons between Siberia and Canada persisted in the Russian perception of Canada. He listed historical similarities in terms of discovery and occupation by Europeans, and geographical likenesses, such as the comparable roles of the Amur and St. Lawrence River systems.

The most spectacular boost to the Russian public perception of Canada at the end of the century, however, had come with the Doukhobor emigration, the details of which will be discussed in Chapter three. Their removal to Canada generated an astonishing explosion of comment in Russia. Within a few months after the first group of Doukhobors stepped off a ship in Saint John, New Brunswick, on 20 January 1899, the Russian press was filled with stories of their new trials and tribulations, their beliefs and, of course, their new homeland. The combination of Leo Tostoy's involvement, and the fact that it represented the first voluntary mass migration of ethnic Russians, made it an extraordinary event in Russian life.[48]

Long accounts of the migration appeared in such diverse papers and magazines as *Yuzhnoe obozrenie* (Southern Monitor), which serialized "Russians in Canada" over seven issues, December 1899 to March 1900. These are presumed to have been written by Prince Dmitrii Khilkov, though they were attributed to an "L.L." The much more widely read *Russkie Vedomosti* (Russian News) carried a three-part series "With the Doukhobors in Canada" in 1900, signed by Vera M. Velichkova, a medical doctor who travelled with one of the first boatloads and later married Vladimir Bonch-Bruevich, himself the author of a three-part study "The Doukhobors in Canada." The latter essays were printed in the still influential *Syn Otechestva* in 1900. Accounts of Doukhobor life in Canada showed up in *Novoe Vremia* (New Times), *Moskovskie Vedomosti*, *Pribaltiiskii Krai* (Baltic District), *Severnyi Kur'er* (Northern Courier), and many others.[49] Several books on the 'Doukhobor in Canada' phenomenon appeared quickly, at least one as early as 1900. A final Bonch-Bruevich volume on Doukhobor settlements in the Canadian prairies was printed in Petrograd in 1918.[50] There is not a little irony in the fact that Bonch-Bruevich (1873-1955) became secretary to the Bolshevik Council of People's Commissars (Sovnarkom) and the director of the Soviet Museum of the History of Religion and Atheism.

The earliest monograph was especially interesting, for it evolved out of detailed reports prepared for Pobedonostsev by a Russian who had already been living in the United States for some twenty years. P.A. Demens (Tverskoi) visited Doukhobor communities in Canada in June 1899 and informed Pobedonostsev that they lived in appalling conditions, were "enslaved" by their elders, and their society was disintegrating due to increased drunkenness, dishonesty and even desertion by heads of families. His accounts of internal political and religious discord, disputes with the Canadian goverment, which he blamed on the Doukhobors themselves, and the desire of some to return to Russia were carried in letters to St. Petersurg from 1900 to 1904. Some of these opinions appeared in a book written by Demens and published in St. Petersburg as *Dukhoborcheskaia epopeia* (The Doukhobor Epic) in 1900.[51]

The book opened with a discourse on the harsh Canadian climate. There followed charges against the Canadian Pacific Railroad for exploiting members of the religious sect as labourers and refusing them "any rights." Demens claimed both in his book and in letters to Pobedonostsev that the Doukhobors were demoralized and doomed to a tragic end if they stayed where they were. He urged them to migrate again, to California where some already had found employment through the Southern California Mill Owner's Association, of which he happened to be president and general manager. In his correpondence with Pobedonostsev, Demens accused Bonch-Bruevich and others of lying about the good life in Canada and pointed out that returned Doukhobors would be excellent "propagandists against emigration out of Russia."[52] That these messages were taken seriously by Pobedonostsev was revealed by his willingness to fund the return to Russia of several sectarian leaders without threat of punishment. By "forsaking" their own country for Canada on the one hand and openly considering return on the other, the conservative and private Doukhobors provided Russians with a unusual and sensitive topic of conversation.

After the turn of the century, when the Russian Empire was again caught up in a moment of political turmoil, culminating in the world's first general strike in 1905, near civil war and, finally, a relatively open political system in which limited public debate was institutionalized for the first time, the image of Canada was once more exploited as a political and social message bearer. An historical survey and political commentary by P.G. Mizhuev, *Krest'ianskoe Tsarstvo* (The Peasant Kingdom) was serialized for the journal *Obrazovanie* (Education) in 1904 and then published as a book the following year. A second edition appeared in 1906. Political and social ends were served as well by two small books on Canadian geography and natural life written by Emiliia Pimenova in 1906 and 1917 as part of a series aimed at a youthful readership, and two short studies of Canada's government structure and its relationship to Great Britain by S.A. Korf (1911, 1914).[53]

Krest'ianskoe Tsarstvo had Canadian agriculture as its nominal subject matter. Compared to a study of that sector commissioned from N.A. Kriukov (discussed at length in Chapter 3) by the Russian Ministry of Agriculture in 1897, Mizhuev's effort was primarily a socio-political manifesto. Because of its political bent, the 120-page monograph was to become the pre-revolutionary Russian analysis of Canada quoted most often by Soviet writers.[54] Canada was but one of the subjects represented on his impressive list of publications, which included over twenty titles on the education systems of England, the United States, Germany, Switzerland, France, and Norway; a biography of Gladstone; French-language grammars for Russians; studies of the British Empire, and of New Zealand; and a long piece on the American Revolution in which that event's implications for Canada were outlined.[55]

In the course of writing about Canada, which he never visited, Mizhuev conveyed and lauded social and political messages quite contrary to the practices and principles of the Russian government. Drawing much of his technical information from Kriukov, he characterized Canada as a country "rapidly progressing in all aspects ... settled by well-established 'farmers,' — or landowning peasants — who live in full material achievement and who benefit at the same time from a strong cultural life." Canada's achievement as "one of the most free, well-organized and happy states" in the world was due, Mizhuev announced in an introductory section, to the fortunate circumstance of its territory being conquered from the French by the British. His purpose here was not to praise one colonial system at the expense of another; rather it was to inculcate in readers his own vision of how Russia generally, and Siberia particularly, should be developed.[56]

Even though Canada's political structure changed dramatically during the forty years that separated the Lakier and Mizhuev observations, their positions on some issues corresponded closely. The social and economic development of Canada was so advanced, Mizhuev wrote, that even many thousands of Americans were emigrating there.[57] Throughout the book, he drew the by now familiar analogies between Canada and Siberia, saying that though their climates and geography were almost identical, it was their dissimilar histories of colonization by a central government — Moscow and London — that most warranted comparison. In all aspects, including treatment of native populations, access to education, and regional political autonomy, Canada was portrayed as much more progressive than Siberia. Furthermore, Canada's administrative agencies were ranked far ahead of their Russian counterparts in efficiency and accomplishment. Since the book was published openly in Russia, its author still had to take some care about criticizing his own government. The comparisons were made either indirectly or by means of statistics. His conclusion that "both the history and current situation in Canada provide perfect material" for Russians to ponder was about as direct as he would get.

The historical section covered Canada's growth only to 1867, but was still noteworthy. Mizhuev wrote glowingly of the advantages derived by Canada from the English conquest. Constitutional monarchy, entrepreneurial incentives, and a milieu attractive enough to draw settlers to an area previously governed by the highly centralized, autocratic government of France, were among the benefits he listed. Mizhuev commended the overall British policy towards the French-speaking population in Canada, who, he claimed, remained loyal during the War of 1812 and for the most part even during the troubles in the 1830s.

Mizhuev told the tale of the rebellions of 1837-1838 in some detail, treating them as the result of actions in Upper and Lower Canada taken by "small groups of dare-devils and irreconcilables" whom the "great majority" of the population failed to support. Instead, the majority chose to call for change by legal and parliamentary means. The history of Canada "demonstrated, it seems, the correctness of the latter point of view."[58] In describing the political structure of Canada after 1867, he wrote that "Canada represents both one of the most democratic countries of the contemporary world and has at the same time a very strong government only nominally subordinated to British parliament."

The last four of Mizhuev's fourteen short chapters were devoted to immigration policy, economic progress, living conditions, education, "the Indian population," and the press. He was especially impressed with an immigration policy that made it possible for "peasants" to obtain and work their own land, enabling Canada to provide even its newest population with a standard of living higher than Russia's own middle gentry. His statistics on Canada's economic development demonstrated that its production, trade, and annual growth rate were far ahead of Russia's on a per capita basis, for which he congratulated the Canadian Pacific Railway system. Kriukov was quoted to the effect that "the splendid Massey-Harris harvesting machines have opened the way even into South Russia."[59] Finally, while emphasizing that Canada had many more newspapers than Siberia and a much more broadly-based educational system, he concluded that,

> [a] still more significant contrast with old Europe is the development in Canada of local self-government, not only for the provinces as outlined in the Constitution, but also for town and village communities. This last fact makes Canada one of the most democratic countries in the world — the first 'peasant kingdom' — since on the one hand competent local power is spread widely, and on the other hand the entire mass of the population participates in elections to this power.

Comparing Canada to the United States, the author noted that the industrialization of that country saw the creation of large syndicates and trusts which effectively kept "peasants" out of political power.[60] In Canada the localized "ruling aristocracy" made such an adverse development far less likely. There was a noticeable echo of the old Karamzin perspective here, and even more of Lakier. In discussing the lot of native peoples Mizhuev ranked Canada unequivocally ahead of the United States, Europe and even his own country. The reservation system, schooling and funds set aside for Indians were unparalleled anywhere, he said, heaping praise on Canadians both for their practices and their moral position in such matters.[61]

Books for Russia's youngsters provided other perceptions of Canada during the Russian Empire's final decades. The first volume by Emiliia Kirillovna Pimenova in 1906 helped corroborate the existing image. She too was prolific, completing monographs on the British colonies, New Zealand, the French Revolution of 1848, and travel stories on the Antarctic, Tibet, and elsewhere. Her main work on Canada was titled *Kanada, Strana velikikh Ozer'* (Canada, Country of Great Lakes). Printed first in 1906, a second edition appeared in 1913. In 1917 she added a smaller and more political booklet, *Strana khleborobov (Kanada)* [Land of Grain Growers (Canada)] to her list of titles.[62] The earlier monograph was published by a society called "Social Benefit" in a series for "young readers." Despite (or because of) the youthfulness of her intended audience, Pimenova described historical political issues in Canada much more specifically than Mizhuev had done, making her book very much a political tract. She insisted, for example, that the rebellions in Canada of 1837 had been beneficial for both England and Canada because they persuaded the British parliament to change the political structure of Canada, giving the country much more freedom and at the same time assuring that the crown would not lose another valuable colony. On the other hand, after devoting more than a dozen pages to Louis Riel, Pimenova called him "wise and talented" and insisted wrongly that he was supported even at the end by the "majority of Canadians."[63] She compared Riel in socio-political significance favourably with the American John Brown, the anti-slavery activist who was captured by federal troops and hanged in 1859. Pobedonostsev was out of office by 1903 and, after the revolution of 1905 in Russia and the formation of fairly representative, if not powerful, parliamentary structure, open support of revolutionary thought was possible, though still risky.

Praising Canada as "for the most part, a democratic republic" and one in which "equality" was a reality, Pimenova emphasized the country's natural attractions for settlers. Among the newcomers to Canada she described were the Doukhobors who, she said, were firm

believers "in the full equality of all people" and who did not recognize the authority of governments. The Doukhobors had already
prospered in Canada and, like all other Canadian farmers, lived
"incomparably better than peasants and even better than many small
landholders in Russia."[64] In this, she was probably right, although
her vision of the Doukhobor idyll in Canada ignored completely
a contrary view about which much already had been written in
Russia.

While she was greatly impressed with both the standard and availability of education in Canada, Pimenova pointed out that in Quebec
the greater part of learning was controlled by the Catholic clergy, in
contrast to the mainly secular schooling everywhere else in the country. This was to the clear disadvantage of Quebec youth, she implied.
Her concluding remark that "for young, strong, and energetic people,
thirsting for self-reliant work and a free, independent life, Canada
will appear to be the promised land," was both a powerful advertise-
ment for Canada and a none too subtle criticism of Russia. To be sure
that her point was not missed, she added a footnote explaining that a
democratic republic was "a state structure in which supreme power
belongs neither to one person, nor to a class, but to the entire people
who govern by means of elected representatives."[65] Her messages —
Canada is a promised land, welcoming to immigrants; and possessing
an ideal ruling system — were still subversive notions to ruling circles
in the tsarist state, though it was now much easier to publish such
opinions than it had been in either Karamzin's or Lakier's time.

S.A. Korf's writings about Canada were very different from those
of Mizhuev or Pimenova. His special interest in federalism had
resulted in a major treatise on federalist forms of government in 1908.
A 1911 booklet, *Gosudarstvennyi stroi Kanady* [The State Structure of
Canada] was limited to a chronological constitutional history of this
country and a remarkably thorough analysis of the 1867 Act of
Confederation. Attributing the "principle of absolute power of crown
and church" to the early French administration, and the idea of constitutions and independence to the "Anglo-Saxon" regime, Korf left
little doubt as to the type of system he preferred. He described Lord
Durham's "solutions" to Canada's problems thoroughly and with
obvious admiration and in a full chapter analyzed the 1867 Act liter-
ally chapter and verse. Korf's study of Canada's federalism, judicial
systems, provincial powers, and so on, was itself a political manifesto
for Russian readers.[66]

As a concluding note to this opening chapter, it is worth mentioning that the Russian vision of Canada was shaped as well by a few

samples of Canadian literature translated into Russian. Though I have had little success in tracking down such works, the two authors of whom there is evidence were of a singular type: Charles G.D. Roberts and Ernest Thompson-Seton. Thompson-Seton (1860-1946) was, in fact, an American citizen and a founder of the American Boy Scouts. But he grew up in Canada and most of his stories about wild animals and boys in the forests were set in the Canadian wilderness. His tales were translated as early as the late 1890s and they remained popular in the Soviet era. *Wild Animals I have Known* was particularly well known. First printed in Russia in 1904, it was to go through more than a dozen editions. In 1910 a complete edition of Seton-Thompson's writing appeared in ten volumes and by the 1950s Russian language editions of his stories numbered in the millions of copies.[67]

Charles G.D. Roberts (1860-1943) was a well known Canadian poet, historian, and writer of animal stories. According to Soviet scholars, a number of his children's tales of animals and the wilds of Canada were translated between 1910 and 1915 and widely read, introducing the wild life of Canada's animal kingdom in story form. He too was a popular author during the early Soviet era.[68] These two writers therefore contributed to the romantic vision of Canada circulated among Russian readers in a variety of formats by Karamzin, Studitskii, Lakier, Pimenova and others.

Writing about Canada's wilderness and native peoples was one thing, for the practice fit into a continuum that began with the Russian pre-romanticism of which Karamzin was the central figure and evolved into a century-long fascination with travel literature. The latter type of writing was popular everywhere, but had a special place in Russia where the right to travel was sometimes restricted even for members of the aristocracy and at the best of times difficult for the gentry because of its cost. Political writing was another matter, and one for which Canada was unusually well suited. It looked, or could be made to look, like Russia; its realities were much more of a mystery to Russians than Europe was. Canada had a large republican neighbour for purposes of comparison and it was itself part of a constitutional monarchy, the government of choice for most Russian advocates of political change, at least before 1905.

---

[1] See especially G.-F. Müller, *Voyages from Asia to America for Completing the Discoveries of the Northwest Coast of America* [1764], translated from the original German (London: T. Jeffreys, 1984). Raymond H. Fisher, *Bering's Voyages. Whither and Why*, edited and translated by Carol Urness (Seattle:

University of Washington Press, 1977), p. 9. *Bering's Voyages: the Reports from Russia* (Fairbanks: University of Alaska Press, 1986), pp. 50-51.

2   "Propozitsii Fedora Saltykova," in *Pamiatniki drevnei pis'mennost i iskusstva*, 83, No. 5, Series 4 (St. Petersburg 1891), pp. 22-24. Saltykov advocated building ships at the mouths of major eastern Siberian rivers and proceeding from there to North America and Japan.

3   See "Pis'mo odnogo Anglichanina iz Kvebeka" [Letter of an Englishman from Quebec], *Vestnik Evropy*, 16 (1803), pp. 272-76; "Pis'mo odnogo molodago Frantsuza iz Monrealia" [Letter of a Young Frenchman from Montreal], *ibid.*, 20 (1803), pp. 279-83. Karamzin founded the journal in 1802, but relinquished his post as editor after only two years. It remained the most widely-read journal in Russia until it closed in 1830.

4   Karamzin's (1766-1825) *Istoriia gosudarstva Rossiiskago* [History of the Russian State], 12 vols (St. Petersburg, 1818-29) was the official history and went through many editions, the last before the 1917 revolution appearing in 1894. The first Soviet edition began to appear only in 1988. On Karamzin as an historian, see J.L. Black, *Nicholas Karamzin and Russian Society in the Nineteenth Century* (Toronto: University of Toronto Press, 1975). On Karamzin as a literary writer, see A.G. Cross, *N.M. Karamzin. A Study of His Literary Career (1783-1803)* (London: Feffer & Simons, 1971).

5   Karamzin, "Obshchestva v Amerike" [Society in America], *Vestnik Evropy*, 24 (1802), pp. 315-18. The Rusian word for "society" had been banned from use by Paul I and only recently had been allowed back in print.

6   Karamzin, *Izbrannye sochineniia* [Collected Works], Vol. I (Moscow-Leningrad, 1964), p. 593. He wrote this in 1801, in the final part of the *Pism'a*. On Karamzin's views on monarchy, see Richard Pipes, "Karamzin's Conception of the Monarchy," in *Essays on Karamzin*, edited by J.L. Black (The Hague: Mouton, 1975), pp. 127-147.

7   "Obshchestva v Amerike," p. 315. The italics were Karamzin's, who claimed to have translated this essay from an unidentified manuscript.

8   See "Pis'mo iz Baltimora" [Letter from Baltimore], *Vestnik Evropy*, 3 (1802), pp. 87-90. In "Korol' Tsesar, Negre v Amerike" [King Caesar, Negro in America], *ibid.*, 2 (1802), pp. 35-37; 6 (1802), pp. 272-76; 16 (1803), pp. 272-76; 20 (1803), pp. 179-183, he translated a piece from the *Salem Gazette* about a "Negro" named Caesar who escaped from slavery in America to become a "noble brigand."

9 Karamzin, "Priiatnye vidy, nadezhdy i zhelaniia nyneshnego vremeni" [Pleasant Views, Hopes and Wishes for the Present Time], *Vestnik Evropy*, 12 (1802), pp. 314-330.

10 Karamzin, "O liubvi k otechestvu i narodnoi gordosti," *Vestnik Evropy* (1802), *Izbrannye sochineniia, op. cit.*, Vol. II, pp. 280-287.

11 See V. Orlov, *Russkie prosvetiteli 1790-1800-x godov* (Moscow: Nauka, 1953), pp. 298f. The Vol'noe obshchestvo liubitelei slovesnosti, nauk i khudozhestv was founded in 1801, the first such society in Alexander's reign, and continued until 1825.

12 Yu.F. Lisianskii, *Puteshestvie vokrug sveta* ... (St. Petersburg, 1812), was translated into English as *A Voyage Around the World in the Years 1803, 4, 5 & 1806 Performed in the Ship "Neva"* (London, 1814). On this, see Glynn R. DeV. Barratt, "Halifax Through Russian Eyes. Fleet-Lieutenant Iurii Lisianskii's Notes of 1794-96," *Nova Scotia Historical Quarterly/ Review*, 12: 2 (1992), pp. 47-65. Pavel Svinin, *Opyt' zhivopisnago puteshestviia po severnoi Amerike* [The Experience of a Picturesque Voyage Across North America] (St. Petersburg, 1815). See p. 6, 12 (on "Cananade," meaning Canada), pp. 162-73 (On Niagara Falls), pp. 205-19 (on Newfoundland). Svinin's work was the first eyewitness accunt of America published in Russia.

13 See, for example, *Moskovskii telegraf* [Moscow Telegraph], edited by the historian and publicist, N. Polevoi, where ethnographical articles on the "Eskimoes" were printed in 1832, comparing native peoples who lived in Russia's Arctic to those who lived in Greenland, Labrador, on the mouth of the Mackenzie River and in the Canadian arctic: "Eskimosy," *Moskovskii telegraf*, No. 9 (May 1832), pp. 554-561.

14 On this, see Cynthia H. Whittaker, *The Origins of Modern Russian Education. An Intellectual Biography of Count Sergei Uvarov, 1786-1855* (De Kalb: University of Illinois Press, 1984), and Alexander M. Martin, *Romantics, Reformers, Reactionaries. Russian Conservative Thought in the Reign of Alexander I* (De Kalb: University of Illinois Press, 1997).

15 "Chto takoe svoboda? [What is Freedom?], *Biblioteka dlia Chteniia*, V, No. 2 (1834), pp. 28-68. On Canada, Senkovskii, "Skandinavskiia sagi" [The Scandinavian Sagas], *Ibid.*, I, No. 3 (1834), pp. 1-77, here p. 21.

16 On censorship in Russia, see A.M. Skabichevskii, *Ocherki po istorii russkoi tzensury (1700-1863)* [Outline History of the Russian Censors] (St. Petersburg, 1892); Leon I. Twarog, "Literary Censorship in Russia and the Soviet Union," *Essays on Russian Intellectual History*, The Walter

Prescott Webb Memorial Lectures, V (Austin: University of Texas, 1971),
pp. 98-123; Charles A. Ruud, *Fighting Words: Imperial Censorship and the
Russian Press, 1804-1906* (Toronto: University of Toronto Press, 1982).

[17] "Inostrannyia izvestiia' [Foreign News], *Moskovskiia vedomosti*, No. 19
(3 March 1838), p. 157. This paper carried much information on
Canadian events in its January to early March issues. The information
was usually about three weeks out of date. Later spelling was *Moskovskie
vedomosti*.

[18] "Letopis sobytii za...." [Chronology of Events for ...], *Syn otechestva*, each
month, in Part 5. Entire reports and proclamations were sometimes
included, among them Durham's proclamation in Quebec, in May 1838,
and Sir John Colborne's official report from Montreal (November).
      Syn otechestva (1812-1852) was a prestigious and narrowly patriotic
Moscow magazine. It and *Severnaia pchela* (1825-1864) were both edited
by Russian nationalists and supporters of Nicholas I's "Official
Nationality." For the ideology of this reign, see especially Nicholas
Riasanovsky, *Nicholas I and Official Nationality in Russia, 1825-1855*
(Berkeley: University of California, 1967), and Sidney Monas, "Shishkov,
Bulgarin, and the Russian Censorship," *Harvard Slavic Studies*, 4 (1957),
pp. 127-148.

[19] See, for example, *Syn otechestva* II, pt. 5 (February 1838), pp. 118-19; III,
pt. 5 (April 1838), p. 125; V, pt. 5 (August 1838), pp. 59-60. For the daily
life of the reign, see W. Bruce Lincoln, *Nicholas I. Emperor and Autocrat of
All the Russias* (Bloomington: Indiana UP, 1978), Chapters 7-9.

[20] "Letopis sobytii za Iiun', 1838," *Syn otechestva*, Vol. IV, pt. 5 (July, 1838),
pp. 102-04; "Letopis ... Iiul'," pp. 139-40.

[21] Although the account referred to above was not attributed to any particular source, it appears to have been taken from *Mackenzie's Gazette*, a
very unusual source for Russian editors to be reading. The *MG* carried
several feature pieces on "Bill" Johnson (or, more often, Johnston), in
which he was built up as a hero, especially for sinking the *Sir Robert Peel*.
See, e.g, a long open letter, "To William Johnson, Now Encamped in
Upper Canada on the Islands in the River St. Lawrence, Contending for
the Liberty of his Native Country," *Mackenzie's Gazette* (21 July 1938).
Mackenzie referred to him as Canada's "Jefferson." Earlier it was said
that Johnson "has a daughter about 19 years of age, very handsome, and
said to possess equal courage with himself. She often goes into a boat
alone, armed, and seeks her father with supplies of provisions." *Ibid.* (30
June 1838), p. 58.

[22] "Khronika russkago v Parizhe" [Chronicle of a Russian in Paris], *Sovremennik*, Vol. X, pt. 2, (1838), p. 28. Because of the Decembrist revolt, Turgenev stayed in Europe almost without interruption, 1825-1845, but his observations often were printed in Russian journals. *Sovremennik* was founded by A.S. Pushkin.

[23] "Istoricheskii ocherk mekhovoi torgovli v Severnoi Amerike" [Historical Outline of the Fur Trade in North America], *Syn otechestva*, 10 (1839), pp. 36-54. The piece was a translation from the *North American Review*. *Syn otechestva* also carried historical pieces about the opening up of America's Pacific coast by Russians, and reports from Baron Ferdinand von Wrangel (Vrangel), who later became a director of the Russian American Company.

"O parokhodstve i ozerakh v Severnoi Amerike" [Steam Ships and the Lakes in North America], was carried in *Otechestvennye zapiski*, 3:4 (1839).

[24] On this, see especially J.L. Black, "Rediscovering Siberia in the Eighteenth Century: The Monthly Compositions, 1755-1764," *Siberica: A Journal of North Pacific Studies*, 1:2 (Winter, 1990-91), pp. 112-126.

[25] Several of Chateaubriand's essays were translated for *Vestnik Evropy* in the 1820s.

[26] See Sidney Monas, *The Third Section. Police and Society in Russia under Nicholas I* (Cambridge: Harvard UP, 1961).

[27] Lakier, *Puteshestvie po Severo-amerikanskim' Shtatam', Kanade i ostrovu Kube* [Travels In the North American States, Canada and the Island of Cuba], 2 Vols (St. Petersburg: K. Vul'fe, 1859). On Canada, Vol. 1, pp. 304-374, translated below; and on Cuba, Vol. 2, pp. 268-335. For the "great experience of the Americas," see his introduction, Vol. 1, p.2.

[28] Lakier, *Puteshestvie*, Vol. 1, pp. 352-53.

[29] *Ibid.*, p. 310.

[30] On the arguments over railroad-building in Russia in the 1859s and 1860s, see Walter Mckenzie Pintner, *Russian Economic Policy Under Nicholas I* (Ithaca: Cornell UP, 1967), and Steven K. Marks, *Road to Power. Building The Trans-Siberian Railway, 1850-1896* (Ithaca: Cornell UP, 1991).

[31] Lakier, *Puteshestvie*, Vol. 1, pp. 308, 339-40, 353.

[32] *Ibid.*, pp. 307, 312; "dollars and cents" were written as in the English, but transliterated into Cyrillic.

[33] In addition to Lakier's description, see e.g., "Most' chrez Niagaru" [Bridge Over Niagara Falls], *Moskvitianin*, No. 24 (December), Bk. 2 (1850), p. 128, and also description by Captain (1st Rank) I.A. Shestakov, footnote No. 42, below.

[34] [Dobrolyubov], "Novyia knigi. Puteshestvie po Severo-Amerikanskim Shtatami, Kanade i Ostrovu Kube, Aleksandra Lakiera" [A New Book. Travels ... of Lakier], *Sovremennik*, Vol. 74, Section 3 (March 1859), pp. 25-48. For proof of his authorship, see Dobrolyubov, *Sobranie sochinenii*, Vol. 4 (Moscow-Leningrad, 1962), pp. 217-239. Dobrolyubov died in 1861 at the age of 25.

[35] "Pchelka: gazetyia zametka" [The Bee: Newspaper Notes], *Severnaia pchela*, No. 31 (9 February 1859), pp. 121-122; *Otechestvennye zapiska*, Vol. 123, Section 3 (1859), pp. 135-150; *Sovremennik* (March 1859), *op. cit.*, pp. 47-48.

[36] On stereotyping of the United States in mid-century Russia, see Hans Rogger, "Russia and the Civil War," *Heard Around the World. The Impact Abroad of the Civil War*, edited by Harald Hymen (New York: Knopf, 1969), pp. 177-256.

[37] Studitskii, *Puteshestvie vokrug sveta. Severnaia Amerika* [A Trip Around the World. North America] (St. Petersburg: Yakov Trea, 1855). With drawings.

[38] Studitskii, *Puteshestvie*, pp. 32-36.

[39] Studitskii, *Puteshestvie*, p. 19. In this case, he was commenting on French Canadian "peasantry."

[40] Romanov, "Monreal'" [Montreal], *Morskogo sbornik*, No. 8 (1862), pp. 1-23. I have not been able to identify the author, but gather from the introduction that he had toured the United States before arriving in Canada. The journal was published by the Ministry of the Navy.

[41] For scattered and difficult to read pages from his diary of the trip, see RGAVMF, Fonds 1247, opis 1, delo 40, pp. 108-120r. Aleksei Mikhailovich, who died in 1895, was the 4th son of Grand Duke Mikhail Nikolaevich, younger brother of Alexabder II.

A Russian geographer toured "America" at about the same time and recorded a few details about Canada's climate and soils, see A.I. Voeikov, "Russkii puteshestvennik v Amerike" [A Russian Traveller in America], *Izvestiia russkogo geograficheskogo obshchestva*, Vol. 10, No. 1 (1874), pp. 59-61.

42 Shestakov, "Polveka obykhovennoi zhizni" [Half-a-Century of an Ordinary Life] (1858), RGAVMF, Fonds 26, Opis 1, delo 17, pp. 52-70; "Vypiska iz pis'ma kapitana I. Ranga Shestakova o nadzore za rybnymi promyslami i na N'iu-Faundlenskikh bankakh ..." [Extracts from a Letter of Captain (1st Rank) Shestakov on Surveillance of the Newfoundland Banks Fisheries (March-July 1859)], ibid., Fonds 6, Opis 1, delo 36, pp.1-13.

43 "Episod iz vozstaniia v Kanade" [Episode from the Rebellion in Canada], Vokrug sveta, No. 20 (1885), p. 306; "Lui Riel' " [Louis Riel], Ibid., No. 45 (1885), p. 716; "Poslednie trappery. Episod iz vosstaniia Rielia" [The Last Trappers. Episode from the Rebellion of Riel], Ibid., No. 13 (1887), pp. 194-196; No. 14, pp. 211-214; No. 15, pp. 229-234; No. 16, pp. 247-250; No. 17, pp. 252-265.

44 Journal de St. Petersbourg, 1884-1885, passim.

45 A translation of an article originally from Svet was carried in the Yarmouth Tribune (22 November 1892).

46 Zavalishin, "Sibir' i Kanada," Vostochnoe obozrenie: gazeta literaturnaia i politicheskaia, No. 34 (1882), pp. 3-4, was translated and reprinted in David N. Collins, "Dmitrii Zavalishin and Canada," Musk Ox, 29 (1981), pp. 47-54.

47 Ibid., p. 49

48 Slightly more than 2,000 Doukhobors were conveyed to Saint John on the Beaver Line steamship Lake Huron. They boarded six passenger trains chartered by the Canadian government and left for their new home-steads on the prairies. By July 1899 about 7,500 Doukhobors had come that way. See John Woodsworth, Russian Roots & Canadian Wings. Russian Archival Documents on the Doukhobor Emigration to Canada (Manotick: Penumbra Press, 1999), p. 1.

49 There are too many of these titles to be listed fully here. The CRCR has a large collection of them. Translations of the Velichkova and Khilkov essays can be found in Woodsworth, Russian Roots & Canadian Wings. One account not included in these lists is a short story written by the Russian prose writer and ethnographer Vladimir Bogoraz in 1899. His little tale about immigration included a conversation with immigrants in New York who already knew of the arrival of Doukhobors in Canada, believing them to be "Circassians." See Bogoraz, "U vkhoda v novyi svet" [At the Entrance to the New World], Sobranie sochinenii, Vol. 5 (St. Petersburg 1911).

[50] Bonch-Bruevich, *Dukhobortsi v Kanadskikh Preriiakh* [Dukhobors in the Canadian Prairies], (Petrograd, 1918); V.M. Skvortsov, *Dukhobory v Amerike i graf L. N. Tolstoi* [Dukhobors in America and Count L. N. Tolstoy] (St. Petersburg: A. A. Porokhovshchikov, 1901), reprinted from the journal *Missionerskoe obozrenie*; and Skvortsov, *Dukhobory v Amerike i Tolstovtsy* [Dukhobors in America and the Tolstoyans] (St. Petersburg: Kolokol, 1912).

[51] P.A. Tverskoi, *Dukhoborcheskaia epopeia* [The Dukhobor Epoch] (St. Petersburg: A. A. Porokhovshchikov, 1900). Demens, originally Dement'ev, took the pseudonym "Tverskoi" because he had gone to the United States from the province of Tver.

[52] The letters of Demens (Tverskoi) from Los Angeles to Pobedonostsev (30 September 1900-3 October 1904), are contained in GARF, Fonds 1574, Opis 2, delo 154, pp. 1-114, *passim*. On Demens, see George Bolotenko, "The Recovery of Doukhobor records from Russia and their Historical Significance," in *The Doukhobor Centenary in Canada*, edited by Andrew Donskov (Ottawa: Slavic Research group, 2000), pp. 187-199.

[53] Editions held by the CRCR are as follows: Mizhuev, *Krest'ianskoe Tsarstvo. Ocherk' istorii sovremennago sostoianiia Kanady* [The Peasant Kingdom. Outline of the History of Current Conditions in Canada] (St. Petersburg: T.F. L'vovich, 1905); Pimenova, *Strana Velikikh Ozer' (Kanada)* [Land of the Great Lakes. (Canada)], 2nd edition, with drawings (St. Petersburg: Obshchestvennaia Pol'za, 1913), and *Strana khleborobov' (Kanada)* [The Land of Grain Growers (Canada)] (Petrograd: Kniga, 1917); Korf, "Gosudarstvennyi stroi Kanady," in *Avtonomnye kolonii Velikobritanii* (St. Petersburg, 1914).

[54] It was the sole pre-revolution source cited in the *Bol'shaia Sovetskaia Entsiklopediia* [Great Soviet Encyclopedia], Vol. 11 (Moscow: BSE, 1973), p. 299. The Pimenova and S.A. Korf works were sometimes noted, but only in passing by Soviet writers.

[55] Mizhuev, *Veliki raskol' anglo-saksonskoi rasy. Amerikanskaia revoliutsiia* [The Great Schism in the Anglo-Saxon Race. The American Revolution] (St. Petersburg, 1901).

[56] *Krest'ianskoe Tsarstvo*, p. 3.

[57] *Ibid.*, Intro.

[58] *Ibid.*, pp. 52-53.

59 *Ibid.*, p. 88. In citing Kriukov here, Mizhuev added his own "(sic !)" as if to express surprise that the government appointee would recommend such a thing to his own government.

60 *Ibid.*, pp. 97-98, 105.

61 *Ibid.*, pp. 116-118. His data on "Indians" were taken mostly from Kriukov.

62 I have used Pimenova, *Kanada, Strana Velikikh Ozer'* (St. Petersburg: Obshchestvennaia Pol'za, 1913), with drawings, 103 pages. The *Strana khleborobov. (Kanada)*, (Petrograd: Kniga, 1917) had only16 pages and carried a more distinctly social democratic tone. Translated below.

Another contemporary work on Canada, printed a few years later than this book calls for, was a study on peasant life in North America by N.A. Karintsev. Fully half of the 150-page 1917 book was devoted to Canada: Karintsev, *Zhizn' krest'ian v raznykh stranakh. Severnaia Amerika* (Petrograd, 1917). He devoted 10 pages to the Doukhobors, and spread a message like that of Kriukov and Mizhuev; that is, that Canada was an ideal country in which to live, especially for agricultural people.

63 Pimenova, *Kanada. Strana ...*, pp. 53-65; on the 1837 rebellion, pp. 43-44; on "equality," p. 108.

64 *Ibid.*, pp. 71-76.

65 *Ibid.*, p. 103. The book contained drawings of towns, rivers, mountains, and native peoples.

66 Korf, *Gosudarstvennyi stroi Kanady* [State Structure of Canada] (Moscow 1911), reprinted in *Avtonomnye Kolonii Velikobritanii* (St. Petersburg, 1914), pp. 1-97. See also his *Federalizm* (St. Petersburg, 1908).

67 On this see A.I. Golysheva, *Sovremennaia Anglo-kanadskaia poeziia* [Contemporary English-Canadian Poetry] (Leningrad: LGPI, 1975), pp. 3-4.

68 For a partial listing of translated titles, see *Istoriia i kul'tura Kanady* [History and Culture of Canada], a bibliography of Russian-language titles on Canada prepared for the Group on Canadian History, Russian Academy of Sciences, by V. A. Koleneko and others, Moscow, 1994.

Montreal Nov. 27th 1838.

Sir,

Having been honored with the commands of His Excellency Sir John Colborne to furnish You with a letter explanatory of the cause of the seizure of Your papers, I am now to acquaint You that this step was adopted upon written information previously submitted to the consideration of His Excellency, the particulars of which I do not consider myself at liberty to disclose.

In making this communication I am further commanded by His Excellency to express his regret if in the execution of this duty You should have suffered any inconvenience. In the peculiar position of this Province the Executive must exercise the same vigilance which under corresponding circumstances would be justly exerted in any country in Europe.

I am happy to have it in my power to add that the result of the examination of Your papers has been such as to exonerate You from the suspicions which, I cannot but repeat, fully justified the proceedings which were adopted.

I have the honor to be, &c

(signed) C. N. Ogden
Attorney General.

P. A. Kitchen Esquire
Montreal.
183

2

The "Canada Card" in Russian Diplomacy and War

ALTHOUGH ALEXANDER I ABANDONED most of his reformist inclinations within a few years of taking the throne in 1801, the first exchange of ambassadors between Russia and the United States in 1809 continued to cause disquiet for Karamzin and others among Russia's conservative intelligentsia. An apparent empathy between America and France, whose Napoleon Bonaparte had only recently forced an unpopular alliance on the Russian emperor (at Tilsit, 1807), reinforced their concern. John Quincy Adams, from one of the "aristocratic" families distrusted by Karamzin and his avid readers,[1] served in Russia as ambassador from 1809 to 1814. On his arrival in St. Petersburg Russia was fighting Britain in league with France, and the United States was friendly with Britain. As he prepared to return home five years later, Russia and London were allied against France and a British-America war was winding down. These were very confusing times in the international arena.

As an ally of France, 1807 to 1810, Russia suffered doubly. It had to forego its most lucrative trade, with Britain, while Napoleon's Continental Blockade drastically limited Russia's exports. Because France and her other allies could not provide the sorely-needed textiles which Russia usually imported from Britain, St. Petersburg lost heavily in customs revenues. On the other hand, Russia maintained its trade with neutral United States. It was made plain to Adams by the francophile foreign minister, Count Nikolai P. Rumiantsev, that their relationship was vital to Russia's interests — just as Napoleon was pressuring Russia to close its ports to neutral ships because they routinely carried British goods. Rumiantsev was appointed foreign minister in 1807 and from 1809 combined the position with that of Chancellor, so his tenure in office was linked inextricably with the French alliance.

The revolving door of diplomatic associations continued to swing and Adams found himself in 1812 condemning the French for their invasion of Russia and bemoaning losses inflicted upon Americans by British forces in North America.

It was in this period as well that the idea of Canada as a buffer, pawn, or arena of conflict between Britain, the United States, and Russia first became a topic of conversation at court in St. Petersburg. Adams was a cautious advocate in Russian conversations of the cession of Canada to the United States and he carried this opinion with him on his return to Washington to 1814.[2] The implications of an American attempt to annex Canada were mooted by senior officials in Russia as the unusual ebb and flow of diplomatic arrangements moved inexorably towards a renewed Russian war with Napoleon in 1812.

Alexander I severed relations with Britain nearly six months after the 1807 accord with Napoleon and gradually began to expand his country's borders with the help of France — at great cost to Russia in lives and resources. While Finland was won from Sweden, war against Turkey in the Romanian Principalities and Azerbaijan continued with only brief respites throughout the entire period, as did fierce resistance by Georgians to Russia's annexation of their lands in 1801. Russia even declared war on Austria in 1809, in part because of obligations to Paris but also to forestall the emergence of an enlarged Polish state under the protection of France. The resurrection of Poland, the Continental Blockade, and Russia's debilitating military commitments compelled Alexander gradually to withdraw from association with France and turn again to Britain for succor. By late 1810, the question of Canada's future suddenly was raised in St. Petersburg as a "card" to play in the ever-changing Russian, British, American and French relationship. That "card" was to re-surface from time to time as the century unfolded.

North America actually had been drawing the attention of the Russian court for some years already and had been a centerpiece of a major policy proposal in 1806. In that year, Alexander's Grand Chamberlain Nikolai P. Rezanov, son-in-law of the chief founder of the Russian American Company, Grigorii I. Shelekhov, was in Sitka planning to expand his country's holdings on the Pacific coast of North America. After visiting Spanish-held San Francisco for six weeks, he recommended to Rumiantsev, then the minister of commerce, that all of what is now California be "brought permanently under Russian control" by fortifying existing Russian America and strengthening its fleet. This must be done right away, during Alexander's reign, he urged, or "we will never accomplish it."[3]

Back in Europe, as Russia pulled away from France and towards Britain, London and Washington moved towards war. Britain's military deployments were even more widely dispersed than Russia's because it stood practically alone conducting campaigns against Napoleon around the world. Aggressively anti-British circles in the United States pushed for war, railing against British impressment and blockade policies. Moreover, they saw that British over-extension opened up a window of opportunity in Canada. From the Russian perspective, war between the United States and Britain over Canada was a potential disaster, for it could draw British troops and resources away from the European continent, where they were needed in the struggle against Napoleon.

America's declaration of war against Britain was issued on 18 June 1812, just six days before Napoleon invaded Russia without declaring war. Many Russian officials suspected collusion between the American and French governments, though little was said about it in public. The war atmosphere in the United States had been reported back to St. Petersburg in great detail by the Russian minister to Washington, A.Ya. Dashkov, and the consul-general in Philadelphia, N. Ya. Kozlov. They told of ringing calls for the annexation of Upper and Lower Canada and described proclamations and boasts from America's "War Hawks" that Canada would fall to American forces without resistance. High in the ranks of the Hawks were such luminaries as John C. Calhoun, who later became the Secretary of War, and Speaker of the House Henry Clay. Despatches to Russia exude a faint aura of puzzlement, for the Russian representatives noted also that the United States was not really prepared for the war its leaders were exhorting them to wage. A rush for territorial aggrandizement seemed to carry the day. In one letter filed in June 1813, Dashkov insisted that the American desire to acquire Canada was the only compelling reason for the war and cited speeches in Congress and newspaper rhetoric in support of this opinion. The neutrality issue was merely a pretext Dashkov concluded, insisting to Rumiantsev that "la disposition ostensible du gouvernement américain de s'agrandir dans ses possessions."[4]

Russian diplomats linked the urge to add Canada to a new American empire to the recent Louisiana Purchase (1803), which had relieved the United States of a possible armed dispute with France. On the other hand, subsequent American pressure on Spain to give up Florida pushed Washington and London to the brink of conflict by 1809-10, because an uprising against Napoleon in 1808 made Spanish rebels vital cogs in the British war effort. The expansionist mood in the U.S. Congress was exhilarating to American politicians and clearly posed a threat to Canada. This mood was relayed to St. Petersburg, where the relationship with France was beginning to pall.

Russian foreign policy advisers had some important decisions to make.

Rumiantsev urged Alexander to act as mediator in the British-American war of 1812.[5] The foreign minister had been informed by Kozlov that the aggressive rhetoric from American political leaders did not reflect the opinion of most Americans. Kozlov had written as well that the American volunteer army was small and that it was having trouble recruiting men for an invasion of Canada.[6] Kozlov's belief that America was not prepared for war and that the northeastern states, particularly, would quickly support a peaceful resolution to avoid crippling trade losses, and the expectation that Russia's commerce with the United States also would be brought to an end, were good reasons for St. Petersburg to facilitate peace efforts. Kozlov's suggestions were still being digested when Napoleon crossed into Russian territory in June 1812. Rumiantsev's long commitment to France cost him the tsar's confidence and by November Count Karl Robert Nesselrode had taken over the duties of foreign minister, a position he was to hold for most of the next half century (though Rumiantsev kept the title until February 1814). A German who began his service in Russia at the age of 16, Nesselrode's ties abroad were with Austria and Prussia, and he was also anxious to re-establish trade with Britain.

As it happened, the War of 1812 in North America did not prove fatal to the British war effort in Europe and, in fact, its results helped solidify British North America, at least in its opposition to annexationist inroads from the United States. The small force of about 5,000 British regulars had been strongly augmented by English and French Canadian militia units and Indian allies. With the British fleet patrolling the coast, "Canada" as the Russian diplomats defined it, successfully defend itself against the invaders. Kozlov kept the Russian foreign ministry informed of almost frantic American efforts to annex Canada before Napoleon was defeated.[7] By the time fighting in North America was stopped by the Treaty of Ghent in December 1814, Russian observers had learned an important strategic lesson. Britain could become overextended and therefore weakened in other parts of the world if deploying troops to Canada became a priority, but they would have to commit more soldiers than they did in 1812-1814 and the British fleet would have to be challenged effectively.

The immediate preoccupation of Russia's foreign ministry with the fate of Canada faded, in part because war and civil strife in Spain made that country less threatening to Russia's holdings on the Pacific coast of North America. Nevertheless, the activities of the Russian

American Company kept North American questions alive in St. Petersburg. The Company, which continued its bitter rivalry with the Hudson's Bay Company, was able to establish a trading post at Fort Ross (name taken from *Rossiia*), close to Mexican (Spanish) possessions in California, in 1812. The fort was dedicated in a religious and military ceremony at almost precisely the moment of Napoleon's march into Moscow. In light of Peter the Great's aggressive encouragement of Russian exploration of and expansion into the north Pacific Ocean and North American coast, the attitude of Alexander I in that regard would appear strikingly passive if one were not aware of his singular interest in Europe. Even the "Monroe Doctrine," promulgated in December 1823 to ward off any further European expansion in "the American continents," was not challenged by Russia though its interests in northwest America were then still large. One contentious issue was settled without much fuss when a Convention limiting Russia's holdings in Alaska to areas north of the 54° 40′ latitude was signed with the United States in April, 1824. The treaty included an agreement to recognize freedom of navigation on the Pacific Ocean. The next year an Anglo-Russian Treaty guaranteed British acceptance of the same boundary, leaving the borders of the Alaskan Panhandle open to question and eventually a matter of dispute between Canada and the United States. The American claim to that area was not finally accepted in Canada until 1903, after a tribunal (carefully stacked by the Americans and the British) yielded to the American position.

There was a subsequent, less direct, attempt to invite a Russian emperor to arbitrate a British-American territorial argument related to Canada's borders. In 1826 the American ambassador to London asked his Russian counterpart, Kh. A. Lieven, if Nicholas I might mediate in an issue related to fishing rights and borders. Nesselrode rejected the idea unequivocally, noting that Russia did not wish to strain its relationship with either side.[8] Russia's diplomats continued to monitor events in Canada, on the lookout for American expansionist tendencies.

During the mid-to late 1820s, for example, Baron F.P. de Maltitz, a Russian diplomat in Washington, kept Nesselrode informed of American legislation limiting commerce between the United States and Britain (and British colonies), making Canadian ports important as conduits for American goods. De Maltitz was able to acquire copies of petitions sent by Canadian Chambers of Commerce and merchants asking the British government to prohibit the import of any goods to the British Antilles from any port south of Halifax. St. Petersburg was thereby forewarned of new disputes looming on the North American horizon. Tensions within Canada were duly reported as well. De Maltitz enclosed copies of anti-government newspaper clippings as he relayed accounts of swelling strains between executives, legislatures and populations in the Canadas.[9]

Nowhere was St. Petersburg's interest in Canada more evident than when rebellions in Upper and Lower Canada in 1837-38 focused Russian attention on North America with an intensity no previous event had evoked. Tsar Nicholas I took a direct hand in the diplomatic manifestations for Russia of the rebellions, and in North America rumours of Russian meddling in Canadian domestic affairs were widely circulated for the first time. Contemporary sources as divergent as American newspapers, for example, the New York *Morning Herald* and the Washington *Chronicle*, the ambassador from France to the United States, and the partisan *Mackenzie's Gazette*[10] all insisted late in 1838 that Russia had helped finance the rebellions. Even American president Martin Van Buren was reported to have said that Russian funds were sustaining the rebels.[11]

T.R. Preston, a British visitor to Canada between 1837-1839, took up the refrain at some length in a two-volume memoir on political conditions in Canada. He quoted but did not name officials, newspapers, and rebels in devising a complex picture of Russian agents with "experience" in Circassia (Georgia), secretly funded societies, and diplomats, all involved in events in Canada. Acknowledging that Van Buren's government loudly trumpeted neutrality, Preston judged it "perfectly incompetent or unwilling to enforce even the semblance of neutrality."[12] He insisted that the majority of American politicians still wanted complete control of the entire North American continent, and that that ambition partly explained Russia's apparent involvement. Preston's findings were based mostly on hearsay. Still, his conclusion that there was "a strong degree of plausibility" of Russian involvement because the pattern in Canada was similar to Russia's activities elsewhere, especially in "British India," would have made sense to contemporary readers.[13]

Russian officials quickly denied the accusations of interference, but there is no doubt that at least some of the rebels were led to believe by their own leaders that Russian help was forthcoming. Dr. Robert Nelson, a founder of the secret organization of Patriotes established in the United States during the spring of 1838 to continue the struggle for the independence of Lower Canada, informed his associates that the Russian Consul in New York had promised funds.[14] He was probably the unnamed source referred to in *Mackenzie's Gazette* (June 1838), where it was claimed that Russia had decided to help the rebels. The Russian ambassador in Washington, A.A. Bodisco, posted a copy of this notice to St. Petersburg, at the same time calling rebel leader William Lyon Mackenzie "shameless" and capable of stooping to anything to achieve his goal. Bodisco, who had just taken up his position in 1837 and kept it until his death in 1854, was soon to be implicated in stories of Russian intrigue.

Later that year at the state trial held in Montreal, one of the accused rebels made a voluntary deposition describing Nelson as the chief fund raiser for the movement, having been sent to New York explicitly for that purpose. "On his return from New York," the deposition continued, "[Nelson] told us that he had an interview with the Russian Consul at New York, who had promised him assistance — that the Imperial Government of Russia would seize with pleasure this occasion to avenge in Canada the deep wounds which the Circassians, sustained by English money and engineers, had inflicted, he said, on the Muscovite armies."[15]

The statement made at the trial coincided with another item in *Mackenzie's Gazette*, on 10 November, charging that "a foreign mercantile house . . . is . . . the agent of the ambitious Nicholas [I] and every movement of the disorganization in society is affirmed to be directed from head quarters at St. Petersburg. . . . Russian gold is freely distributed all along the borders and Russian muskets are deposited by the thousands at convenient depots."[16] The meeting between rebel leaders and Russian diplomats was called mythical by later commentators. They were quite mistaken.

The Russian Consul in New York, E.I. Krehmer, had apprised St. Petersburg of serious unrest in Canada as early as October 1836, as did the Russian Consul in London, Count Charles André Pozzo di Borgo, a few months later. Krehmer never mentioned any meeting with Canadian rebels. In December 1837, Pozzo di Borgo informed Vice-Chancellor Nesselrode that the real aim of the Canadian rebels was independence from Britain. Bodisco filed a similar report in January 1838. The tsar, worried about confrontation with Britain in the Caucasus, clearly was pondering the significance of events in Canada. Preparing for a Caucasus campaign that same month, he wrote Field Marshall Prince I.F. Paskievich (Paskiewicz) that they would have to "wait and see what will happen with the rebellion in Canada."[17]

At that time, the British and the Russians were competing for influence in Constantinople and were hovering on the brink of war in the Black Sea and the South Caucasus. Any circumstance that might sap

British military strength was therefore encouraging to the Russian court. Remembering the lessons offered by the War of 1812, Nicholas recognized that Britain's ability to move against Russia would be compromised by the need to maintain troops in Canada. He told his Minister of Marine, Admiral Prince A.S. Menshikov, and Paskievich that, according to Pozzo, Britain had few troops available to contribute to an expected British-French assault on the Dardanelles and Constantinople: "Whatever England and France do, we are prepared." Pozzo's report confirmed that there are "only up to 40,000 troops in England, more are either in North America or do not exist." Confident that Russia's interests were safe on the Black Sea, he ordered troops into Moldavia and Wallachia.[18] A Russian attempt to manipulate events in Canada to raise the odds in their favour elsewhere should not have surprised anyone.

More to the point perhaps was Russia's re-establishment of good economic relations with the United States in 1832 by dint of a Russian-American Commercial Treaty. The Russians had for some time hoped to use America as a diplomatic and strategic counter to the predominance of Great Britain at sea, especially at the time of the Russo-Turkish War, 1828-29. They were encouraged to look to Washington for diplomatic support when, in contrast to actions undertaken by the French and the British, the United States government did not lodge official protests against Russia's ruthless repression of Polish insurgents in 1830-31.[19]

The "Eastern Question" had taken a new turn in the 1830s, leaving Russia and Britain suspended in a state of mutual hostility and suspicion over the fate of the Turkish empire. The Russian emperor and his diplomatic corps on several occasions tried to accommodate British concerns, with little success. Their relations grew even more tense after 24 November 1836 when a British schooner, the *Vixen*, was caught trying to run a Russian blockade and deliver arms to rebellious tribes in the Caucasus.[20] These are the events to which Robert Nelson claimed that the Russian representative in New York referred. *Mackenzie's Gazette*, which kept readers posted on Russian adventures in Poland and Transcaucasia, and England's reaction to them, carried a feature article on the *Vixen* in 1838 claiming that it was the British who did not wish "to hazard a rupture with Russia."[21] At any rate, it was obvious that by 1838 anything that might draw British troops to North America, and away from the Black Sea and the Dardanelles, would be very helpful to Russia.

The advantage to Russia of rebellions in Canada was such that when the new United States Minister to Russia, George Mifflin Dallas, was first presented to the tsar on 6 August 1837 the Russian ruler almost immediately inquired about the "disturbances in Canada." Astonishingly for a Russian autocrat, he went on to express the opinion that, in Dallas's words, "when a government became oppressive, and forgot the tender care to which a colony was entitled, she justified resistance and separatism." Almost exactly a month later, the Grand Duchess Yelena, wife of the Grand Duke Mikhail Pavlovich, asked Dallas about the possibility of Canada being annexed to the United States.[22] Obviously, the Canada question was again a topic of conversation at the Russian court.

To the extent that they were recorded in his diary, the American's responses were ambiguous. In August 1837, he replied to Nicholas that Canadians were not "energetic or united enough" to seek independence from England. A few months later Dallas changed his tune, warning a diplomat from London at the Russian court that the "character of the Canadian population" might lead to a much more prolonged conflict than the Englishman seemed to expect.[23]

The tsar's remarks justifying resistance must have been a diplomatic nod to the common interest held by Russia and the United States in the future in Canada. Nicholas was, in fact, far better known for his intense dislike of rebellion than he was for justifying resistance to tyranny. His reputation as the "Gendarme of Europe" was a manifestation of his willingness to help other rulers battle insurgents and of his vindictive reaction against any outbreak within his own domain. The Convention of Berlin, a secret agreement signed by Russia, Austria and Prussia in 1833 "to strengthen the conservative system" in Europe, serves as testimony to the tsar's desire that the existing order in Europe be preserved.[24]

Defence of the status quo signified much the same to Nicholas I as it had to Karamzin. They defended legitimism, which in theory meant that republicanism in Switzerland and autocracy in Russia both deserved to remain intact. When push came to shove, however, Russia's national interest as Nicholas saw it took priority over any philosophical inclination against rebellion and explained the tsar's support of the Greek uprising against Turkey in 1828-29. Reviling the Greeks "as revolted subjects,"[25] Nicholas went to war anyway in expectation of reaping huge strategic and territorial benefits at the expense of Turkey. In the case of the Canadas, though Nicholas complained to his brother in February 1837 that "the English continue to growl at us,"[26] his diplomatic behaviour was much more circumspect and typical than his remarks to ambassador Dallas. In December that year Nesselrode instructed Pozzo di Borgo to inform the British government that "the sincere wish of the emperor" was that rebellion in Canada would be brought to a "quick and decisive end" and that respect for law and the "power of Queen Victoria" be renewed.[27]

Barely a month later, on 31 January 1838, Nicholas again told Dallas that the Canadian colonists were right to resist oppressive and unjust treatment. He recognized the names of Louis Papineau, George Brown, William Lyon Mackenzie, and Robert Nelson. The tsar had been thoroughly briefed on recent discussions Nesselrode had conducted with the American representative, who made it plain but unofficial that he thought England should consent to the separation and independence of Canada. While revealing his Canadian card to the American ambassador, fully aware that his remarks would be reported in Washington, Nicholas still avoided commitment by adding that Russia had no interest in the "misfortunes of other countries" even when those misfortunes offered Russia an advantage. To the American's observation that if Canada separated from Britain, Russia might be able to replace Canada as a supplier of timber to the English fleet, Nicholas replied that, "she might, but perhaps not of such good quality, nor as cheap."[28]

Privately, the Russian tsar was of two minds. Two weeks after his comment to Paskievich about the dearth of British troops for deployment to the Black Sea, he wrote again that the "circumstances in Canada are still not clarified, but the sending of [British] troops [to Canada] shows that it is an important matter; 7,000 men for England is the equivalent of 70,000 for us — and that many fewer to oppose us!"[29] Obviously, when he reiterated his startling support of rebellion to Dallas at the end of that month, he had concluded as he did earlier on the Greek situation that circumstances in Canada could provide Russia with a strategic edge in its, to date, cold war with Britain. It was also to Paskievich that Nicholas continued to re-affirm his passionate dislike for revolution, referring to it in 1841 as a "diabolical spirit, which tries to overthrow everything."[30] Paskievich certainly was the person in whom to confide on such matters: he had been a successful commander in the Caucasus Wars of 1827 and defeated the Polish rebels in 1831. As Viceroy of Poland for the next twenty-four years, with the title Prince of Warsaw, Paskievich administered and worked hard to russify the Polish kingdom.

Doubtless, the Canadian rebels knew that Russia hoped to distract the British from the Caucasus. This was obvious enough from the pages of *Mackenzie's Gazette*. In addition to a number of short notices on British/Russian haggling, there were longer pieces: for example, the June 1838 article "Russia and Circassia" described how the

English were trying to smuggle arms to a potential army of 300,000 Circassians so that they might fight Russians, and in November documents from France reported that an English-Russian war "cannot much longer be deferred."[31]

Russia's lively interest in Canada's crisis heightened in November 1838, when officials in Montreal arrested and briefly detained the Russian Consul in Boston, P.A. Kielchen (Kil'khen in Russian). Kielchen had come to retrieve his wife and two daughters who were living in Montreal for the purpose of their children's education. He planned to leave his son, Peter, to finish his schooling. In a letter to his wife in November, Kielchen had written: "The accounts from Canada are again alarming; there appears to be so much trouble and agitation in store for the winter that I can no longer subdue my uneasiness about you." Kielchen asked her to prepare for departure on very short notice. He feared the "danger of detention by the marauding parties who infest that part of the country [from St. John's to Burlington] at present."[32]

One can assume from his arrest that officials in Lower Canada expected clandestine Russian consular involvement in their internal affairs. *Mackenzie's Gazette* and T.R. Preston, who detested the "notorious Mackenzie," agreed on this one matter. Both were quick to proclaim that Kielchen had ulterior motives for his trip to Montreal.[33]

This potentially explosive situation, especially in light of the *Vixen* crisis, remained a point of contention between Russia and Britain for months. Kielchen's written authorization to visit Canada from the British vice consul for the State of Massachusetts notwithstanding, his wife's house was surrounded by police and his private papers were seized. Even though he was released within a few days, a flurry of despatches between Bodisco, Nesselrode and Pozzo di Borgo illustrated the seriousness with which Russian diplomats treated the incident.[34] Bodisco was quick to blame a Polish "adventurer" for telling officials in Montreal that Kielchen was intervening in Canadian affairs. In their turn, authorities in Canada saw the matter as a test of their efficiency. In a rather lame letter of apology written on Sir John Colborne's behalf by C.N. Ogden, Attorney General in Montreal, the Canadian official insisted to Kielchen that their "suspicions" were "fully justified." They were exercising "the same vigilance which under corresponding circumstances, would be justly exerted in any country in Europe."[35]

Although no evidence has been found to implicate Kielchen, there is little mystery why he was regarded with such suspicion. It is clear from Bodisco's missives to St. Petersburg that the Russian diplomatic corps hoped to see the situation in Canada deteriorate further. They saw little likelihood of official American intervention, Bodisco having written in July that Washington was no longer interested in annexation. Among other things, he had been told by the Secretary of State that the addition of Canadian territory would cause a great imbalance in the Union itself. The full text of President Van Buren's proclamation on American neutrality in the dispute and copies of a warning that his government would not come to the assistance of American citizens caught meddling in Canadian affairs were hurried to St. Petersburg in November. Sporadic raids and harassment of commerce by private groups were inevitable, however. Diplomatic despatches mentioning William (Bill) Johnson's forays carried an image of him and his activities quite at odds with the heroic tales borne by the popular press: in Bodisco's reports Johnson was a "brigand" leading insurrectionists of Canadian, American and Polish citizenship, who deserved his capture and ultimate fate. American official unease over border demarcation disputes stirred up by Canadian rebels and their friends in the United States, including the governor of Maine who was threatening to redraw the border between his state and New Brunswick, was such that Russia refused even to discuss the renewal of the 1824 Convention with Dallas.[36]

Information on events in Canada and the level of support for the rebels from segments of the American population was relayed to Russia in great detail. In December 1838, for example, Nesselrode was informed that habeas corpus had been waived, the Canadian press was loudly protesting martial law, several French judges had been dismissed from their posts, and the jury system in Canada was suspended. More significantly for St. Petersburg, Bodisco reported that American citizens were planning to invade Canada, compelling the British to deploy still more troops to North America.[37] Shortly after these reports arrived in the Russian capital, the emperor took a personal hand in the Kielchen affair. On 21 February 1839, Nesselrode wrote his agent in London that: "our Auguste Master, [Nicholas I] . . . has taken into consideration that in an epoch when our two governments intend to strengthen the harmonious relations which exist between them, by means of the most frank and amicable discussions, . . . obviously he must doubly regret that so natural a thing as a trip by an agent of Russia [Kielchen] to visit his family in the main city of Lower Canada would give offence to the local authorities." On the other hand, "His Majesty" recognized the necessity of such actions: he would expect similar "vigilance" on the part of his own officials in rebellious Poland. Nesselrode asked Pozzo di Borgo to inform

Palmerston of the tsar's standpoint. The Russians, then, took exactly the position represented in Ogden's letter to Kielchen. On that same day, the Russian Foreign Minister also wrote Bodisco and cautioned him in much less diplomatic language that "Mr. Kielchen and our other consular agents in the United States must use the greatest circumspection in their language and their conduct."[38]

Pozzo di Borgo promptly met with Palmerston and, after a "very serious" conversation, pointed out that his emperor had been at first inclined to require a public apology but in his wisdom requested only an "unofficial and friendly explication." Palmerston was reported to have appreciated the gesture and promised to convey his displeasure "with the injustice and hastiness of the conduct by authorities in Canada," asking in return only that if an Englishman was ever to be found in a similar situation that the Russians would treat him "with the same moderation."[39] There were no serious diplomatic repercussions from this event and the door was now open to a Russian-British accommodation.

Meanwhile, in December 1838, after several times telling Nesselrode that he did not know the source of the rumour that Russia had decided to help the rebels, Bodisco finally admitted that it had been he, and not Krehmer in New York, who invited Papineau and Robert Nelson into his home. The meeting had been arranged on 9 December by John L. O'Sullivan, editor of the *Democratic Review*, mouthpiece of a very aggressive American expansionism, and Henry D. Gilpen, whom Bodisco called "le confident intime du Président." At that time Gilpen was U.S. District Attorney for Eastern Pennsylvania, a post he took in 1831 after his political patron left to become a U.S. Senator. That patron was none other than Dallas, who at the time of Bodisco's session with the Canadian rebels was the American ambassador in St. Petersburg. Links between Dallas and the American "Hawks" help explain the unusual observations on the efficacy of rebellion offered him by Nicholas I.

Bodisco agreed that the British themselves were supporting rebels everywhere in the world and that such deeds needed avenging, but insisted to Nesselrode that he had qualified his response to O'Sullivan as follows: "We are at peace with England and interference in its troubles in Canada would be contrary to this principle line of behaviour." Diplomatic propriety out of the way, Bodisco then told O'Sullivan that he would be at home each morning if Papineau and Nelson still wished to see him. They showed up the next day.[40] Speaking "with animation," Mackenzie provided Bodisco with an historical account of the situation in Lower Canada. "According to [Mackenzie] systematic

oppression by the British government" had caused "implacable
hatred for the English on the part of the more than 600,000 Canadians
of French origin." Nelson confirmed this opinion, adding that the
British had no support in Canada other than its army.[41] Bodisco ack-
owledged the partisan nature of such accounts, yet was well aware
that the British were vulnerable in North America. He noted that
whereas Papineau and Nelson seemed not to have "established relations with the revolutionary French [in France], they count mostly on
the sympathy of Americans." Russian diplomats now had a Canada
card to play in their own negotiations with Britain, as Nicholas I's
quid pro quo offer in the Kielchen matter made clear.

It was on the basis of the meeting with Bodisco that Nelson claimed
that Russian assistance was forthcoming, the Russian envoy's subsequent denial to Nesselrode notwithstanding. A misunderstanding
was possible, but it is more likely that either Nelson or Bodisco was
lying — or that they both exaggerated for strategic reasons. Given the
time that it took to relay information between North America and St.
Petersburg (usually about a month), Bodisco would have had to make
some kind of commitment, no matter how vague, if he wished to keep
Russia's stake in the Canadian affair alive. But he could not afford to
admit such indiscretion later, after the tsar changed the rules of the
game. In November 1838, the level of tension between Russia and
Britain had risen to the extent that Dallas wrote in his diary that the
two countries were poised on the brink of war, that "Russia would re-
excite the Canadians," and that his own country would be drawn into
the conflict politically. This turn of events would hand the United
States an opportunity to settle both the northeast and the northwest
boundary questions in its favour.[42] Dallas thus exposed the American
interest in pitting Russia and Britain against each other in North
America. In the end, the American ambassador's prognostications
proved to be wishful thinking. The Russians were not to be drawn in.
Moreover, according to Bodisco, the United States was enmeshed in
political deadlock and was in no position to wage war anyway. The
issue of annexation would not fade away, of course. A few years later
Bodisco reported conversations with members of a new generation of
American Hawks who promised to "wage a war of extermination"
against Loyalists in Canada if Britain were to grant independence.[43]

Nesselrode was adamant in communications with Russia's representatives in London and Washington in February and March, 1839,
that they must not appear to be meddling in British affairs in Canada.
His despatch to Bodisco was unusually stiff, reproving the diplomat
for exceeding his authority and doubtlessly misleading the rebels into

thinking that Russia might help them. This letter was seen by Nicholas I, who endorsed its reproving tone with a terse "so be it." By that time, the relationship between Russia and Britain had begun to change for the better. Nesselrode had been especially concerned because he knew that British foreign secretary Palmerston had held discussions with Prince Adam Jerzy Czartoryski, a prominent leader of the Polish rebels against Russia in 1830.[44] The Russians knew Czartoryski well. Boyhood friend and member of Alexander I's Unofficial Committee of advisers, the Pole had served as Russian foreign minister from 1804 to 1806. Czartoryski was instrumental in creating a constitutional regime for the Kingdom of Poland in 1815, with Alexander as its king. When Polish nationalists rebelled against Alexander's successor in 1831, he served as head of a Polish court in exile in Paris and lobbied for support among Europe's leading statesman and royalty. The Russian court recognized in Czartoryski a dangerous and influential opponent. London and St. Petersburg now both had a rebel "card" out on the table.

The Russian foreign ministry was worried as well about a delegation from Egypt that, from December 1838 to April 1839, actively negotiated in London for help in a new war against the Ottoman Empire. Nesselrode did not want the British retaliating against Russia by offering support to émigrés in the struggle for Polish independence, or by making special arrangements with the Egyptians.

Though his peek into the future turned out to be mistaken, Dallas had good reason to believe in the likelihood of open hostilities between Russia and Britain. War had been a real possibility since the mid-1830s. Their strategic interests had reached world-wide proportions, clashing in Asia, the Near East, and on the Pacific coast of North America. Economic competition between them intensified and national pride, fueled by Britain's remarkable economic expansion and Russia's unbroken string of military victories since 1812, gave their leaderships a sense of invincibility and destiny. Influential officials in both imperial centres urged their governments to act aggressively against threat, real or perceived. The Russian Minister of Finance, Count E.F. Kankrin, for example, so disliked England that he sponsored prohibitive tariffs against British goods.[45] The nationalist military commander in the Near East, Count Alexei Orlov, predicted war with England in 1836 and exhorted the tsar to prepare for it.

But Nesselrode was an Anglophile.[46] In 1836, he ignored Orlov and Kankrin and persuaded Nicholas to reduce the tariffs set against British goods. The next year he worked closely with the British ambassador to St. Petersburg, Lord Durham, to smooth over the *Vixen*

affair. It was finally settled in May, 1837, in the face of a furious public clamour for revenge in England and an organized campaign by the
commander of Russia's Black Sea Fleet to claim the schooner as a
prize of war.[47] In short, Dallas's subtle hope that the British might be
over-extended as a result of Russia's activitieas, enabling the United
States to avail itself of an undefended Canadian border, was doomed
to disappointment well before he expressed it. But the English attitude towards Russia continued to puzzle Nicholas. In November
1838, precisely when Dallas thought that England and Russia were
poised for war, Nicholas complained to Paskievich that "in England it
is said that they are strengthening their shores against us! What
idiots! As their affairs in America continue to deteriorate, it would be
wiser of them to clean up this matter, or else they will suffer forever
by losing Canada."[48] Less than a year later, Russia and Britain
reached a modus vivendi, for which Nicholas I was personally
responsible. His eldest son, Grand Duke Alexander Nikolaevich,
enjoyed a successful visit to London in May of that year and Nicholas
offered to work closely with the British in resolving a new crisis in the
Near East.

On the other hand, Nicholas informed Paskievich that the visit in

Like Nesselrode, Nicholas respected England and this respect was
magnified by his distaste for France's Louis Philippe. Not trusting
France, Nicholas ignored the opinions of his advisers and decided to
negotiate with England. He believed that country to be founded on
legal principles and institutions and therefore worthy of Russia's
friendship. Louis Philippe's revolutionary government, based on
what he believed were illegal principles and institutions, was not.[49]
His anger against Louis Philippe for the European crisis of 1830 was
rekindled in 1838-39 when Belgian independence finally was agreed
upon at the expense of King William II of the Netherlands, who happened to be Nicholas' brother-in-law. Having taken the initiative
away from his diplomats, Nicholas was relieved and delighted by the
success of his son's tour of England. The twenty-one year-old heir to
the Romanov throne was treated "with great indulgence," Nicholas
wrote his sister. "Everyone is receiving him with incredibly kind
attentions . . . . I thank God to have inspired me to demand that my
son go to England . . . against the unanimous advice" of everyone but
his own wife and son.[50] Pozzo di Borgo reported that the Grand Duke
Alexander's tour had a "magical" political effect on London. All political and most press attacks on Russia ceased while he was there.[51]

On the other hand, Nicholas informed Paskievich that the visit in
October 1839 to London of Baron F.I. Brunnov, a diplomat charged with
offering an accord on the Eastern Question in return for guarantees of

Russia's interests in the Straits connecting the Black Sea to the Mediterranean, had not been a complete success. Several issues were left unsettled, Brunnov informed Nesselrode, while congratulating himself for at least "opening the eyes of England to our position and stimulating the dissatisfaction between it and France."[52] The emmisary had risked diplomatic censure by raising directly with Palmerston the question of "rumours" that Russia was involved in Canadian affairs. According to another secret despatch to Nesselrode, dated 24 August 1839, Palmerston then read from a confidential letter stating categorically that Russia was funding Papineau. They were assisted in this conspiracy by the Prussians, who were providing military advice to the rebels. Palmerston refused to divulge the letter-writer's name and made it obvious that the British government believed the accounts. Brunnov claimed that he had been able to dissuade Palmerston of such "absurdities."[53] He must have been right. In November, Nicholas wrote more encouragingly to Paskievich that "we are managing very well with the English and it seems that they are arguing with the French about it," and in December he said that he would like nothing better than a successful treaty with England.[54]

The upshot of the tsar's patience was the Treaty of London, 15 July 1840, in which Russia, Great Britain, Austria and Prussia collectively imposed a settlement on Egypt, again saving the Ottoman Empire. France had little choice but to join the group a year later in a Straits Convention (13 July 1841). Among other things, the Convention closed the Bosphorus and Dardanelles to foreign warships during times of peace. Russia's special interest in the Black Sea and its potential for influencing affairs in Turkey were again assured. At least for awhile, the fate of Canada once again became irrelevant in St. Petersburg.

There were other strands to the intricate web of Russian diplomacy involving Canada. The fact that John George Lambton, 1st Earl of Durham, was sent to Canada in May 1838 to find a solution to its troubles may also have been instrumental in shaping the new Russian-British relationship. Durham had been British ambassador to St. Petersburg in 1832, and again in 1835-37. While in Russia he grew to admire Nicholas I, who in his turn appreciated Durham to the extent that he appointed him to the Order of St. Andrew in 1837, a quite unusual act. England's King William IV wrote at one time that Durham "really appears to forget that [he] is the servant of His Britannic Majesty and not of the Emperor of Russia."[55] Earlier, Brunnov had written Nesselrode that, "When Lord Durham went to Russia as ambassador from Great Britain, he was filled with dislike for Russia and hostility towards the ruler Nicholas. On leaving his post after three years, he was an ardent defender of the Ruler." On another occasion, Brunnov claimed that "all the Durhams are Russians."[56]

Durham did take a hand in nurturing the British relationship with Russia. In October 1839, it was he who persuaded Brunnov to raise the question of Canada with Palmerston: "Durham did not fail to give me new evidence of his goodwill towards us and revealed to me spontaneously a fact which, in his opinion, will contribute to stimulate the distrust of the English government towards us and impede the rapprochement between the two countries that, on our part, has been always our main priority," the Russian envoy apprized Nesselrode. Durham, who worked very hard to facilitate Brunnov's mission, had referred to the letter that Palmerston eventually read to Brunnov.[57]

Bodisco kept his ministry well informed of Durham's activities in Canada, noting the "remarkably conciliatory tone" of his proclamations. The Russian diplomat detailed Durham's organizational plans for Canada, above all the advantages of a federation that would include the two Canadas, New Brunswick, Nova Scotia and Newfoundland. He especially noted anger in the United States at Durham's apparent plan to "raise French Canadians up to the same level as the English." Durham's recall and the harm the politics of his angry resignation might do to Canada, were all treated thoroughly and with evident sympathy.[58]

The connection between Durham and the Russians certainly was not lost on the Canadian rebels. *Mackenzie's Gazette* commonly referred to Durham as "young Nick" and in September 1838 condemned him for using dictatorial "processes so familiar to [him] since his visit to St. Petersburg." Segments of the mainstream American press also blamed the crisis in Canada on "Russian politics and money." Stories such as these were all dutifully forwarded to St. Petersburg in Bodisco's despatches.[59] Paradoxically, Nicholas was later reported to have said that he would like to hang Durham "with his own hands" for proposing responsible government in Canada,[60] a statement that well-illustrated the opportunism of the tsar's earlier remarks to American ambassador Dallas.

When a paper on the possibility of Russian interference in Canada commissioned by the British minister in Washington was submitted in July 1839, no action was taken on its judgement that the Russian government was engaged "in a criminal conspiracy against the British Crown" in Canada.[61] British authorities and their representatives in Canada arrived at the conclusion, for public consumption at least, that the stories about Russian involvement were either exaggerated or deliberately disseminated by American provocateurs. The actual extent to which Russian diplomatic personnel might have been meddling in North American politics was signalled by the tone of another, very strongly worded, memorandum to Bodisco from Nesselrode in October 1840. Implying that his officials still were still not behaving with enough "circumspection," Nesselrode ordered the envoy to stress Russia's neutrality in regards to any further unrest in Canada. The intriguing diplomatic story ended there.

The long standing Siberian and Pacific connection provides yet another key to understanding the quick deflation of official Russian concern for the potential for rebellion in Canada in the late 1830s. The trade accord reached between Russia and the United States in the 1820s had become strained by 1838 as the Russians tried to prevent Americans from trading with the native peoples of Russian North America. Russian merchants with business in the Pacific were again worried about American expansionism and, as their lobby's profile grew in St. Petersburg, the Russian American Company began to agitate for a settlement with the Hudson's Bay Company.

Discussions in February 1839 between George Simpson, governor of the Hudson's Bay Company's holdings in North America, and Baron Ferdinand Wrangel, a director of the Russian American Company, were to have long-term significance for Russian-Canadian associations. The agreement signed by them that month benefitted both organizations.[62] The Hudson's Bay group leased the entire Alaskan panhandle for a ten-year term for a fixed payment in otter pelts and became the provisioners of food and other supplies to the Russian company's administrative headquarters in Novo Archangel'sk, on Sitka Island. The two companies agreed to combine their efforts against Americans in the fur trade. After the arrangement was reached, the working relationship between the two companies improved to the extent that Simpson visited Novo Archangel'sk regularly and even made a spectacular journey from Alaska to St. Petersburg by sled and carriage in 1841-42.[63] Wrangel, who was appointed governor of Russian America in 1840, and Simpson became close friends; Simpson was the Hudson's Bay Company's governor in North America from 1826 to 1860.

In the long run, the great significance of the 1839 agreement, which divided the operations of the two companies into what we would now call "spheres of influence," might be that it helped prevent American control of the entire Pacific Northwest coast south of Alaska. This consequence was noted at the time by Bodisco, who warned his superiors in St. Petersburg that, by opting to accommodate the British in this matter and within a few years liquidating the Russian American Company holdings in California, Russia was encouraging America be more aggressive in the region.[64] The Americans will be angered, he warned Nesselrode. The region that became a province of Canada as British Columbia in 1871, just four years after the sale of Alaska to the United States and Canadian Confederation, had been part of the Hudson's Bay Company's "sphere."

There had been worry in St. Petersburg about the possibility of new British expeditions to discover the northwest passage, just as Russians had been seeking a northeast route since the 16th century. In 1837, I.F. Kruzenshtern, by this time a Vice Admiral, proposed and supported strongly a Russian expedition to make the discovery first. The purpose of the venture, he wrote the Admiralty in St. Petersburg, would be to map the Arctic waterway, compile astronomical readings, and bring "glory to Russia's naval officers." The expedition was approved in 1838 under Wrangel's administrative leadership. This was not a time to engage Britain in dispute, especially one with potential military ramifications.[65]

Diminishing chances of conflict between Britain and the United States in North America and tenuous accommodation between Russia and Britain in the North Pacific, both with Canada in the middle, did not mean that Russian diplomats in Washington stopped watching events unfold north of the border. The arrest of Canadian Alexander McLeod by American authorities in 1840 and his subsequent indictment for burning the United States steamer *Caroline* in December 1837, caused some excitement in St. Petersburg. Because the *Caroline* was smuggling arms to Canadian rebels, it was considered fair game in London, and because McLeod claimed to have been somewhere else when the event in question took place the British minister in Washington demanded his immediate release.

Political disputation on this and other issues in the United States, continuing bloodshed and border raids in Canada, and even the moderate approach taken by Lord Sydenham (Charles Poulett Thomson), Lord Durham's replacement as Governor General, were the stuff of Bodisco's reports in 1841. Still, the Mcleod affair was the subject to which he kept returning. In one missive from his superior Bodisco was told that the Mcleod business "made a deep impression on the spirit of the Emperor" who hoped that a peaceful resolution could be found. The tsar could not remain indifferent to the prospects of war in North America, for it would again impede commercial relations between North America and Europe. Bodisco was instructed to pass on the tsar's "words of peace and conciliation" directly to the American president.[66] It is not clear from this particular message if the ministry was again putting the tsar forward as mediator. At any rate, McLeod's eventual acquittal came as a relief to the Russian court.

As Canada moved towards Confederation, Russia's presence in North America dimmed. Indeed, the British North America Act and the purchase of Alaska from Russia by the United States almost coincided. Both were agreed formally in March 1867, though Canada's official day of Confederation was set at 1 July. Among other things, that sale spelled the end of the long contest between the Russian American Company and the Hudson's Bay Company, a competition that had been ameliorated significantly by the agreement of 1839, but not entirely curbed. From the Russian perspective, the sale of Alaska was a relief. The lucrative fur trade had been reduced to a trickle by indiscriminate slaughter of the sea-otter and Alaska was not then seen to have any great strategic value.

The Russian ambassador in Washington had been instructed to negotiate the sale already in 1857, and the Russian American Company's charter expired and was not renewed in 1862. The sale of Alaska finalized the Company's retreat from North America. Because there was strong opposition to the purchase in the United States, mostly due to its $7 million price tag, the Russian government even paid money to newspaper editors and congressmen to influence the vote on ratification — and Secretary of State William H. Seward became famous forever as architect of "Seward's Folly." In light of the Russian American Company's incorporation in 1798 precisely to make Russia master of commerce, settlement and religious proselytizing "on the American mainland to the northeast [of Russia] and on the Aleutian and Kuril islands, and in the North Pacific Ocean, which belong to Russia by right of discovery," it could be said that the enterprise had been a spectacular failure.[67]

Though the Russian American Company had issued shares and conducted wide ranging business ventures, it was above all an agency of the Russian government. Its three charters (1799, 1821, and 1841) had granted the Company a monopoly on commerce in the Aleutian, Kuril and other Pacific islands, and it had been in charge of settlement there and on the west coast of North America. It also had the right to develop trade with Japan and China, and claim protection from the Imperial Russian Navy. The fact that the Tsar was the Company's patron and major share holder ensured such protection. The official demise of the Company in 1868 left only the Orthodox Church as an active agent of Russia on the Pacific coast of North America.

The American purchase also checked whatever ambition the Hudson's Bay Company had in Alaska, where its ships now had to recognise American port authorities. Some Canadian organisations began to worry about the Alaskan Purchase as part of a broader American design on British Columbia, with Russian support.[68] As insurance against such an eventuality and even before Confederation year was out, the Canadian government petitioned Britain to transfer both Rupert's Land and the Northwest Territory from the Hudson's Bay Company to Canada. By 1870 this had been done.

It was not until after the turn of the century that Canada would achieve some autonomy in foreign affairs. A Canadian Department of External Affairs was established in 1909, but in the big questions of international affairs it was still very much a colony.[69] That is not to say that direct contacts between Canada and Russia were not being made, or that mutual public interest was absent. Well before the sale of Alaska, there were international situations in which the Canadian government participated with Britain in opposition to Russia's interests. Quite a few Canadians had urged their government to send armed forces to help the British against Russia during the Crimean War, 1854-1856, a conflict that spread after a Russian-Turkish war in 1853 over control of the Black Sea. At that time, there was a flurry of voluntary militia activity in Anglophone Canada, and the small port at Esquimalt on Vancouver Island was used by the British Admiralty as a way station for its limited war with Russia in the Pacific. On that coast, Governor James Douglas offered to arm and lead Indians against Russian trading posts, "if only the order came."[70] There was a public call in Montreal to raise Canadian land forces to help the British fleet conquer and annex Russian America, and the famous Nova Scotian politician and journalist, Joseph Howe, actively recruited Canadians and, illegally, Americans to fight against the Russians. In December 1854, the British Parliament adopted the Foreign Enlistment Act, allowing foreigners to sign up against Russia. But American neutrality laws countered the act for U.S. citizens. Howe recruited them in the guise of railway workers. His contemporary friends worried that in recruiting forays to American cities, there were "Russian agents and Russian sympathizers all round him."[71]

The Crimean War was the first to be covered by war correspondents, who roused the public in both Europe and North America. The seige of Sevastopol, a name virtually unknown in North America before the war, took two long years and cost thousands of British and French lives, long enough for a hatred and fear of Russia to be nurtured by inflammatory journalism.[72] In Canada, tales of tsarist plots against British domination of the seas and threats to Canada's coast-lines were believed. The "Russian Bear" and above all the iniquities of tsardom were caricatured in the Canadian press in the style of Britain's *Punch* magazine, and suspicions were raised against immi-grants or visitors from the Russian Empire. Several small towns in Ontario were named after battle sites in the Black Sea region, and in 1857 Aleksandr Lakier wrote rather wistfully of seeing Russian can-non on display in Montreal as war prizes ("our eagles, which came to earth so far from their native land . . ."). Typically, of course, there were Canadians who saw a renewed threat from the south as well.

Although the war was confined mostly to the Crimean peninsula on the Black Sea, British and French flotillas attacked the Russian naval base at Petropavlovsk in Kamchatka in consecutive years, and also engaged Russian American Company and Russian navy vessels. Russia responded by occupying the Amur Basin, Maritime Territories, and the northern half of Sakhalin Island with troops, ensuring that competition would intensify in the North Pacific between the British, Russians, Americans, and later the Japanese. Interestingly, an appen-dix to the Russian American Company and the Hudson's Bay Company contract of 1839 had included a tacit agreement that their territorial holdings would be regarded as neutral during any conflict between Russia and Britain and, for the most part, this was adhered to in the Crimean War.[73] Indeed, from that time until the American purchase of Alaska, the two great trading companies colluded to maintain the commercial status quo even in the face of what officials in St. Peterburg believed was a serious British effort to grab the Russian coastal strip south of Alaska and join it to Canada.[74]

Neutrality agreement or not, the Crimean War had made the "Russian threat" a reality for employees of the Hudson's Bay Company, as well as for other merchants and inhabitants of British Columbia. British warships were refitted and recoaled at Esquimalt, where a temporary hospital was built to provide for wounded British seamen. The navy presence was therefore established, not so much against danger from the United States as had often been predicted, but against Russia.[75] Interestingly, the resilience of the American men-ace to Canada's west coast was corroborated in St. Petersburg by Russian observers in the late 1850s. Captain A.I. Shestakov, whose presence in New York was described in the first chapter of this vol-ume, reported to the Admiralty that strong expansionist tendencies were characteristic of the United States. The Monroe Doctrine, "or the dogma of 'manifest destiny'," represents a "cynicism" common even to the youngest generation in that country, he said, "fed to them with their mother's milk." For that reason, America poses a great threat to the Russian colonies of North America and "defence against it is impossible."[76] British North American holdings on the Pacific may have been in less danger than Shestakov believed because of the powerful British fleet, but the primal urge of American expansionism was clear to everyone.

Seriously weakened and humiliated by its embarrassing performance in the Crimean War, briefly leaderless on the death of Tsar Nicholas I in 1855, and caught up in sweeping domestic reform throughout the early 1860s, Russia was both vulnerable and temporarily isolated. Canada's own rapid movement towards political integration kept it looking inward as well. At any rate, as we have seen, the sale of Alaska brought closure to one chapter of British-Russia competition off Canada's western coastline and, geographically at least, cut Russia and Canada off from each other at least for the time being.

Trepidation about American ambitions on the Pacific notwithstanding, the potential for war between Russia and Britain resurfaced as a pressing danger in the late 1870s when Prime Minister Disraeli sent the British Mediterranean fleet through the Dardanelles to help defend Turkey against advancing Russian troops. Russia had defeated Turkey again in 1877 and by the Treaty of San Stefano forced the Ottomans to relinguish large parts of their Balkan and Black Sea empire. Western European countries, which themselves had no special liking for Turkey, combined to keep Russia out of southeastern Europe by forcing changes in the Treaty at a Congress held in Berlin, June 1878. This ad hoc 'solution' to Russian expansionism had a familiar ring to it in Europe. The government in Ottawa paid attention as well, for in contrast to the period of the Crimean War, Canada now stretched from ocean to ocean and Russia was seen by some as a neighbour whose international ambitions would bear watching. Rumours of pending Russian expeditions against Canada were heard once again. The Russian Ministry of Foreign Affairs, already re-awakened to Canada because of a substantial Mennonite emigration from Russia in the mid-seventies (see Chapter 3), once more had to consider the Canadian west coast as a potential battleground.

John A. Macdonald, then a member of the opposition, among others used the Russia issue to propose an expansion of Canada's small standing force into a regular national army. By 1880, however, with the Russia crisis fading and negotiations underway for a very expensive coast to coast railway construction programme, Prime Minister Macdonald (having won an election in September 1878) gave up on

his earlier vague commitment to spending on the military.[77] But a
new conciousness of Canada as an arena for a British-Russian conflict
was born, just as a recognition of the strategic importance of Canada
was resurrected in a new format in St. Petersburg. The construction of
the Canadian Pacific Railway from the early to mid-1880s would soon
augment that picture.

The fact that the Balkan crisis was resolved, temporarily, did not
mean that tensions between Russia and Britain subsided to any great
extent. Britain judged that Russia's expansion into Central Asia challenged its predominance in India and a clash between Russian and
Afghan soldiers in Afghanistan, a British protectorate since 1878,
nearly brought war in 1885. A few Canadians rallied to the British
cause this time, but pressing domestic issues such as the North-West
Uprising helped persuade Macdonald's government to avoid foreign
entanglements. Nevertheles, the Russian press was observant enough
to note in 1885 that Canada finally had created a standing army.[78]
Civil unrest in Canada may not have been as interesting to the new
government in St. Petersburg as it had been a half-century earlier, but
the story of the Riel rebellion still created a bit of a popular sensation.
More significantly, both the real and fancied role played in quelling
the rebellion by Canada's expanding railroad system was cited regularly in arguments over constructing the Trans-Siberian Railway (see
Chapter 3).

For strategic reasons, the Russian Admiralty had been filing information on approaching rail links to British Columbia from as early as
1879, even in the face of the famous "Pacific Scandal" and the delay in
actual incorporation of the Canadian Pacific Railway until February
1881.[79] Detailed reports on Canada's coastal defences were maintained from the early 1880s and in at least one of these it was assumed
that war with Britain was inevitable. Admiral I. Likhachev insisted in
a paper entitled "How We Should Wage War with England" (1885)
that "animosity towards Russia is at the very core of the patriotic principles" of Britain. He recommended the strengthening of Vladivostok
and, though Canada was not mentioned, logic assumes that preparation for attacks from, and assaults on, Esquimalt were essential. The
same archival files include a rejection of the Likhachev thesis by
Admiral N.M. Chikhachev, who disagreed that war with Britain was
inevitable. Chikhachev's opinion was important because he was to
serve as the Minister of the Navy from 1888 to 1896. Reports submitted by Russian naval officers who visited Esquimalt spoke highly of
the facility's potential and of the great advantages it could render the
British fleet.[80]

In 1887, Lt. Col. Baron A.E. Tizengausen provided his superiors with a long accounting of British naval forces in the Pacific and the importance to it of the CPR. Though Russian interest in Canada's railway system is dealt with more broadly in the next chapter, it is worth mentioning here that the Russian fleet fretted greatly that the line brought "the Pacific Ocean closer to Great Britain." It furnished the British with a military highway to Vancouver from London in a fourteen day trip (7 by ship, 7 by rail), as opposed to about four months by sea. The military implications of this potential were obvious to Tizengausen, as were the commercial benefits of the CPR, for India, China and Japan were "easily reached" from Vancouver. So was Russia's Far East!

Esquimalt is being upgraded, he reported, with dry dock facilities and fortifications. There was some light for Russia in this darkness, however. The 1885 report in Russia's press notwithstanding, Canada has no permanent army as of yet, Tizengausen wrote, continuing that its militia is badly trained and "very poor in quality." His assumption was that Canada wished to spend little on military matters and, even though most political parties wanted "complete independence" from Britain, they still expected Britain to defend Canada so as to protect its own interests there. England is strong enough to blockade the Russian maritime region and to conduct raids on its coast, but not strong enough to occupy it. Canadians (and Australians) may not even want to help Britain in a war with Russia. Instead, he predicted, Britain was likely to look for some sort of an alliance with Japan and continue to strengthen its coastal ports in Canada. Senior officers commenting on Tizengausen's assessments generally agreed, adding that even with a strengthened Esquimalt Britain's fleet was overextended in the Pacific. Russia could defend its Amur region easily enough with the addition of a few more cruisers,[81] or so they thought before the advent of Japan's show of strength on the Pacific.

Two years later, a Russian clipper, the *Kreiser*, arrived in Esquimalt to take on coal. Reports from its commander described the port in considerable detail, suggesting that it was not much improved since Tizengausen was there. He was plainly surprised that in light of rumours that Britain hoped to make the facility as "inaccessible [to its enemies] as Gibraltar," the port was still "absolutely defenceless."[82] The Russian Admiralty seemed to have got it right: the very real potential for absolute British dominance in the Pacific was blunted seriously by the absence of political or economic cohesion among London, Ottawa, or Victoria.

Admiral Likhachev continued to urge preparation. Nearly twenty years after his first call to arms, he warned his ministry that Russia was threatened in the North Pacific — this time by the United States and the Japanese, against whom Russia had just opened another debilitating war. In February 1904, Likhachev submitted a paper "On Securing and Improving the Dominant Position of Russia on the Coasts of the Pacific Ocean." In contrast to his earlier suggestions, he was now very defensive, pointing out that further conflict with Japan would be disastrous ("they need but one fleet, we need three") and recommending only that Russia's own coast be strongly fortified. Britain had been hostile to Russia, to be sure, but perhaps now was an appropriate time for both sides to work toward accommodation. Implicitly, Likhachev called for closer association with the British on the Canadian west coast.[83] The relationship did, indeed, vastly improve.

The seizure of Canadian sealing vessels on the Bering Sea by the Imperial Russia navy in 1892 proved to be a complication. Long and often acrimonious negotiations among Russia, Britain, and Canada about this action were conducted at the diplomatic level for more than a dozen years. They were intricately connected to the ongoing debate, which included the United States, on the future of the fur seal and sea otter industry.[84] Fishing disputes between Canada and the United States were old hat by that time. When yet another major fisheries storm gathered force in 1885, both sides were more or less prepared for it. The United States unilaterally abrogated certain clauses of a treaty signed in Washington in 1871, causing Canadian authorities to seize American ships caught fishing within the 3-mile limit on the eastern sea board, and the U.S. navy to take in Canadian vessels on the Bering Sea.

The American fleet claimed the right to protect the Alaska Commercial Company's monopoly on the Pribylov Islands' fur seal rookery and of another American company with a lease bought from Russia allowing it an exclusive right to hunt seals on the Kommandorskii islands. These two companies amalgamated their very lucrative leases in the mid-1870s, angering competitors. Poaching — often by Canadian ships and crews — was rampant by the 1880s. A natural consequence of this phenomenon was the rapid depletion of the herd, already endangered by legal American and Russian fishing. The American company tended to side closely with the Russians against the British in disputes over the fishery. The Russian navy cooperated by busily hauling in seal hunting ships discovered anywhere near the Kommandorskii islands. In fact, when the lease was up for renewal in 1890, it was picked up by a Russian-American team, that is, the previous American group with an added-on Russian co-administration.

In 1892, as the first general outcry about the protection of a species began to grow in volume, Washington agreed to bring the question of pelagic fur-sealing to an international arbitration tribunal sitting in Paris. The tribunal broke up the American monopoly, but also pro-hibited any sealing within a 60-mile range of the Pribylovs. In the meantime, more Canadian vessels originating from British Columbia and Nova Scotia had been gathered in by the Russian Pacific Fleet. Almost at the same time, Russia switched sides in the fur sealing dispute.

The change of allegiance came in part because St. Petersburg was not invited to participate in the Paris tribunal and in part because it did not want a dispute with Britain while it was still reeling from the results of a major famine. Moreover, the expensive and complex Trans-Siberia Railway construction programme was just getting underway, so Russia needed a hiatus in its long standing rivalry with the British Empire. A new fishing deal was signed with London in 1893. Among other things, Russia agreed to listen to compensation claims from owners of seized ships and an appeals Commission was established in Vladivostok for that purpose.[85]

The captured ships were a mixed lot. The *Marie* and the *Rosie Olsen*, both registered in Victoria, the latter with a crew of "six Europeans and 16 Chinese," the *Vancouver Belle*, and the *Carmolita* were all caught with many pelts and some unskinned dead seals. The *Tupper* and *Hall* had plenty of skins aboard but were released after a short time because they were sailing under a British Flag. The strength of Russia's case against the captains and crews depended upon where the seals were taken, the accuracy (or absence) of data in the ships' log books, and where the actual fishing boats from each schooner were apprehended. The Russian position, stated by Commission member Pavel P. Tyrtov in a letter to the deputy foreign minister, Count Vladimir N. Lamsdorff, five years after the capture of the ships, was still that "the detention even of one boat because of illegal hunting in the territorial sea is sufficient for the lawful detention of the ship of which this boat [in this case, the *Marie*] is part."[86]

Two of the Canadian ship owners were compensated for their losses in 1897; the others received nothing from Russia until 1907, shortly after Russia and Britain found themselves allied in the ever-shifting European diplomatic game of coalitions. Captain of the *Carmolita*, William Otis Hughes from Digby, Nova Scotia, later described his ordeal, claiming that he and his men were imprisoned briefly in a roofless chicken house in Petropavlovsk. Their ship was looted of everything that could be removed, and they were delivered, penniless, to Vladivostok after a month. From there they were expected to make their own way home with one ruble each in their pockets. Apparently their misadventure served as the basis for Rudyard Kipling's story "The Devil and the Deep Sea" (1899).[87]

The negotiations over compensation were themselves long and often bitter. The original instructions to the Russian navy on seizing ships, issued from St. Petersburg in 1891, had been explicit: "confiscate all ships caught in this unlawful trade [fur sealing] with non-Russians or fishing in our waters, and escort them to Vladivostok. If it appears for some reason impossible [to do this] you should sink them. The crews of the confiscated ships may be set free if they do not resist."[88] Though the sailors were to be treated "according to the law," no real law had been established. Another Commission was appointed in 1892 in the Ministry of Foreign Affairs, St. Petersburg, to hear the Canadian cases. British officials represented the ship owners. As the discourse proceeded, the Russian documentation referred to the sealers as "thieving," "lying," and drunken, yet acknowledged that the evidence against them was difficult to verify.

The international politics of the final decision were obvious. Owners of the Canadian schooners *Ariel* and *Willie MacGowan* had been compensated in 1897 in the sum of $40,078.75,[89] but as late as 1904, the Commission adamantly refused payment for six remaining claimants, insisting that "weighty evidence" had been presented against them.[90] Because their fishing boats were picked up within Russia's territorial waters the host schooners were considered good "prizes." The Commission concluded as well, in June 1893, that not only were the claims of mistreatment mostly untrue, the "conduct of these seamen [in Petropavlovsk] was most disorderly." Even the captains of *Rosie Olsen* and *Willie MacGowan* were guilty of a "state of intoxication ... and abusive language."[91]

In March that year the Russian representatives proposed to the Canadian delegate to a meeting of the Commission in London that compensation for damage done to the sealing schooners be combined with a general ban on fur seal hunting. The Canadian government rejected the proposition. By this time Japanese poachers were far more dangerous to the herds than the Canadians. Wanting to get the Canadian issue out of the way and be freed up to concentrate on the Japanese problem, the Commission recommended that compensation be awarded anyway. But it still would not be until April, 1907, that a compromise was reached: Canada renounced its claims for damages done to four of the ships and the Russian government paid up for another two, *Annie Moore* and *Sayward*. By that time, the payment, which included 6 percent interest for each year since the original detention, had reached an amount of over $80,000.[92] The Russian press was not so accommodating and still referred to the "thievish" and "drunken" behaviour of the Canadian crews and captains.

Such squabbles were minor in so far as the overall Russian vision of Canada was concerned, but provided added reason for the Russian Ministry of Foreign Affairs to recommend, in August 1899, that a consulate be established in Canada. The Russian Empire had greatly expanded its consular representations in 1893 to facilitate participation in world trade. The idea that Russia should have an official presence in Canada was first discussed in St. Petersburg in April 1894, on the basis of a report submitted by Councillor A. K. Bentkovskii, "On the Necessity of Establishing a Russian Consulate in Canada."[93] He pointed out that Canada was a strategic centre for the British Empire. With strong bastions in Halifax and Cape Breton on one coast and in Esquimalt on the other, the British fleet would never be without coal. Moreover, the recently completed CPR system of rail and steamship connected Canada with England, China and Japan, making it clear that "Canada deserves our attention, especially in view of the current federative direction of British colonial policy." Alexander III read the Bentkovskii submission in May 1894 and had still done nothing about it by the time he died in October of that year. Russia's relationship with England had been tense since the mid-1880s, so a consulate in Canada, Bentkovskii's appeal notwithstanding, looked to be more trouble than it was worth. Five years later the notion was taken much more seriously.

Diplomatic circumstances had changed greatly for Russia by that time. The dismissal of Bismarck by Kaiser Wilhelm II in 1890 resulted in the lapse of Russia's benevolent neutrality agreement with Germany, signed in June 1887. Yet even that Reinsurance Treaty had come a little too late, for Russia's ties with Germany, a cornerstone of Russian foreign policy since 1863, were undermined the same year by prohibitive financial edicts on both sides. In May 1887, Russia forbade foreigners from holding land in its border territories, an act which fell hardest on German subjects living in Russia's part of Poland. In retaliation, Bismarck ordered the German state bank not to accept Russian securities as collateral for loans. Though German private investment in Russia, especially in Siberia, remained substantial and Germany was Russia's main trading partner, the Russian government turned to

France for large credits. This move was to have very important long-range consequences. Moreover, Bismarck's political demise brought Russia and France closer together strategically. Massive financial assistance from Paris stimulated the ambitious industrialization programme initiated by Minister of Finance Count Sergei Witte in 1892. A year prior to that, a formal Russian-French military accord had been reached and, in January 1894, a full military convention between them was confirmed. Russia had switched sides on continental Europe once again. In the meantime St. Petersburg remained at odds with London. They stood against each other in most Black Sea affairs and competed for influence in China and Afghanistan. More ominous was an event of January 1902, when Japan and Britain agreed to an alliance just as relations between St. Petersburg and Tokyo deteriorated to the brink of war. On the other hand, while Russia was playing the international great power game, it desperately needed world markets for its goods. Britain was potentially a large consumer of Russian grains and lumber, but these were precisely what Canada was providing. The consulate in Canada was a by-product of all these pressures, antithetical though they might appear to have been.

Two trends of the mid-nineties helped persuade the Russian Ministry of Foreign Affairs that Bentkovskii's recommendation of 1893 should be re-visited. One of these was the obvious growth in Canadian autonomy in matters of trade. The Russian ambassador in London kept St. Petersburg informed of this development in reports on a major Colonial Conference held in Ottawa in 1894 and subsequent trade agreements between Canada and France.[94] At the same time, German-Canadian trade had grown exponentially. That situation was reversed when a trade war was opened between Britain and Germany in 1897, leaving room for other European countries, including Russia, and Japan to pick up the slack. In the winter and spring of 1898, Russia's ambassadors in London (Ye. Ye. Staahl) and Washington (Count A.P. Cassini) urged their department to open a consulate in Canada, informing St. Petersburg that the British and American governments concurred. Their reasoning was consistent with Bentkovskii's. Canada was a logical location for the expansion of Russia's consular services because of its growing trade in agricultural and other machinery, the ever-increasing "Russian" emigration to Canada, and as an ideal site for monitoring American-British relations.[95] As a vantage point for all three of these developments, Montreal was proposed as the consulate's location.

The turning point came in April, 1899, when Minister of Foreign Affairs, Count M.N. Murav'ev, informed Witte that Russia's ambassadors in London and Washington now agreed that Canada "had acquired great importance for us both politically and economically." In the rationale accompanying the message to Witte, Murav'ev described Canada as the largest and wealthiest colony of England, representing "great convenience for trade relations with the rest of the world" by dint of its natural wealth and location. He added that Canada had been for sometime "almost an independent state." Britain's efforts to maintain a monopoly on trade with its colonies meant, he continued, "the fate of trade relations of Russia with England depends to a significant decree on the greater or lesser strengthening of trade relations with its colonies, and so the study of the circumstances of its trade with Canada . . . is absolutely essential . . . to the future of Russian exports."[96] Murav'ev referred as well to Canada's "statesmen" already participating autonomously in British Imperial affairs, as the Bering Sea question demonstrated.

Canada was said to have "very important strategic significance" for England. With its wonderful ports and railroad, it would provide Britain with crucial access to the Pacific if, in time of war, the Suez Canal was closed. Placed "at the disposal of British squadrons in the Pacific and Atlantic Oceans," Canada's coal could be the only means whereby England might preserve "world sea domination." Russia needed an on-site "observation point" from which to monitor the activities of both the British and the Americans generally and their movements in the North Pacific Ocean in particular, Murav'ev explained. Furthermore, a Consulate was necessary to safeguard the interests of Russian immigrants in Canada. For the most part, Murav'ev was re-stating Bentkovskii's recommendations. After reading this report from Murav'ev, Nicholas II ordered him to set up a permanent Consulate in Canada.

In November 1899, State Councillor Nikolai B. Struve was named Consul-General in Montreal and Henry Mathers, a Canadian citizen, the Honourary Consul in Halifax. According to instructions handed them, their tasks were to provide regular services to Russia's citizens in Canada and to keep close track of the Canadian-American and American-British relationship. They were to record carefully all circumstances in Canada that might prove informative for the development of Siberia. The similarities in nature and purpose of the Trans-Siberian Railway and the CPR systems were singled out for attention, as was the settling of people in both countries' hinterlands.[97]

Because he was already *in situ*, Mathers began his service in the summer of 1899. The Consulate in Montreal was opened officially in

May 1900 by Struve, who almost immediately set out across the country on the CPR, following a trail blazed by Kriukov and Kropotkin. On his return to Montreal Struve submitted a substantial general report on Canada to his bosses in St. Petersburg. After a century of informed observation, government to government relations were now institutionalized.[98]

[1] See, e.g., "Pis'mo Soedinennykh Amerikanskikh oblasti" [Letter from the United American Region], *Vestnik evropy*, 2 (1802), pp. 75-77.

[2] See *The Diary of John Quincy Adams, 1794-1845*, edited by Allan Nevins (New York: Ungar, 1969), pp. 60-109, 138-39. On Rumiantsev, see P.K. Grimstead, *The Foreign Ministers of Alexander I. Political Attitudes and the Conduct of Russian Diplomacy, 1801-1825* (Berkeley: University of California Press, 1969), Chapter 5.

[3] "Confidential Report from Rezanov to Rumiantsev, 17 June 1806," in *The Russian American Colonies. A Documentary Record*, edited by Basil Dmytryshyn, et al., Vol. 3 (Portland: Oregon Historical Society, 1989), pp. 112-148. Rezanov died in Krasnoyarsk on his way to deliver this report personally.

[4] Dashkov to Rumiantsev (30 June / 12 July 1813), AVPRI, Fonds Kantseliariia, delo 12170, p. 261; also in VPR, 1st Series (1801-1815), Vol. 7 (Moscow: Politlit, 1970), pp. 630-31. See also Dashkov to A.B. Kurakin (5 / 17 January 1812), *Ibid.*, Vol. 6, pp. 259-260. These diplomatic documents were, for the most, written in French.

     For further details of the Dashkov and Kozlov letters to St. Petersburg, see N.N. Bolkhovitinov, *Stanovlenie russko-amerikanskikh otnoshenii 1775-1815* [Establishing Russian-American Relations], (Moscow: Nauka, 1966), pp. 490-601.

[5] Grimstead, *The Foreign Ministers of Alexander I*, p. 176.

[6] Kozlov letters to Rumiantsev, March-April 1812, AVPRI, Fonds Kantseliariia, Opis 468 (1812), delo 9242, pp. 3-4, 63-64.

[7] Kozlov letters to the foreign ministry, April to August 1814, AVPRI, Fonds Kantseliariia, Opis 468 (1812), delo 9243, pp. 25-70.

[8] Nesselrode to Lieven (21 November / 3 December, 1826), VPR, 2nd Series (1815-1830), Vol. 4 (Moscow: Nauka, 1980), p. 158.

[9] For the detailed correspondence between De Maltitz and Nesselrode in 1827, see AVPRI, Fonds Kantseliariia, Opis 468 (1827), delo 12235,

pp. 13-282, *passim*. The petitions referred to here were sent from Saint John, New Brunswick.

[10] *Mackenzie's Gazette. Devoted to the News and Politics of Canada and the Other N.A. Colonies, England and Wales, Ireland, Scotland and the Continent of Europe*, was a weekly published by Canadian rebel leader William Lyon Mackenzie in the United States. Its main purpose was to raise support for the rebel cause in Upper and Lower Canada. Its first "Prospectus" was issued on 17 April 1838.

[11] Summaries of contemporary newspaper items are included in L.S. Stavrianos, "The Rumour of Russian Intrigue in the Rebellion of 1837," *The Canadian Historical Review*, 18:4 (1937), pp. 367-73. Stavrianos' summary rejection of any Russian involvement was challenged in 1942 by Thomas H. Le Duc, who cited a small fraction of the Russian archival sources used here. See Le Duc, "The Rumour of Russian Intrigue in 1837," *The Canadian Historical Review*, 23: 4 (1942), pp. 398-400. For a Soviet view of this intriguing possibility, see V.A. Tishkov, "Rossiia i vosstanie 1837-1838 gg. v Kanade" [Russia and the 1837-38 Rebellion in Canada], *Amerikanskii ezhegodnik*, 1976, (Moscow, 1976), pp. 283-99. Stavrianos denied the possibility of Russian involvement outright, but he used no Russian sources. Tishkov examined Russian archival materials and also concluded that there was nothing to the rumours, because the tsar and his foreign ministry, though they monitored the affair closely, decided to stay neutral in what they saw as a conflict between England and the USA.

[12] T.R. Preston, *Three Years' Residence in Canada from 1837 to 1839*, Vol. 1 (London: Richard Bentley, 1840), p. 202. In his Preface, Preston noted that the troubles between the United States and England had prompted his travels, and that he hoped to promote the welfare and strengthening of Canada so as to keep it within the British Empire.

[13] *Ibid.*, pp. 231-242. L.S. Stavrianos shrugged off Preston's arguments and ignored completely the realities of Russia's activities elsewhere.

[14] See Oscar A. Kirchen, *The Rise and Fall of the Patriot Hunters* (New York: Bookman, 1956), pp. 32-33. The organization, which had secret rituals and codes, was founded in the name of Frères chasseurs or Hunters' Lodges.

[15] *Report of the State Trials Before a General Court Martial Held at Montreal in 1838-9: Exhibiting a Compete History of the Late Rebellion in Lower Canada*, Vol. 2 (Montreal: Armour & Ramsey, 1839), p. 551. The "Voluntary Deposition" was said to have been provided by Jean Baptiste Henri

Brien, a "physician and surgeon," who pleaded guilty to a charge of treason and was sentenced to be hanged (Vol. 1, pp. 352-53). The fact that Brien's execution was stayed and he was released under orders not to come closer than 600 miles "from the province" would suggest that his deposition (Vol. 2, pp. 548-556), in which he informed on many of his colleagues and portrayed himself as a reluctant rebel who spent most of his time heroically saving other people from his brutal associates, was taken as an authentic account.

[16] *Mackenzie's Gazette* (10 November 1838), p. 214. The item was a summary from the New York *Commercial Advertiser*, and typified newspaper conjecture.

[17] Nicholas I to Paskievich, 3 January 1838, TsGIA/RGIA, Fonds 1018, Opis 5, delo 185, pp. 1-2; Krehmer to Nesselrode, 11/23 October 1836, AVPRI, Fonds Kantseliariia, Opis 469, delo 222, pp. 38-40.

[18] Nicholas I to I.F. Paskievich, 3 July 1838, in A.P. Shcherbatov, *General'-Fel'dmarshal' Kniaz' Paskevich'. Ego zhizn' i deiatel'nost'* [General-Field Marshal Prince Paskevich. His Life and Activities], Vol. 5 (1832-1847) (St. Petersburg, 1896), Appendix, pp. 365-66; Nicholas to Menshikov, 2 July 1838, *Russkaia starina*, XC (1902), p. 232.

[19] For a Russian version of the trade agreement of 1832 and its significance, see N.N. Bolkhovitanov, *Russko-amerikanskie otnosheniia, 1815-1832 gg.* [Russian-American Relations, 1815-1832], (Moscow: Nauka, 1975), Chapter 8.

[20] On the *Vixen* affair, see Harold N. Ingle, *Nesselrode and the Russian Rapprochement with Britain, 1836-1844* (Berkeley: University of California Press, 1976), pp. 63-72; John C.K. Daley, *Russian Seapower and the "Eastern Question" 1827-41* (London: Macmillan, 1991), pp. 123-127, and *Sobranie Traktatov i Konventsii Zakliuchennykh Rossieiu s Inostrannymi Derzhavami* [Collection of Tracts and Conventions Concluded by Russia with Foreign States], edited by F. Martens, Vol. XII (St. Petersburg, 1898), pp. 62-70.

[21] "Seizure of the Vixen," *Mackenzie's Gazette* (25 August 1838), p. 127.

[22] See *Diary of George Mifflin Dallas, United States Minister to Russia, 1837-1839.* Edited by Susan Dallas (New York: Arno, 1970), pp. 34, 11. This is a reprint of an 1892 edition. Mikhail Pavlovich was Nicholas' younger brother. The Grand Duchess originally was Helene of Württemberg. It was their son who toured Canada in the 1870s, see Chapter 1.

[23] *Diary of George Mifflin Dallas*, p. 63. The entry was made sometime in early January 1838.

24 The Convention of Berlin and Russia's part in it can be found in *Sobranie Traktatov i Konventsii*, Vol. IV (1888), pp. 460-462.

25 Quoted in Nicholas Riasanovsky, *Nicholas I and Official Nationality in Russia, 1825-1855* (Berkeley, CA: University of California Press, 1967), p. 239.

26 "Pis'ma Imperatora Nikolai I i Velikago Kniazia Mikhaila Pavlovicha" [Letters of Emperor Nicholas I to Grand Prince Mikhail Pavlovich], (14/24 February 1837), *Russkaia starina*, No. 5 (1897), p. 227.

27 Nesselrode to Pozzo di Borgo (30 December 1837), AVPRI, Fonds Kantseliariia, Opis 469, delo 125, pp. 270-278.

28 *Diary of George Mifflin Dallas*, p. 65.

29 Nicholas I to I.F. Paskievich, 18 January 1838, RGIA, Fonds 1018, Opis 5, delo 185.

30 Nicholas I to I.F. Paskievich, 22 September 1841, in Shcherbatov, *General'-Fel'dmarshal' Kniaz' Paskievich'*, Vol. 5, Appendix, pp. 487-88.

31 "Russian and Circassia," *Mackenzie's Gazette* (2 June 1838), p. 31; (17 November 1839), p. 223.

32 Kielchen to his wife (14 November 1838), AVPRI, Fonds Kantseliariia, Opis 468 -1839g, delo 217, pp. 24-25. Letters from Kielchen to his wife ("My dearest love"), reveal deep affection though she is not named.

33 Preston, *Three Years' Residence in Canada*, Vol. 1, pp. 231-32, on the "notorious Mackenzie," p. 181. "Mr. Kielchen, the Russian Consul at Boston, was arrested by Sir John Colborne's orders, while attending mass at the Cathedral Church, Montreal. His house was ransacked by the military and his private papers seized and carried to the police office," *Mackenzie's Gazette* (15 December 1838), p. 252.

34 The British vice consul in Massachusetts was R.C. Manners. His authorization of the trip can be found in AVPRI, Fonds Kantseliariia, Opis 468-1839g, delo 217, pp. 23, 26.

35 S.N. Ogden to Kielchen (27 November 1838), AVPRI, Fonds Kantseliariia, Opis 468 -1839g, delo 217, p. 27.

36 See, e.g., Bodisco to Nesselrode (25 July 1838), AVPRI, Fonds Kantseliariia, Opis 469, delo 222, pp. 61r-62r; Despatch No. 15, (11/23 June 1838), *ibid.*, 133r-135r, 136.

37 Bodisco to Nesselrode (16/28 December 1838) [received 31 January 1839], AVPRI, Fonds Kantseliariia, Opis 469-1839g, delo 217, pp. 35-36.

38 Nesselrode to Pozzo di Borgo (21 February 1839), AVPRI, Fonds Kantseliariia, Opis 469, delo 121, pp. 188-191; Nesselrode to Bodisco (21 February 1839), *ibid.*, delo 217, p. 354.

39 Pozzo di Borgo to Nesselrode (24 March/5 April 1839), AVPRI, Fonds Kantseliariia, Opis 469, delo 119, pp. 335-336.

40 Bodisco to Nesselrode (17/29 December 1838), AVPRI, Fonds Kantseliariia, Opis 469-1839g., delo 217, pp. 37-43.

41 Bodisco despatch from Washington (17/29 December 1838), [received 31 January 1839], AVPRI, Fonds Kantseliariia, Opis 469-1839g, delo 217, p. 37.

42 *Diary of George Mifflin Dallas*, pp. 124-125.

43 Bodisco to Nesselrode (19/31 January 1839), AVPRI, Fonds Kantseliariia, Opis 469, delo 217, pp. 48r-49r, 330r-342r.

44 Nesselrode to Bodisco (21 February 1839), AVPRI, *op. cit.*, p. 354. Nesselrode told Bodisco of the Czartoryski-Palmerston meeting. See also Kenneth Bourne, *Palmerston. The Early Years, 1704-1841* (London: Allen Lane, 1982), pp. 353-54, 431. Czartoryski viewed the 1830 Polish uprising as useless, but nonetheless accepted a leading role in the rebel government so as to be in a position to negotiate a return to the status quo. See esp. W.H. Zawadzki, *A Man of Honour: Adam Czartoryski as a Statesman of Russia and Poland, 1795-1831* (New York: Oxford UP, 1993).

45 See Walter Mckenzie Pintner, *Russian Economic Policy under Nicholas I* (Ithaca: Cornell UP, 1967), pp. 107, 111, 239-40.

46 See especially F.F. Martens, "Rossiia i Angliia v tsarstvovanie Imperatora Nikolaia I," *Vestnik Evropy,* Vol. 189, No. 1 (1898), pp. 5-31; No. 2 (1898), pp. 465-502; and Ingle, *Nesselrode,* pp. 58-59.

47 Ironically, one of the accused in the 1839 trials in Montreal, Charles Hindenlang, a citizen of France who had participated in the revolution in Paris of 1830, used the *Vixen* issue as part of his defence. His participation in the rebellion in Canada was a question of helping a people achieve independence, he said, and was no different from the help offered by British officers to the "Circassians dans leurs projets d'indépendance." Even the Emperor of Russia had returned the British soldiers and the ship to England: "L'Angleterre serait-elle donc moins

juste qu'un prince absolu et cruel? ou voudrait elle n'imiter de lui que ces actes sanguinaires dans la malheureuse Pologne," Hindenlang asked rhetorically. He was hanged anyway. *Report of the State Trials . . . 1838-9*, Vol. 2, p. 31.

[48] Nicholas I to I.F. Paskievich, 29 November 1839, in Shcherbatov, *General-Fel'dmarshal' Kniaz' Paskievich'*, Vol. 5, Appendix, p. 375.

[49] See Mosely, *Russian Diplomacy and the Opening of the Eastern Question* (Cambridge, MA: Harvard UP, 1934), pp. 56-60; 134-38; *Sobranie traktatov i konventsii*, Vol. XII (1898), 107-08, 112; Lincoln, *Nicholas I*, pp. 214-15; Ingle, *Nesselrode*, pp. 114-15, 124-27.

   Nicholas' letters to various family members and to his confidantes were filled with anger at Louis Philippe and France. In January 1838, for example, he wrote Paskievich that the "impotent pleading in France on behalf of Poland is ridiculous! and shows only their weakness and ill-will." Nicholas I to I.F. Paskievich, 18 January 1838, RGIA, Fonds 1018, Opis 5, delo 185.

[50] See letters of Grand Duchess Anna Pavlovna to Nicholas, 10 May 1839, and Nicholas to her husband, William, King of Holland, 23 May 1839, in *Romanov Relations*, edited by S.W. Jackman (London: McMillan, 1969), pp. 287-88; and "Imperator Nikolai Pavlovich v ego pis'makh k kniaziiu Paskievichu" [Emperor Nicholas Pavlovich and his Letters to Prince Paskievich (1832-1847)], *Russkii arkhiv*, No. 1 (January 1897), pp. 5-44, in which he vented fury at France and Belgium.

[51] *Sobranie Traktatov i Konventsii*, Vol. XII (1898), pp. 107-08.

[52] Nicholas I to I.F. Paskievich, 17 October 1839, in Shcherbatov, *General'-Fel'dmarshal' Kniaz' Paskievich'*, Vol. 5, Appendix, p. 395.

[53] Brunnov to Nesselrode (11 October 1839), AVPRI, Fonds Kantseliariia, Opis 469, delo 122, pp. 242-244; Pozzo di Borgo, Notes for Despatch to Bodisco (1839, n.d.), AVPRI, Fonds Kantseliariia, Opis 469, delo 217, pp. 382-384r.

[54] *Ibid.* (12 Nov 1839, os), p. 396; Nicholas I to I.F. Paskievich, 11/26 December 1839, *Russkii arkhiv*, No. 1 (January 1897), p. 27.

[55] Cited in Sir Charles Webster, *The Foreign Policy of Palmerston, 1831-1841*, Vol. 2 (London: G. Bell, 1969), pp. 560-62. Durham was allowed to accept the gift from the Tsar, an exception to the rule that British ambassadors not accept foreign Orders.

[56] *Sobranie Traktatov i Konventsii*, Vol. XII (1898), p. 114.

57 Brunnov to Nesselrode (11 Oct 1839), *op. cit.*

58 Bodisco despatches from Washington, No.'s 15, 16, 27, 29, 38-48 (May-October 1838), Fonds Kantseliariia, Opis 469, delo 222, pp. 219r-222, 223-228, 2303-234r, 235r, 239r, 240r-243r.

59 "Russian Policy in Lower Canada," *Mackenzie's Gazette* (15 September 1838). This was a piece on Durham's behaviour, not on "Russian policy" per se. On "young Nick," see for example, *ibid.* (7 July 1838), p. 69. See Bodisco Despatch from Washington, No. 46 (7/19 November 1838), Fonds kantseliariia, Opis 469, delo 222, pp. 241r-242r, for copies of articles.

60 Quoted in Webster, *The Foreign Policy of Palmerston, 1831-1841*, Vol. 2, p. 562.

61 Quoted in Stavrianos, p. 368. The report was prepared by Stewart Derbishire, a London attorney commissioned by Henry Fox, British Envoy to Washington. It is available in the National Archives of Canada.

62 See James R. Gibson, "The 'Russian Contract': The Agreement of 1839 Between the Hudson's Bay and Russian-American Companies," *Russia in North America*, edited by Richard A. Pierce (Fairbanks, Alaska: Limestone Press, 1990), pp. 157-180.

63 See Sr. George Simpson, *An Overland Journey Around the World* (Philadelphia: Lea & Blanchard, 1947); and J.S. Galbraith, *The Little Emperor: Governor Simpson of the Hudson's Bay Company* (Toronto: Macmillan, 1976).

   Much has been written on the Hudson's Bay and Russian American Companies. For documentation on the latter organization, see *To Siberia and Russian America. Three Centuries of Eastward Expansion*, edited by Basil Dmytryshyn, et al., Vol. 3: *The Russian American Colonies, 1798-1867* (Portland: Oregon Historical Society, 1989). On the relations between the two companies, see R.A. Pierce, *Russia and British Columbia to 1967* (Calgary: Glenbow Museum, 1973).

64 Bodisco to Nesselrode, 10/22 August 1839, 18-30 May 1839, AVPRI, Fonds Kantseliariia,(1839), delo 217, pp. 238-241, (1840), pp. 143-144. In 1841, Fort Ross was sold to John A. Sutter, a German who settled in California in 1839 and took out Mexican citizenship.

65 RGIA, Fonds 18, Opis 5, delo 1302, pp. 1-12. Kruzenshtern (1770-1846) was co-founder of the Russian Geographical Society and a member of the Royal Society in London.

[66] Draft Despatch to Bodisco (18 March 1841), AVPRI, Fonds Kantseliariia, Opis 469, delo 195, pp. 282r-384r, 385. For the sequence of reports on the McLeod affair, *ibid.* (January-October 1841), pp. 69-305, *passim.*

[67] Charter cited in S.B. Okun, *The Russian American Company*, edited by B.D. Grekov. Translated from the Russian (Cambridge, MA: Harvard UP, 1951), p. 50. See also N.N. Bolkhovitinov, *Russko-Amerikanskie otnosheniia i prodazhe Aliaski, 1834-1867* [Russian-American Relations and the Sale of Alaska], (Moscow: Nauka, 1990).

[68] See on this Joseph Tarnovesky, "Canadian Press Reactions to the Sale of Alaska," *Eastern Europe: Historical Essays* (Toronto: New Review Press, 1969), pp. 191-210.

[69] See John Hilliker, *Canada's Department of External Affairs*, Vol. 1: *The Early Years, 1909-1946* (Montreal/Kingston: McGill-Queen's Press, 1990).

[70] James Douglas' offer was cited in Desmond Morton, *A Military History of Canada* (Edmonton: Hurtig, 1985), pp. 79-80. See also W. Kaye Lamb, ed., "Correspondence Relating to the Establishment of a Naval Base at Esquimalt, 1851-1857," *British Columbia Historical Quarterly*, 6 (1942), 277-296; G.P. deT. Glazebrook, *Canadian External Relations. An Historical Study to 1914* (London: Oxford UP, 1942), p. 56, and C.P. Stacey, *Canada and the Age of Conflict* (Toronto: Macmillan, 1977), p. 41.

[71] J. Murray Beck, *Joseph Howe*, Vol. 2 (Montreal: McGill-Queen's, 1983), pp. 79ff. *The Speeches and Public Letters of the Hon. Joseph Howe*, edited by William Annand, Vol. 2 (Boston: John P. Jewett, 1858), p. 221. On the Montreal appeal, see, for example, A.R. Roche, *View of Russian America in Connection With the Present War* (Montreal, 1855). This was an address delivered to and published by the Literary and Historical Society of Quebec, 7 March 1855.

[72] See Trevor Royce, *The Great Crimean War, 1854-1856* (New York: St. Martin's, 2000).

[73] See W.L. Morton, *The Critical Years. The Union of British North America, 1857-1873* (Toronto: McClelland and Stewart, 1964), p. 26.

[74] See, for example, the long commentary associated with a request from the Russian American Company for naval vessels to protect Russian holdings in the Stikine River (September 1862-September 1863). Reports by Captain Prince Maksutov are especially revealing in this regard: RGAVMF, Fonds 410, Opis 2, delo 2585, pp. I-Ir, 1-35.

[75] On this, see Glynn Barratt, *Russian Shadows on the British Northwest Coast of North America, 1810-1890* (Vancouver: University of British Columbia Press, 1983), Chapter 3.

[76] AVPRI, Fonds Gl. arkh. I-9 (1857-1868), delo 4, pp. 50-55, cited in Bolkhovitinov, *Russko-amerikanskie otnosheniia i prodazha Aliaskii*, pp. 116-117.

[77] Donald Creighton, *John A. Macdonald. The Old Chieftain* (Toronto: Macmillan, 1979), pp. 236, 295.

[78] See, e.g., *Journal de St. Petersbourg*, No. 4 (5/17 Janvier 1884), p. 2.

[79] See, for example, "Kanadskaia tikhookeanskaia zheleznaia doroga" [Canadian Pacific Railway], RGAVMF, Fonds 24, Opis 1, delo 171 (1879), pp. 4-41, which opened with "Everything is being done to speed up the construction of the Canadian Pacific railway from Lake Superior to the Red River." The Russian author of this particular memorandum was convinced that rail links between Canada's eastern and western coasts were imminent and strategically very significant.

[80] Likhachev, "Kak nam voevat' s Anglieiu?" [How Should We Wage War with England?] (1885), with observations on the subject by Admiral N. Chikhachev (May 1885), RGAVMF, Fonds 16, Opis 1, delo 230, pp. 23-50; "Prikazaniia i rasporiazheniia komanduiushchego otriadom sudov v Tikhoi okeane kon-admir. Aslanbegova" [Orders and Instructions for Commander of the Pacific Ocean Squadron, Vice-Admiral Aslanbegov (19 January 1880-1 July 1882), RGAVMF, Fonds 41, Opis n/a, delo 38, pp. 45-48; "Zametka o stroitel'stve sukhogo doka v Eskvaimopol'skoi gavani . . ." [Observations on the Construction of a Dry Dock in Esquimalt], RGAMVMF, Fonds 24, Opis 1, delo 171, pp. 1-9.

[81] "Zapiska podpol. General'nogo shtaba A.E. Tizengauzena, 'O voennoi polozhenii Anglii v Tikhoi okeane i o znachenii Kanadskoi zheleznoi dorogi' i proekt ee dopolneniia . . ." [Memorandum of Lt.-Col. A.E. Tizengauzen of the General Staff, "On the Military Position of England in the Pacific Ocean and on the Significance of the Canadian Railroad . . .," (1887), RGAVMF, Fonds 417, Opis 1, delo 296, pp. 1-24. Tizengausen did say that the Suez Canal would still be a better route for British forces going to the Pacific, mostly because of the unpredictable nature of Canadian weather.

[82] "O krugosvetnoi plavanii . . ." [On the Circumnavigation of the World by the Clipper, *Kreiser*, from Kronstadt to the Pacific Ocean . . .], (July 1888-August 1891), RGAVMF, Fonds 417, Opis 1, delo 408, pp. 150-160r, describes in great detail the ports of Esquimalt, Vancouver and Victoria.

[83] Likhachev, "Ob'obezpechenii i uprochenii preobladaiushchago polozheniia Rossii na beregakh Tikhoiu Okeana" [On Securing and Improving the Predominant Position of Russia on the Shores of the Pacific Ocean], RGAVMF, Fonds 16, Opis 1, delo 251, pp. 1-5. Japan launched its first attack on the Russian fleet at Port Arthur on 8 February 1904. The Russians were completely unprepared, though fleet commander Vice-Admiral Stark believed hostilities were imminent. He had asked the Russian Viceroy for Asia (Admiral Alekseev) for permission to put his fleet in a state of readiness, but was turned down. It would appear therefore that the fleet's detailed and often astute reports were not attended to very carefully in St. Petersburg.

[84] Canadian vessels were taken by American authorities regularly in the 1880s. On the long negotiations over fishing rights in the Bering Straits, see R.C. Brown, *Canada's National Policy, 1883-1900. A Study in Canadian-American Relations* (Princeton: Princeton UP, 1964), pp. 42-62; and lengthy Russian documents found in RGAVMF, Fonds 410, Opis 3, delo 327, pp. 1-185; delo 207, pp. 1-218. See also *Novoe vremia* (9 June 1904).

[85] On this entire issue, see the unpublished paper by Norman E. Saul, "The United States, Russia, and Seals, 1867-1911," read at the Pacific Coast Branch, AHA, Hawaii (5 August 1995). I am grateful to Professor Saul for sending me a copy of his interesting paper.

[86] P. P. Tyrtov to Lamsdorff, 23 September 1897, RGAVMF, Fonds 410, Opis 3, delo 327, pp. 86-87, 69-79. Lamsdorff was deputy foreign minister 1887 to 1900, and minister from 1900 to 1906.

[87] For the Hughes account, see the *Digby Weekly Courier* (4 March 1910). The "Devil and the Deep Sea" was published as part of Kipling's *The Day's Work* (London: Macmillan, 1899), pp. 148-180.

[88] From "Vypiska iz raporta Nachal'nika Eskadrn sudov v Tikhom Okeane, Vitse-Admirala Nazimova, ot 1 Iul' 1891" [Extracts from a Report of the Commander of the Squadron of Ships in the Pacific Ocean, Vice Admiral Nazimov" (1 July 1891), RGAVMF, Fonds 410, Opis 3, delo 207, pp. 65ob-66ob.

[89] Minister of Foreign Affairs Count M. N. Murav'ev to P.P. Tyrtov, 15 December 1897, "on receipt of this sum, it [British government] will consider the matter closed," RGAVMF, Fonds 410, Opis 3, delo 327, p. 98.

[90] *Ibid.*, pp. 149-50.

[91] In addition to the Russian archival files on this matter, see *Despatch from Sir R. Morier, inclosing the reply of the Russian Government in regard to the*

Seizures of British Sealing vessels by Russian cruizers in the North Pacific Ocean, presented to both Houses of Parliament by Command of her Majesty, June (12), 1893 [sic]. This 15-page paper includes a translation of the 1893 Russian Commission report.

[92] Foreign Minister A.P. Izvolskii to His Excellency I.M. Dikov, 9 April 1907, RGAVMF, Fonds 410, Opis 3, delo 327, p. 182. Izvolskii replaced Lamsdorff as foreign minister in 1906 and retained the post until 1910.

[93] "O neobkhodimosti uchrezhdeniia russkogo konsul'stva v Kanade," AVPRI, Fonds II departament, 1-5, Opis 407, delo 1202, p. 17. This report and Bentkovskii's subsequent commentaries are cited in G.I. Luzianin, *Rossiia i Kanada v 1893-1927 gg.* (Moscow: Magnitogorsk GPI, 1997), Chapter 3. These documents were not available to this writer at the time of writing, but since then they have been acquired by the CRCR. Apparently the idea of a Russian Consulate originated with a Doctor W.H. Walton-Johns (as transliterated from the Russian), a Canadian in Montreal who wrote directly to Alexander III in 1893. The suggestion was rejected on the advice of the Russian envoy to the United States, G.L. Kantakuzin, on the grounds that it might prompt Britain to increase its representation in areas where it and Russia competed, AVPRI, *Ibid.*, pp. 14-15.

[94] AVPRI, Fonds II departament, 1-5, Opis 407, delo 1202, pp. 25-38.

[95] AVPRI, Fonds II departament, 1-5, Opis 407, delo 1202, 76-85.

[96] Murav'ev, "Zapiska o russkikh interesakh v Kanade" [Memorandum on Russian Interests in Canada] (8 March 1899), RGIA, Fonds 565, Opis 4, delo 14456, pp. 1-6; "Ministerstvo Inostrannykh Del'. Ob uchrezhdenii dolzhnosti konsula v Kanade" [Minister of Foreign Affairs. On Establishing the Duties of a Consul in Canada] (9 October 1899), *Ibid.*, p. 9. For more detail, see RGIA, Fonds 1149, Opis xii-1899, delo 110, pp. 1-19. Negotiations had been going on for some time. The final judgement was marked "approved" by the tsar on 1 April 1899, though the administrative process went on until November. The new Consul was conferred at the "6th class in rank, 6th category in uniform, at an annual salary of 10,500 rubles." Office expenses budget was set at 1,500 rubles.

    The "Zapiska" can be found also in AVPRI, Fonds II departament, 1-5, Opis 407, delo 1202, pp. 88-91.

[97] AVPRI, Fonds II departament, 1-5, Opis 407, delo 1202, pp. 95-96.

[98] Struve's first report, "Ocherk Kanady" [A Sketch of Canada], can be found in the *Sbornik konsul'skikh donesenii. God tretii* [Collection of Consular Reports. Year Three], Issue VI (Ministry of Foreign Affairs: St. Petersburg, 1900), pp. 473-496; and in translation below.

Первые поселенцы среди дѣвственнаго лѣса.

"First settlements among the virgin forest"

3

Canada as a Place to Live: Haven and Economic Model

One of Friedrich Engels' many letters to the German socialist Friedrich Adolph Sorge was sent from Montreal in September 1888. Engels was touring America and, like Aleksandr Lakier, spent a short time in Canada. The Engels correspondence would not have been known in Russia at the time, but his comments on Canada were to be echoed for 70 years with only slight interruption, by his Marxist-Leninist protégés in the Soviet Union.[1] He wrote:

> It is a strange transition from the States to Canada. First one imagines that one is in Europe again, and then one thinks one is in a positively retrogressing and decaying country. Here one sees how necessary the feverish speculative spirit of the Americans is for the rapid development of a new country (presupposing capitalist production as a basis); and in ten years this sleepy Canada will be ripe for annexation — the farmers in Manitoba, etc., will demand it themselves. Besides, the country is half annexed already socially — hotels, newspapers, advertising, etc., all on the American pattern. And they may tug and resist as much as they like; the economic infusion of Yankee blood will have its way and abolish this ridiculous boundary line — and when the time comes, John Bull will say "Yea and Amen" to it.[2]

These opinions ran counter to almost every Russian observation on Canada in the 19th century, whether it be from radical or reactionary.

A few years after the Engels tour, a differently radical traveller penned an impression that was much more typical of the Russian perspective. The analogy with Siberia, drawn so often by Zavashilin and others from the 1880s onward, helped persuade the famous Russian anarchist-geographer, Prince Peter Kropotkin, to visit Canada in 1897. He accepted an invitation from the British Association for the Advancement of Science to read papers at its annual meeting, sited that year in Toronto. Journeying from his home in exile in England,

Kropotkin first spent two weeks with his friend James Mavor, a Professor of Political Economy and Constitutional History at the University of Toronto who had arranged the invitation. After the professional meetings, Kropotkin and twenty-three international geologists were transported across the country to Victoria on the Canadian Pacific Railway. The CPR organized the excursion to promote Canada's immigration policies, from which the Railway company benefitted financially. The Russian observed with astonishment the large quantities of wheat produced in Manitoba and noted that this production came "not . . . on mammoth farms, but by no less than 27,000 farmers."[3] On his return to Mavor's home, where he stayed for nearly another month, Kropotkin wrote a piece on Canada and its resources, with special insights on Mennonite communities. Published in 1898 by the British journal *Nineteenth Century*, the essay impressed upon readers the geophysical similarities between Canada and Russia, most specifically the striking resemblance between Canada's western regions, Northwest Siberia, and the Siberian steppe lands. They had "the same millions of acres of unoccupied prairies; the same rivers teeming with salmon on the Pacific borders; the same inexhaustible mining resources." Kropotkin likened Quebec City to Tobol'sk, both seen as fortress gateways to vast hinterlands.[4] The essay was read with interest by Vladimir Chertkov, another Russian-in-exile in Britain who in turn passed it on to his friend, Leo Tolstoy — symbolic leader of the Doukhobors.

Kropotkin's extensive unpublished notes on Canada reflect even more clearly the way in which he juxtaposed Western Canada and Siberia and reveal his fascination with the subject of French-English relations, the system of federalism, and the Canada's native peoples.[5] He left detailed descriptions of all three issues in his private papers and, with an eye to his anarchist beliefs, called Louis Riel an "agitator without parallel." Lengthy examinations of the links among railway systems, capital investment, settlement, and successfully managed agricultural development in Canada foreshadowed reports and the books written shortly afterwards by Kriukov and Mizhuev, and observations relayed to St. Petersburg by Russian consuls after they began staffing offices in Canada. Among other things, Kropotkin favoured Canada's system of federalism over the American version because, he claimed, it provided for a far greater degree of regional autonomy.

The anarchist had first-hand knowledge of Siberia, having served as an aide-de-camp to the Governor-General of Eastern Siberia as a young man. Like Zavashilin, he attributed many of the problems faced by Siberians to excessive centralization from St. Petersburg and the delays caused by distance and an incomplete rail system. In the 1860s Kropotkin was assigned the task of investigating Siberian prisons, a duty which apparently turned him against all forms of state-directed discipline and set him on his way towards becoming a self-styled "anarchist."[6] He therefore had personal experiences in both Canada and Siberia which helped shape his comparative survey.

The trip to Victoria from Toronto and back, during which Kropotkin visited communities established by the Mennonites who had arrived in Canada from Southwest Russia in the early 1870s, convinced him that Canada was the ideal location for Doukhobors.[7] "On approaching a Mennonite village," he wrote, "one is transported to Russia." In contrast to the quality of their lives in Russia, Mennonites in Canada were said to be prosperous and wealthy, able to revere Leo Tolstoy's name openly, and reject any participation in state functions and all subsidies from the state. "They are not communists; they recognize private ownership," Kropotkin continued. Warning that the "land monopolies" — that is, the CPR and Hudson's Bay Company — might destroy the future of Canada, he still lauded this country as a haven for emigrants driven from their own country by "social conditions."[8] In an earlier published article on "Recent Science," Kropotkin described in great detail experimental farms operated by the Canadian government. Comparisons to Siberia were drawn in that study as well, with special emphasis upon the types of crops and farming practices in both regions. He noted particularly the important experiments that Canadians were conducting with varieties of North Siberian wheat (Ladoga and Onega) and apples.[9]

The experimental farms and the seriousness with which Canada it took scientific agricultural work were featured prominently in Kropotkin's private notes. The compatibility of grains and fruit grown in Siberia and Canada was the subject of conversations he had with Dr. William Sanders, the first director of the Dominion Experimental Farm System, at the Central Branch in Ottawa. The fact that seeds for these products were exchanged between Vancouver and Vladivostok prompted the Russian to write about the immense potential of communications link-ups between Canada and Russia by ship, rail and telegraph.[10]

His personal connection with Mavor was important for further Russian-Canadian associations. Mavor was a central figure in the settlement of Doukhobors in Canada and later served as a liaison for several Soviet scientific overtures to Canada in the 1920s.[11] In 1914, he produced the first scholarly English-language history of the Russian economy, which was greeted with enthusiasm in Russia.[12] Kropotkin and Mavor had been introduced to each other in the 1880s; the Canadian professor also befriended Sergeius Stepniak (S. M. Kravchinskii) in London, where the Populist revolutionary fled after he assassinated the chief of the Russian gendarmerie in 1878.[13] Although Mavor was to become disenchanted with the Doukhobors, he remained close to Kropotkin and wrote him sympathetically in 1905 about the great unrest in Russia: "Daylight must come soon and I feel that these hours must be a time of deep anxiety to you and excitement too. I hope with you that the end will be in new awakening and the beginning of a new and better era for your country."[14]

It is unlikely that very many people in Russia outside the limited circles of Doukhobor supporters and a few scientists paid much attention to material on Canada published by Kropotkin in England. The Third Department (secret police) still watched him closely, however, and a police report in St. Petersburg charged that he went to North America solely "to spread the idea of anarchism abroad."[15] Be that as it may, his opinions mirrored and helped confirm images of Canada already commonly held in Russia: lots of 'free' land, open spaces, and a government that was not oppressive. This image was strengthened in the 1890s by the Canadian government's policy of attracting immigrants to open up Western Canada. The Ministry of the Interior, under Clifford Sifton in a Liberal government that came to office in 1896, introduced an unusually aggressive immigration policy. Sifton encouraged peasants from the Austrian and Russian Empires to come to Canada and is still remembered (not always kindly) for his statement to the effect that "peasants in sheep-skin coats" would be ideally suited to develop agriculture in the prairies. He made it abundantly clear in memoranda to the prime minister that the purpose of immigration should be limited to developing natural resources and increasing the production of wealth related to them. According to Professor M.F. Timlin, Clifton "clung to the idea of the agricultural immigrant as the only good immigrant" during his entire period in office, from 1896 to 1905.[16]

Kropotkin's timing was right, then, when he wrote Mavor in 1898 asking him to intercede with Clifton on behalf of the Doukhobors. Mavor contacted the minister soon afterwards and also corresponded with Chertkov and Tolstoy, hearing from the famous writer that the Doukhobors were "the best farmers in the world." After going to Ottawa and making arrangements himself for Doukhobors, Mavor was able to claim success. Doukhobor representatives Ivan Ivin, Petr Makhortov and Prince Dmitrii Khilkov came to Canada that year and chose a site in what was then called Assiniboia (Southern Saskatchewan). In March 1899, Tolstoy's eldest son, Sergei, arrived in Canada with one of the first boatloads of Doukhobors and called on Mavor in Toronto. A few months later Mavor was able to go to Russia to talk with the great man himself at Yasnaya Polyana.[17]

Arranging for Russians to emigrate was not an easy matter. In spite of rural over-crowding and terrible famines in 1891-92 and again in 1911, Russian emigration laws remained highly restrictive. There had been an important episode of accommodation in the emigration relationship between Russia and Canada in the 1870s after Alexander II began to withdraw privileges once used to attract German-speaking Mennonites to Russia. In 1870, the tsar issued a decree allowing Mennonites and other non-conformists ten years in which either to leave Russia or to submit to conscription. Mennonites were threatened as well with the loss of regional autonomy and the free use of German as the language of instruction in schools.

During the next few years a competititon arose between the American, Canadian, and even Russian governments, as they all came to realize that Mennonite settlers would prove beneficial to their agricultural sectors. When it became obvious that many Mennonites preferred leaving Russia to giving up what they assumed to be their rights, the Russian government offered compromises. In the end, about a third of Russia's Mennonites left anyway, mostly to the United States. Between 1874 and 1880, with help from Mennonites already living in Canada, nearly 7000 arrived in Southern Manitoba, where Kropotkin was later to visit. They had been promised land, cultural autonomy and exemption from military service, all appealing conditions to the Doukhobors as well. During the early stages of negotiation, during which several delegations came to Canada and a Canadian German, William Hespeler, went to Russia to act as agent, promotional material on Canada and Manitoba was disseminated extensively in Russia.[18] Within less than two decades, Manitoba came to be recognized in some Russian circles both as a wonderful place in which to settle because of the Mennonites, some 20,000 of whom lived in Canada by the end of the century, and at the same time a site of seething rebellion because of the Riel troubles.

The Russian government continued to prefer that its excess population move to Siberia and develop that vast region to the advantage of the state. The Trans-Siberian Railway facilitated just such a large-scale movement, but only after 1906, when Prime Minister Peter Stolypin explicitly called up the Canadian model as he encouraged peasant migration to Siberia. Stolypin recognized that Russia's system of land use was in desperate need of improvement. Even after they were freed from serfdom, peasants had remained trapped in communes to which they still owed redemption payments for land acquired by the collective in the 1860s. Stolypin's famous Land Reform, first set in motion in 1906, cancelled all redemption payments in 1907, established Land Banks to help finance the modernization of Russian agriculture, removed restrictions against peasant mobility, and provided assistance to peasants willing to migrate to Siberia. According to one biographer, the prime minister told a British diplomat in 1908 that he had studied internal migration in Canada and the United States, concluding that Canada's success story was a product of "adequate capital and well-organized private associations to assist settlers."[19]

That Stolypin was familiar with such activities in Canada has been documented. In December 1906 his office became embroiled in lengthy negotiations with the Grand Trunk Pacific Railway, a competitor to the CPR which hoped to contract Russian workers, mostly Doukhobor, to work on railway construction.[20] The Russian Consul in Montreal, Struve, relayed requests for more Russian workers from the General Manager of the Grand Trunk, Charles Melville Hays, its vice president, Frank W. Morse, several Canadian parliamentarians, and the minister of the Interior, Frank Oliver. Doukhobor leader Peter Verigin signed the final agreement on their behalf.[21] The fact that Russia and Canada had different perceptions of the purpose of emigration caused this project to break down: the Russian government expected the workers to stay in Canada for two years, then bring what they had earned back to Russia; the Canadian government was looking for permanent settlers.[22]

Stolypin certainly had a model to follow as he devised ways and means to provide more local economic autonomy in the Russian Empire. In addition to the CPR example of moving people, he admitted to using a Canadian precedent to justify a division of powers between the Russian government on the one hand, the Senate and Diet of Finland on the other.[23] A Russian law to this effect of 17 June 1910 was opposed by Finnish nationalists who insisted that their country was part of the Russian Empire by contract with Alexander I, and thus deserving of even greater autonomy. Stolypin's position was also the subject of protests by a number of foreign countries, among them England, despite its friendship with Russia by that time.

Approximately seven million Russian subjects crossed the Urals voluntarily to settle the vast reaches of Siberia during the late 19th and early 20th centuries, but this was not enough to satisfy Stolypin's plan to fill the area with productive Russian and Ukrainian peasants. Some of them returned to western Russia; others took up jobs with the Trans-Siberian, or otherwise failed to become productive farmers. The number of Russian subjects who were able to emigrate to Canada legally therefore remained scarce. Nevertheless, successive Russian consul-generals in Montreal, Struve, M.M. Ustinov, N. Passek and S.A Likhachev, continued to process requests for temporary Russian labour to Canada on the assumption that they and much of their incomes would be returned to Russia. There were other schemes devised to bring large numbers of Russian laborers to work on Canadian railway construction projects, and the CPR set up recruiting offices in Siberia. These undertakings achieved only a modicum of success.[24]

The reason for the limited effectiveness of these efforts was revealed very early in correspondence between Struve and the assistant manager of the Canadian Copper Company. In September 1901, Struve was asked to intercede with authorities in St. Petersburg to send the Company more Finlanders. Praising work done by Finnish employees in contrast to other nationals "who expect to earn large wages and give nothing in return," the Copper Company (later Inco) was doomed to disappointment. Struve's reply encapsulated the standard Russian position: "I am unable to intercede with emigration officials in my country . . . It is not in the interests of Imperial Russia to induce immigration out of our country."[25]

In Russia the message was less clear. Attempts to regulate emigration by rejecting petitions from Russian companies wanting to open up ticket agencies failed miserably because German and British shipping lines became the chief carriers of emigrants leaving Russia. By 1907, so many complaints had reached the Ministry of Trade and Industry that it, and the Ministry of Foreign Affairs, had little choice but to grant Russian "shipping businesses the possibility of participation in the profitable organization of such trips."[26] Russian shipping lines were given the right to open ticket agencies, though they remained subject to strict regulations about conditions of sales, passport rules, and the character of their agents. The Ministry of Foreign Affairs, for example, issued a "categorical demand" that all agents who "display criminal character" be immediately dismissed. The shipping lines then zealously distributed Canadian Ministry of the Interior and CPR brochures, translating them into Russian and even recommending changes to make them more appealing to a prospective Russian audience.[27]

Entire associations for the purpose of emigration had already been formed. One of these, the Jewish Colonization Society, distributed a

25-page booklet on Canada filled with general information for "any-one who wishes to go to that country." Data on Canada's major urban centres, its population, climate ("dry and healthy, only people with throat and chest diseases should not go") and geography, prices for food and other supplies, where work was to be found, and even what clothing to take on the boat were part of the wide range of advice offered in the informative little pamphlet. Locations of earlier Jewish settlement in Canada, railway fares, and a large full page map of the country also were provided.[28]

Immigration chaos was not solved by the new regulations, or by well organized private facilitating agencies. Consul General Struve reported in 1909 that he had too little information about the number of people travelling from Russia to Canada and back. No differentia-tion was drawn between regular passengers and emigrants, and statistics for the latter group were "extremely dissatisfactory," he complained. Emigrants from Russia still arrive from German, Dutch, Belgian and English ports, in the summer to Quebec and in the win-ter to St. John's or Halifax; some Russian "subjects" come to Canada via New York. The statistics "are silent," for example, about which country Poles and Jews come from. Of the 262,000 settlers arriving in Canada in 1907, Struve calculated that about 14,000 were from Russia. In addition to the earlier mass migration of Mennonites and Doukhobors, there is now, he said, a large Jewish migration from Russia fleeing "mainly from the former disorder in our fatherland." This was probably an allusion as much to the pogroms of 1903 and 1905 as it was to the rebellion of 1905. They have settled in Montreal, Toronto, Ottawa and Winnipeg, he continued, and already have "suc-ceeded in taking control in Canadian cities light industries and trades, such as tailoring, shoe making, wood working, metal working, clock making, and so on."[29] Struve complained bitterly about "sneaky" travel agents who lie to prospective settlers, making life difficult for them and for consulate personnel who eventually had to straighten matters out. He accused agents mostly from "among the Jewish pop-ulation of Russia" who, among other things, fail to inform settlers about the severity of Canada's winters and provide contracts for employment that did not exist.[30]

The new regulations in Russia prompted the Grand Trunk Pacific to apply again, in 1910, for labourers from Russia to help with the con-struction of its Transnational. This time a request was sent to the Ministry of Internal Affairs, asking that Russians be allowed to come to Canada for periods of two to three years. Under "formal contract" they were to be guaranteed "good nourishment, lodging, treatment and supervision, and also medical services." The request, signed by Louis Kon, Russian-speaking chief of the railway's Labour Department, pointed out that the company was handicapped because it was "prohibited from using workers who are not of the white races." Glossy brochures on the railway were submitted in both the French and English langauges, and Kon offered to ensure that the workers would be returned to Russia when the terms of their contracts expired.[31] He failed to mention that the Grand Trunk Pacific had suffered a debilitating strike in 1910, when Canadian workers had demanded and received a major pay hike and other concessions. Prospective Russian workers would not be informed that they were to serve as "cheap labour," though their circumstances in Canada were likely to be a considerable improvement over their working situation in Russia. As a result of opportunities such as these, the image of Canada as a land of bustling enterprise seems to have set down firm roots in Russia by the time of the outbreak of World War I.

The emigration of labour from Russia grew in spite of the state's reluctance to open its doors more than a crack, but it never approached the scale of migration by ethnic Ukrainians from the Austrian provinces of Galicia and Bukovyna between 1896 and 1914. Nevertheless, in August 1912, the Russian-America Steamship Line reported that the demand in Canada was so great that the company was prepared to transport 1,000 Russian labourers per month. Having delivered 900 already that spring, to Halifax, they complained that Canada was discriminating against Russians by requiring that they demonstrate that they had certain amount of money with them. The Line's recommendation was that the government of Canada provide an exemption for Russians as it had done for emigrants from other European countries. They illustrated how highly Russian workers were regarded in Canada by submitting dozens of letters from satisfied employers and explained their success as other Russians had: "The Dominion of Canada has more or less the same climate, soil and vegetation as in Russia, and there the Russian settler and labourer has a great field in the future, in the waste lands of the Dominion."[32]

After a few months of pressure from the immigrant carriers, both Russian and Canadian, the Department of the Interior in Ottawa gave notice that "Railway and general labourers will be admitted to Canada without money qualifications if coming to assured employment, provided they are citizens of Great Britain or Ireland, or . . . some other European country, provided they come by continuous journey from that country." This memorandum was taken to include citizens of the Russian Empire, if they were not "persons of Asiatic origin."[33] The regulations required documentary evidence of the means to reach their place of employment. Among other things, the rules dictated intricate and binding links between Russian and Canadian shipping and rail companies, and between officialdom in both countries.

The extent of the demand for labourers was obvious to Russia's few official representatives in Canada. On 24 November 1911, Struve complained to the Trade Department of the Russian Ministry of Trade and Industry that the "vast Russian population in Canada and their relations with the federal government in Ottawa takes all my time from morning to evening . . . . I have not one free hour . . . to serve the interests of the Fatherland's trade and industry."[34] The "sleepy Canada" described by Engels in the 1880s was clearly not the same country imagined by Russians twenty years later.

In fact, long before the Stolypin era in Russia and the clamour in Canada for Russian workers and settlers, the Canadian Pacific Railway Company's successes had been cited to exhort the Russian government to spend more on the Trans-Siberian Railway project. In 1891, for example, Col. N. A. Voloshinov of the Army General Staff wrote that the "Canadian government did not begrudge money for the construction of a transit route [to China], and the government of Great Britain did not begrudge funds to develop shipping between Canada and China." Like the proponents of the Canadian Railway, Voloshinov combined his opinion of the Russian enterprise as an important economic investment with the notion of the railway as national unifier. He complained that his own fellow countrymen knew too little about Siberia and its great riches and, unless it was made possible for settlers to move into the region, Russia faced the danger of leaving the area for foreigners to exploit.[35]

Voloshin was but one of the many advocates of the Trans-Siberian Railway who turned to the Canadian experience for support of their argument. Engineers were sent to Canada by the ministry of transport as early as 1889 to study the CPR, and returned with detailed accounts, photos, drawings, and geographic charts. They described how the extraordinary complex of rail, ships, grain elevators, canals, and hotels worked wonders and enthused about what such a system could do for Russia generally, and for Siberia particularly. These reports were published in at least three separate journals in 1890-1891.[36]

The most thorough account was carried over several issues of *Zhelesnodorozhnoe Delo* (Railway Affairs), an organ of the Imperial Russian Technical Society. Engineers N.S. Krugilov and A.I. Imshenik-

Kontradovich left Vladivostok in October 1899 and arrived in Vancouver in November after spending some time in Japan. Their task was to "familiarize [themselves] with all the technical, economic, administrative and operational networks of the Canadian Pacific Railway Company." With letters of introduction from the General Superindendent of the CPR, whom they met in Vancouver, they were able to ride the train eastward, visiting Ottawa first, then Montreal, Toronto and Hamilton. They met with senior Railway officials, ministers of the federal and provincial governments, bridge builders, were hosted briefly by the CPR's founding chairman, William Van Horne, and returned to Russia with masses of statistical data, regulations, schedules and blueprints.[37]

In contrast to most other reports on the CPR circulated in Russia, the Krugilov and Imshenik-Kontradovich account took care to highlight the fundamental differences between the Russian and Canadian projects, noting especially that the geographical circumstance (the CPR runs along a 45°-52° latitude; the Trans-Siberia would have to be constructed in a 50°-60° latitude), and climate ("Canada's weather is significantly less severe"), would have to be taken into consideration. Otherwise, they argued, most conditions were the same and in certain cases construction was more difficult and dangerous in Canada than in Siberia. Similarities and differences were painstakingly elaborated on and the conclusion was drawn that for moving goods and people to and from developing regions the value of a sea-to-sea rail line was inestimable.

The link between rail construction and settlement was clear in both the published and archival sources on railway building in Canada. Files for A.V. Vasiliev, member of the Council of State Comptrol and Administration of the Main Association of Russian Railways, for example, contained a description of Canadian settlement from the 15th century, with detailed analysis of the later period when the west was opened up. The role of the CPR and the Dominion Lands Act of 1872 ("like the Homestead Act in the United States") in this development were thoroughly detailed for Russian officials then hoping to open up Siberia by using the Trans-Siberian to re-settle people from over-populated villages in central Russia.[38] Further, a typed document, "On the Principles of Introducing Private Property to Siberia" (1898), from the files of the Committee of the Siberian Railway, compared land ownership and land use policies in Siberia to practices in Canada and elsewhere. Private landownership and the right to sell or pass land on to heirs have "evidently beneficial results" in Canada and the United States, the compilers of these documents somewhat begrudgingly acknowledged.[39] No reference was made to Kriukov's reports of 1897 but, as will be demonstrated shortly, Committee members must all have known of it. These and other such documents provided Russian officials with a wealth of economic reasons for connecting Siberia to western Russia by rail for the purpose of settlement and development.

A few years after Voloshinov's treatise appeared, a two-part series on the Canadian Pacific Railway and the influence it had on the growth of "economic well-being in Canada" was published as part, and a characteristic part, of efforts by Russia's officialdom to use a Canadian success story to support projects of their own. Appearing in the Ministry of Finance's *Vestnik Finansov, Promyshlennosti i Torgovli* (Journal of Finance, Industry and Trade) in 1894, the piece was a catalogue of reasons to double the number of miles in Russia's railway network.[40]

The opening paragraph of the study demonstrated its purpose especially well:

> The construction of the great Siberian Railway, which has brought to life a vast and nearly inaccessible region, [and] has created new markets stimulated by the natural wealth of Siberia, now has raised and clarified questions about the economic future of that region. In modern history ... the only analogous ... grandiose ... event is the building of the English Canadian railway.

Compiler of the report, D.D. Pokotilov, cited the several similarities between the Canadian and Russian railways and then pointed out that the Canadian venture seemed to have produced far greater benefits for Canada than the Russian system of railways was so far generating for his own country.

To explain this circumstance, the history of the Canadian Pacific Railway, its cost, and its political and economic purposes were outlined. The contract granted to a "syndicate now known as the Canadian Pacific Railway Company" to construct a line from Central Canada to British Columbia engaged Pokotilov's attention particularly. Huge government subsidies, a large land grant, and various special privileges that allowed the company to construct and control branch lines and telegraph systems, and to establish steamship services on the Atlantic and Pacific Oceans and on the Great Lakes, were believed to be especially important. Emphasis was placed on the tax free status of the company's buildings, grounds, and rolling stock and the government's promise not to allow the construction of any competing lines to the United States.

The tremendous early achievements of the CPR, which were out-lined to Russian readers on the basis of financial statistics and quantities of goods transported from one end of the country to the other, were attributed to the "compact network, utilized according to a known and strictly adhered-to programme organized by one gen-eral administration." Through its control of a wide cross-section of enterprises — railways, steamships, telegraphs, grain elevators, land, and the like — the CPR was "a powerful component of the Canadian economy, with influence in government circles from the federal to municipal levels."

The railway and its growing branch lines, it was noted, contributed enormously to the development of Western Canadian towns and cities, facilitated a dramatic increase in grain production and cattle raising, and above all made it possible to attract immigrants from overseas. A "passive attitude towards immigration and the develop-ment of land proved inadequate," and so the Canadian government actively participated in constructing the CPR complex. Ottawa's cam-paign for settlers and the terms granted them were described enthusiastically by the authors of the series, who, it is clear, wished to see a similar programme evolve in Russia.[41]

In March 1891, the government in St. Petersburg made up its mind to build a railway through Siberia in part as the consequence of the terrible famine which exposed the state's inability to transport food and medical supplies across the empire quickly. Early the next year the project was turned over to a newly formed railway department headed by Witte and located within the Ministry of Finance. The deci-sion to build the Trans-Siberian marked the culmination of a process of change in a state policy that had made it difficult for citizens to emi-grate even to Siberia. Had the famine not made the need for change so stark, a reversal in the traditional distrust of a mobile population might been slower in coming. Count Witte, whose department pro-duced the *Vestnik* noted above, was one of the rare senior officials in Imperial Russia who was already persuaded to modernize out of eco-nomic necessity and for strategic reasons. He hoped to penetrate the Chinese market and counter British and Japanese expansion into that region.[42] His goal could not be accomplished without modern trans-portation to Russia's Far East.

Russian military planners, who claimed that the CPR had proven effective in moving troops from central Canada to Manitoba in 1885,[43] promoted the Russian railway system as a means to gain effective sovereignty over northern Manchuria, and to protect the Amur and Ussuri regions in Siberia's Far East. Japan demanded control of southern Manchuria when it defeated China in a war during 1894-95, but Russia forced the victors to give up the area, occupying it themselves by 1898. The Chinese-Eastern Railway, which linked central Siberia via Chita directly with Vladivostok through Manchuria, and a branch line from Harbin straight through the Liaotung Peninsula to the port of Dalnii (precisely the area coveted by Japan), was central to St. Petersburg's strategic maneuvres in the Far East.

A long time railway official and owner himself, Witte was a strong advocate of the industrialization of Russia and recognized that a rail network was essential to the operation of an industrial economy. Later in 1892 he was appointed Minister of Finance, though he also remained in charge of the railway enterprise. It was only well after the Trans-Siberian planning was underway that he realized a still larger administrative apparatus was needed. In 1896 a new office called the Resettlement Administration was established in the Ministry of the Interior to facilitate settlement in areas through which the railway was to pass.

Except for a stretch around Lake Baikal, the Trans-Siberia link to Vladivostok was completed by 1903 and proved its importance to the development of Russia's Far East. But the nature of Russia's bureaucracy and events such as the political chaos which led to and ensued after the general strike of 1905 prevented the completed system from having the impact that the *Vestnik* authors foresaw in their description of the Canadian Pacific Railway.[44] As we have seen, the Canadian model provoked considerable debate: some proponents of the Trans-Siberian enterprise used the Canadian example to further their economic and settlement arguments, others pointed to the military-strategic value of continent-wide rail linkages. Given British-Russian hostilities in Afghanistan, Voloshinov insisted in 1890 that the CPR had been fully financed by England so as to cut some two weeks off the time it took to transport troops to the Far East. He supported the Trans-Siberian as a means to counter the British move.[45] Voloshinov's presumptions about the military significance of the CPR were a published echo of the substantial secret report submitted to the Russian Ministry of the Navy in December 1887 by Tizengauzen, "About the Military Situation of England in the Pacific Ocean and the Significance of the Canadian Railway."[46]

Neither the British nor the Russians were blind, of course, to the military potential of the CPR. As the Canadian cross-country rail line was nearing completion, war between Russia and Britain loomed once again. Russia had acquired the city of Merv in 1884 and its troops clashed with Afghan forces at Penjdeh in March 1885. British Prime

Minister W.E. Gladstone demanded defence credits on the grounds that Russia was edging inexorably towards India by threatening Afghanistan. War was averted when Germany and France pressured Turkey not to allow passage through the Straits to British warships. An accommodation in September 1885 diminished but did not eliminate tensions between the two antagonists, so Voloshinov's strategic warnings were relevant enough the planners of the Trans-Siberian Railway.

It has been determined already that the Riel rebellion did not spark the same level of interest in Canadian affairs at court in St. Petersburg as had the events of the 1830s. Nevertheless, the notice it excited in the Russian press played a part in the wide-ranging debate over the construction of the Trans-Siberian because events in Canada demonstrated how troops could be moved quickly by rail to trouble spots. Russian and British foreign policy makers were equally aware that energetic cross-continent Railway building could place their countries on a collison course more quickly than their navies could. When Lord Salisbury granted a large contract to the CPR for a Pacific Mail service in 1887, he was strongly influenced by Russian expansion on the Pacific and his belief that the Trans-Siberian Railway would make Russia a greater challenge to Britain in the Far East. CPR Chairman Van Horne confirmed this motivation in 1889, explaining to a Canadian Senate Interstate Committee on Commerce why his trans-Pacific steamers were fitted out to be converted easily into armed cruisers.[47] International frictions helped persuade the Russian government to construct the Trans-Siberian in the Canadian manner, that is, along the most direct and fastest route, even though members of the Russian Technical Society strongly advised against doing so. Among other things, they cautioned that Canadian engineers had not been compelled to build on permafrost.

War scares aside, neither country lost sight of the potential for Russian-Canadian cooperation in transportation. CPR representatives arrived in Vladivostok as early as August 1891, discussing with the Tran-Siberian Railway authorities the possibility of passenger and freight exchanges. The recently introduced CPR "Empress" line of steamships, proclaimed to be the fastest way of travelling to the Far East from North America, were central to the discussion. The first three "Empresses" (of *India, Japan,* and *China*) were commissioned in 1889 and an advertising campaign for the CPR's round-the-world tours began the next year. The fact that the *Empress of India* was completed only in January 1891 reveals how quickly Russian-Canadian negotiators found their way to Vladivostok.

For all that CPR steamships carried goods to Vladivostok after 1891, these early negotiations accomplished very little, presumably because the Trans-Siberian was not yet complete and long-standing political discord between Russia and Britain were difficult obstacles to overcome. Ten years later, however, William Whyte, vice-president of CPR's Western Lines, was sent from St. Petersburg to Vladivostok via the Trans-Siberian to study an interchange of both passenger and freight traffic. Count Witte himself provided Whyte with a letter in which all Russian Departments were instructed to assist the CPR representative and provide him with information.[48] Whyte's report, which was submitted in September 1901, rejected the idea of a regular service to Siberia.[49] Soon afterwards, the Russo-Japanese War slowed Russia's renewed and growing presence in the Pacific, and helped reduce tensions between St. Petersburg and London. It also accelerated trade between Russia and Canada, for which the new official London-St. Petersburg relationship and the consulates in Canada proved especially helpful. In April 1908, for example, the Canadian Bank of Commerce established an association with the St. Petersburg Discount Bank and its branches in Kiev, Rostov-on-Don, and Taganrog.[50] The two countries began to investigate the potential for mutual benefit much more seriously than they had in the past.

The CPR later established a recruiting office in Siberia under the auspices of its Colonization Department. Advice aimed at improving the Russian Railway system was invited from CPR officials, and Sir George Bury, CPR vice-president, was in Petrograd for that purpose when revolution broke out in 1917.[51] Before the war and revolution, Russians were especially interested in learning how to take better advantage of their own Far Eastern rail systems. The Chinese-Eastern Railway had proven inadequate during the humiliating war with Japan, and the large Amur-Ussuri region fell into a state of serious economic decline after 1905. Settlers preferred to stay in western or central Siberia, or move further south to Manchuria.[52] In an effort to improve the situation, the Amur branch of the Trans-Siberian was under construction by 1908. Its advocates spoke of the region's "inexhaustible resources," but the central government reacted more readily to reports about the region's vulnerability to Japanese, or even Chinese, military intrusion. Even at that, the branch was not completed until 1916.

The Russian government appropriated huge amounts of money for its Railway and at great cost imported some 15,000 Slavs and Tatars from European Russia and Western Siberia as labour. Japanese and Chinese migrant workers and Koreans already settled in the Ussuri region worked on the Railway, as did thousands of prisoners who were compensated by reductions in their sentences.[53] Economic development and self-sufficiency, national unity, and strategic concerns were the rallying cries behind the enterprise. Imperial Russia and Canada were rushing to tighten links between their centres and their Pacific coastlines almost at the same time, and almost for the same reasons.[54]

There is an epilogue to the story of CPR-Trans-Siberian relationships. Further proposals for closer Canadian-Russian rail and steamship connections were made in January 1917 when George W. Macdonald, a Canadian ammunition manufacturer living in Bridgeport, Connecticut, wrote the CPR president offering to help establish a rail service in Russia. The proposition was rejected immediately, with the explanation that the CPR's "traffic relations with Russia are already established on a satisfactory basis." A few months later another Canadian, Major J. Mackintosh Bell, travelled across Russia on the Trans-Siberian in July 1917 and proposed both trade relations and a direct line of small ships between Vancouver and Vladivostok. His suggestions were taken more seriously than Macdonald's, but a final decision was postponed. By that time the Autocracy had been overthrown in Russia, the Provisional Government's war offensive collapsed in July, and Russia was destabilizing further. By the time order was restored, a new revolutionary government was in place, and no such linkup was possible.[55]

* * *

Whereas the general population of Russia knew Canada as a place for settlement, work and Railway construction, the government in St. Petersburg saw it as a broad pattern of economic experience. The first full-length Russian studies of the Canadian economy appeared near the turn of the century, with the Canadian agricultural sector, its political structures, and its geography attracting the greatest attention. Several of the politically and socially motivated publications of the following few years were discussed in Chapter One, leaving the interest taken in Canada by Imperial Russia's ministries to be dealt with here. Among other things, the government sponsored studies demonstrate that Canada was used as much as a model for Russia's modernization as it was to carry Aesopian political and social messages.

By far the most important of the economic studies was a long report submitted in 1897 to the Russian Ministry of Agriculture by N.A. Kriukov, whose conclusions and recommendations were echoed clearly in reforms introduced later by Stolypin.[56] An agronomist in the employ of the Governor General of the Amur Region (Priamurskii Krai), Kriukov was very widely travelled and the author of some 300 papers on agricultural conditions around the world. Consequently, he had a wealth of experience from which to judge the merits of agricultural practices in Canada. Instructions handed him in Russia were explicit: "In light of the difficult circumstances in certain branches of the Russian agricultural economy," it would be especially useful to gather detailed information from countries similar to Russia geographically. Canada was a uniquely appropriate venue, and Kriukov was ordered there posthaste. He was allocated 800 rubles plus expenses for the task.[57]

Kriukov carried letters of introduction from the secretary of the Royal Agricultural Society of England, of which he was a member, and from the Office of the High Commissioner for Canada in London, Lord Strathcona (Donald A. Smith), who wrote directly to Clifford Sifton on Kriukov's account.[58] Even before he arrived in this country, the Russian investigator was convinced of the merits of private land ownership, especially for Siberia. In addition to its wealth of information, the study's significance lies in the extent of its circulation in Russia. The Ministry in St. Petersburg printed 1200 copies and distributed them to members of the royal family, the State Council, the Chancellery, the Committee of Ministers, Governors and Governor Generals, agricultural units of the zemstvos, representatives of the ministries of agriculture, forestry, fishing and mining in the Russian provinces and their training schools, provincial libraries, geographical and other relevant societies, Railway officials, and so on. Review copies were submitted to nearly 100 professional and popular journals.[59] Kriukov himself was given 300 extra copies to circulate, without the right to sell them. There would have been no one interested in agriculture or other natural resources industries in Russia who did not know this 235-page book about Canada well. Echoes of Kriukov's recommendations were obvious in Count Murav'ev's later proposal for the creation of a consulate in Montreal.

Kriukov's study was remarkably thorough, with sixteen chapters in which Canada's geography, government, natural resources, native peoples, trade and industrial development were carefully described. Aside from the large agricultural sector, the fishing and timber industries were allotted a full chapter each. Appendices that outlined the history and regulations of the Canadian Pacific Railway, Hudson's Bay Company, Canada's tariff regulations, and the mining industry were included. Because Russia and Canada had much the same products to sell, the author hoped that his research would help Russia become a competitor on the international market. The agriculture ministry obviously wanted to break into the British market:

> We not only do not know and do not follow the international markets, but we also ignore our competitors. England is our chief consumer, the English are the wealthiest, the most efficient and the wisest buyers; therefore, in our own interests, for our own well-being, it is important that we become better acquainted with this customer. In the meantime, articles about England appearing in our periodical literature [are shallow], . . . the majority [of our authors] do not know the language and have seen the country only through the windows of a coach. Not knowing our main clients well we are incapable of organizing our export trade and must turn to the Germans and Jews for help.[60]

Kriukov went on to complain bitterly about "unwanted middlemen" who, he claimed, impeded the normal acquisition of information on trade between Russian producers and their English buyers. The reference clearly was to Jews, so his research opened as a mirror of the rampant anti-semitism then prevalent in Russia. Kriukov spent the winter and spring of 1897 in Canada. Stressing the importance of railways, which held the very "weakly united" country together, he credited them with providing Canadians with the means to exploit their country's natural resources, make its population mobile, and open up the prairie lands ("where bison roamed and Indians galloped") to farming. Canada was able to export farm machinery to Australia, South America and Africa. Its "magnificent harvesters made by Massey-Harris have opened the way even into South Russia." Canada's "energetic and industrious population, its practicality, efficiency, and skill in trade has created a faith in Canada on the part of English capitalists," a reputation sufficient to attract credit from London for any business activity. The help that central and provincial bodies were willing to provide for agricultural development was especially important, and government measures generally were said to be among the "main causes of the material progress in Canada." Kriukov added that

> *private ownership of land* and *the high moral quality of its population.* Here are the foundations of the current and future prosperity of Canada. Families of farmers who live on their own land are religious, hard working, and frugal, [and] are the first line of defence of the state's strength and of the industrial forces of the country.[61]

His conclusion included an extraordinary panegyric to the qualities of Canada's people, much in the old Karamzin style. The praise was clearly meant to show that the strength of character represented in his real or imagined Canadians was notably absent in Russia. Kriukov's final word was "*the basic cause of success in agriculture is neither money nor machinery, rather it is the people themselves.*"[62] Of the many countries he studied, it appeared that Canada, and Canadians, served up the examples he most urged Russia to emulate.

Kropotkin's enthusiastic account of Mennonite communities in Canada were corroborated in this contemporary study. Kriukov included data on their numbers, about 20,000 by 1896, and claimed, none too modestly and perhaps with some exaggeration, that they seized an opportunity to converse with a well-informed Russian such as himself. According to Kriukov, many of the Mennonites still spoke Russian and some had revisited their previous country. They told him proudly that Prince Grigorii S. Golitsyn, Governor General of the Caucasus from 1856 to 1904, had visited several of their Canadian villages in 1893.[63] Golitsyn was one of the officials presented with a copy of Kriukov's study.

Detailed and widely-used as Kriukov's volume was, it was by no means the last word on Canada's agriculture prepared in pre-war Russia. The way in which Canada marketed its grain world wide remained a matter of great interest. A lengthy report on the grain trade in North America, mostly on the United states but with many references to Canada, was compiled by I.B. Rozen and circulated in the Yekaterinburg Guberniia (Province) in 1909, and re-worked for publication in book form in 1914.[64] The second edition featured Canada much more prominently, emphasizing grain production methods and the organization of marketing which "recently has attracted special attention from all sides of Russian society." Canadian grain elevator systems were thoroughly analysed, as were government regulations and management. The links between elevator terminals, railway and shipping centres were described with superlatives. It was made plain throughout the book that to be competitive on the world market, Russia would have to adopt many of the practices that worked for Canada and the United States.

Rozen's analysis and others were by-products of dramatic change in Russia. The pre-war decade was momentous: the disastrous war with Japan, 1904-05, demonstrated fundamental weaknesses within the Russian state, just as the Crimean War had done some forty years previously. This time, however, the humiliating loss came at a time when the country's soaring urban population and impoverished peasantry were seething with unrest. Peasant uprisings had been met with brutal police retaliation; strikes, although illegal, were endemic in urban centres; and modern revolutionary ideologies emanating from Europe swept through the country, taking on new forms as they were filtered through Russia's special combination of poverty, illiteracy and authoritarianism. Europe's first general strike occurred in Russia's major urban centres in 1905 and spread like wildfire throughout the land, causing state activity to come to a full halt. This event culminated in the creation of Russia's first parliamentary legislative body (Duma), Count Witte's resignation and, after the dissolution of the first Duma in 1906, Stolypin's accession to the prime ministership. The story of Stolypin's period in charge of Russia's agricultural and industrial modernization has been recounted in more detail elsewhere. Suffice it to say here that the Revolution of 1917 would suggest that his gargantuan efforts resulted in failure — though some would say that his assassination in 1911 by reactionary forces was a sign that he had been on the brink of success.

At any rate, for the purpose of this study, Stolypin recognized that Canada was Siberia's greatest competitor in the expanding wheat export market. He believed as well that, in the long run, Russia held an advantage, primarily because of its proximity to rapidly urbanizing Europe. Before that market could be exploited, however, the Russian prime minister was aware that settlement patterns, transportation of people and goods, and marketing techniques in Russia had greatly to improve.[65] We have seen that he looked to Canada for guidelines.

Karamzin in the first decade of the 19th century and Lakier at mid-century had evoked images of Canada that Kriukov and others now repeated. In the late nineteenth and early twentieth centuries, scientific and practical work on Canada poured forth to complement Kriukov's and other Russian studies of Canadian agriculture. Long and detailed reports on the Canadian Pacific Railway, settlement, land use, forestry, and even fox farming, were published in book or booklet forms. Russian geologists, engineers, and diplomats provided accounts of our mining industries, natural resources, bridge and canal building.[66]

The subject of settlement and efficient land use, which had come up during the debate over the Trans-Siberian, was thought sufficiently important that the Russian Ministry of Land Organization and Agriculture's Land Improvement Department sent N. N. Epanchin to Canada in 1910 to observe land use, irrigation and settlement issues. Epanchin, a "communications" engineer by training, was the eldest son of Major-General N. A. Epanchin, director of the Royal Corps of

Pages and very highly placed on the General Staff. His father's status meant that Epanchin's reports had considerable clout because they were introduced to members of important circles.[67] He arrived in Canada in April 1912 to investigate the irrigation and colonization practices of the CPR in Western Canada, focussing on Alberta. He spent nearly six months in Canada and submitted a report of some 500 pages, plus dozens of drawings and photographs of farms, Railway stations, grain elevators, and irrigation systems. The monograph included a detailed analysis of the Canadian grain trade, public education, and government (federal and provincial) management of the national resources. Above all, it was a glorification to the CPR, which he said was managed by the most capable administrators in the world and which he put forward to his department as the ideal example to follow.

The Ministry's Hydrological Committee studied Epanchin's submission in June 1913 and questioned him and other engineers at great length about its contents. Concluding that the research "had undoubted significance" because of the great similarities between Canada and Russia, the Committee urged that it be published and circulated in Russia — which it was in that same year.[68] Epanchin previously had conducted similar investigations in India and Egypt in 1910 and concluded that Canada provided the best examples for Russia. Copies of Canadian laws on settlement and both water and land management regulations were attached to the published work as annexes. The author acknowledged the assistance of Mr. Dennis, vice president of the CPR in Calgary, and M.M. Ustinov, who served briefly in 1912 as Russian Consul-General in Montreal. In 1914, another Epanchin study of Canada's grain distribution and elevator system was printed in St. Petersburg.[69]

Russian official awareness of Canada in the late 19th and early 20th centuries was expanded greatly by long and thorough reports turned into books such as those by Kriukov and Epanchin. Canada's own campaign to attract agricultural settlers and railway workers contributed to Russia's general sense of its largest neighbour. Continued questions about citizenship and the dissolution of the Doukhobor immigrant community into opposing factions also raised Canada's profile among both official and public observers in Russia of the international scene.

Russian authorities were concerned about the role Doukhobors might play in damaging the image of their homeland abroad. Tolstoy was in disrepute with the Russian government and was excommunicated by the Orthodox Church in 1901, so there was a deep-seated suspicion of the connections between him, Kropotkin and the

Doukhobors among officials in St. Petersburg. Doukhobors were said to have read Kropotkin's published articles on Canada and to have been influenced by them. Tolstoy, who donated the profits of his final novel, *Voskresen'e* (Resurrection, 1899), to the Doukhobor cause, chose engineer Leopold Sulerzhitskii to act as his agent in assisting them to emigrate. Sulerzhitsky came to Canada ahead of the migration and helped Mavor make appropriate arrangements. On returning to Moscow, Sulerzhitskii added a chronicle of his efforts to the already long list of titles on the Doukhobors in Canada. The book was filled with anecdotes, stories, and studies of individuals and groups in their new life in Manitoba and Saskatchewan, all in a much more optimistic tone than that used earlier by Demens.[70]

The arrival of Doukhobors helped lift the "Russian" population in Canada from approximately 1200 in 1881 to nearly 20,000 by 1901.[71] The number of migrants from Russia was to increase by more than four times in the following decade. Hundreds of Doukhobors took up jobs on railway construction to raise money to help build their new villages. The Russian state interest in the Doukhobor story remained strong and their activities in Canada were closely observed by the new Russian Consul. In 1903, for example, Struve filed a report from the Canadian Commisioner of Immigration in Winnipeg that certain Doukhobors "left their villages and marched to Yorkton intending to proceed to other parts over the country in a state of undress which was considered indecent." The marchers were arrested and sentenced to jail with three months of hard labour, he wrongly informed his superiors in the Russian Ministry of Foreign Affairs.[72]

In 1906 Struve wrote A.K. Bentkovskii, director of the Second Department, that if another large contingent of Doukhobors were to come to Canada they would not receive the same "privileges" granted to the earlier migration. Instead, they would be obliged to enter Canada under the same guidelines as all other immigrants. His authority on this point was Canada's new Minister of Interior, Frank Oliver, who acknowledged that the Doukhobors were hardworking and worthy of respect. Yet their "tendency to isolationism and exclusion, and also their evident subordination to the will of one leader [Peter V. Verigin], who has vast influence over them" was a problem for the state and the larger community.[73] Ongoing Doukhobor problems with the Canadian government were fairly widely publicized in Russia. In Canada, by 1907, Mavor had reservations himself about the community, writing Kropotkin that they were "difficult" and explaining that he could no longer help the Doukhobors because of their obstinate behaviour towards Ottawa.[74]

Prince G.E. Lvov, a Constitutional Democrat (Kadet) who was to became premier of Russia as the head of the first Provisional Government after the February Revolution in 1917, visited the Canadian Doukhobor community in 1909. According to Paul Miliukov, foreign minister in that same later government, Lvov remarked that "observing the Doukhobor communes among the Canadian farmers, one is involuntarily gripped by a feeling of pride in the Russian name, in the inner dignity of that people which could produce from among itself such a noble offshoot so full of energy and idealism." Miliukov, however, was not complimentary about Lvov who, he claimed, was very unrealistic and failed to notice any of the less palatable characteristics of the community.[75]

The lively interest within Russia about Doukhobors residing in Canada was matched by the Doukhobors' own resilient attachment to their original homeland. In contrast to Mennonites who were ethnically German, the Doukhobors were, and remained, very Russian in language, customs and religion. From the beginning they retained an affiliation with their native soil, and the notion that they might one day return on their own terms never fully disappeared. Demen's early efforts notwithstanding, the first serious attempt to retrace their steps came only in November 1906, shortly after the general strike of 1905 forced the tsar to grant Russia a constitutional structure. Almost at the same time the Canadian government demanded that Doukhobors take an oath of loyalty, a persuasive instrument in Verigin's request that his followers be allowed repatriation. He led a delegation of six to Russia for discussion, a five-day visit with Tolstoy, and to search for yet another location for his flock. According to the Doukhobor leader's letters, Stolypin took the proposal directly to the tsar, who agreed that they should be allowed to return.

Regardless of the fact that the Russian government set aside free land for Doukhobors in the Altai region, the great restoration was not to be. According to Verigin's letters back to Canada, the conditions of disorder, revolution and hunger in Russia were such that he advised them not to follow up on their own request. The setback did not dampen Doukhobor enthusiasm for Russia and small groups continued to apply for resettlement.[76] Verigin considered other possible homes, such as Bulgaria and Switzerland, and openly distrusted the Canadian government. He complained to Tolstoy in 1907 that Ottawa was offering citizenship to anyone who would agree to work land (15 acres) on an individual basis. Most would not fall victim to this "dirty trick" he said, because they already had decided not to take out citizenship. On the other hand, the Doukhobors were "enjoying full health and prosperity" in Canada and were able even to provide Tolstoy with 10,000 rubles to help resolve the problem of "hunger in Russia." This was a strangely mixed message.[77]

The Doukhobor saga was well known in Russia, though much of the writing about them was inaccurate. Canada itself was far better known in Russia at the turn of the century when Mizhuev was writing than it had been during Lakier's time. Officialdom and the business community were apt to see Canada as a competitor in the world market, yet also one with an industrial and trade capacity worth copying. Canada was regarded by some groups in Russia as a site especially well-suited for emigration and by many others as an ideal place for temporary employment.

As Kriukov demonstrated in 1897, agriculturalists and government agencies throughout the Russian Empire had been familiar with and impressed by at least one famous Canadian product for many years. In 1885, Massey harvesting machinery represented Canada at the International Exhibition in Antwerp, earning gold medals and, more importantly, orders from around the world. One of these came from Saratov, in South Russia. Massey-Harris business in Russia flourished. Its harvesters were introduced to the Crimean Peninsula in the late 1880s and permanent offices were opened in St. Petersburg, Moscow, and Omsk by 1907. Russian agents sold Canadian agricultural machinery in Ukraine (Voronezh and Kharkov), in Warsaw, the Caucasus, and along the Trans-Siberian Railway as far east as Vladivostok. Warehousing facilities were opened in Moscow in 1908, with R.O. Macdonald from Ottawa as their manager.

In August 1912 the Agronomy Bureau of the Russian Department of Agriculture conducted extensive tests of agricultural equipment from several countries. As part of the process a memorandum was sent to the agricultural provinces (gubernii) and districts (uezdy) for commentary on Western European and North American machinery. Responses, as they trickled in during 1913, were overwhelmingly in favour of Massey-Harris products. "Very good," "easy to use," "simple and light," were common evaluations. Massey-Harris won the competititon for binders easily. Another Canadian firm, Frost and Wood (Smith Falls, Ontario), came fourth behind French and German machines, but was still rated very highly. In a final report prepared by the ministry, Massey-Harris equipment was said to be "first class . . . and able to provide a large quantity of machines."[78] A warehouse director in Tula informed the ministry that he already had ordered 19 harvesters and six binders from the Massey-Harris plant, and a chief agronomist in Omsk reported that individuals and associations in his region had been buying Massey-Harris machines because they are "widely used and there are spare parts for them at the warehouses."[79] The final report made it clear that Massey-Harris had dominated the field since 1908, and proclaimed that the

> Massey-Harris enterprise is first class and can produce a large number of machines at its three factories. It could manufacture approximately 10,000 machines for Russia. Presently it sends 4,500 hay binders to Russia. These machines are reliable. Having worked on 23.5 desyatins one such machine did not break and its parts did not wear much, though it worked under very hard conditions: wet wheat, sticky soil and bad handling of the machine.

Frost and Wood, in fact, was judged the manufacturers of the best harvesters for Russia. It too had a factory in Russia and, according to the report, was capable of adding another 2,500 hay binders to the purchasing list. But in terms of quantity and quality, it was Massey-Harris agricultural equipment that most helped Russia make a strong appearance in the world wheat market, contributing to a drop in the world price of wheat.[80] Ironically, the tests were initiated because of an imminent tariff war with the United States, whose International Harvesters had been commonly purchased in Russia.

Wanting to break into the world market themselves, Russia still took care not to allow North American merchants a long-term foothold in the Siberian market when it meant close competititon with Russian producers. In November 1907, for example, the Military Governor of the Primorskii oblast passed on to the Ministry of Foreign Affairs in St. Petersburg a request from an American firm for a two-year contract to supply the Russian Far East with frozen meat from Washington State and live cattle and sheep from Canada. After much discussion and correspondence, and an acknowledgement by the Ministry that there was a severe food shortage in the region, the proposal was rejected. To solve the problem of food shortages, the ministry decided to subsidize the cost of shipping cattle to the Far East from Western Siberia and the steppe region by rail and lower rail prices for the transport of such goods.[81]

In 1913 there was an overture to Canada from the Russian Ministry of Finance for trade and co-operation in the field of agriculture. This request came just as the Russian State Duma was discussing the question of expanding its consulates in Berlin, London, New York, Paris, Breslau, Leipzig, Chicago, and Canada; and instituting new consulates in Nome, Seattle, Pittsburgh, and Honolulu. A law was passed to this effect in June 1913.[82] The Pacific focus of Russia's widening diplomatic and trade service had important manifestations for Canada. The Russian Ministry of Foreign Affairs made discreet enquries in 1913 about lands purchased in British Columbia by wealthy German capitalists and was informed by its Second Department that German interests in the province were vast and included valuable shore line, huge tracts of land, forests and mining concerns. This discovery may have been the incentive behind the formation in November 1913 of a Russo-Canadian Trading Syndicate in British Columbia, with capital assets of $250,000.[83] Vancouver would be added to the list of proposed new full consulates in 1915.

Two years before that, however, the newly-appointed Consul General in Montreal, N. Passek,[84] informed Prime Minister Sir Robert Borden's office that his Ministry planned to send a delegate to Canada to discuss matters concerning "commerce, industry, agriculture, and ways of communication." Shortly thereafter, I. M. Goldstein (Gol'dshtein) arrived from St. Petersburg and presented Borden with two official proposals: first, citing an economic crisis in Russia, he invited Canada to send commercial travellers to help create an export market for Canadian industrial goods; secondly, he proposed a conference of representatives from all countries with a major interest in exporting agricultural products. The meeting to discuss cooperation on grain elevators, farmers co-operatives, and rural credit plans was to be held in St. Petersburg and co-sponsored by Canada and Russia.

In response to a letter of introduction from the Consul General, Prime Minister Borden offered access to all the appropriate federal ministers. Between May and October 1913, Goldstein travelled widely, presenting his ideas to provincial premiers who apparently were enthusiastic about them, as were the Canadian Minister of Trade and Commerce and Minister of Agriculture. On the face of it then, this was a very high level business venture, but Goldstein's own agenda appeared to be to learn Canadian methods of handling and transporting wheat, ultimately to raise the viability of Russian exports.[85] This may explain why negotiations moved so slowly that by the outbreak of the First World War a year later little progress had been made. Neither the conference nor a government sponsored effort to reach new markets in Russia materialized.[86] A professor at Moscow University and a specialist on wheat, Goldstein hoped, as Kriukov had, to adapt the best of Canada's agricultural methods to Russian conditions.

In Montreal Passek was kept busy with matters of immigration. In the spring of 1913, he helped work out an arrangement to bring immigrant workers from eastern Russia on short-term contracts. They were escorted from Vancouver to the prairies under armed guard to prevent desertion from their obligatory jobs with the Canadian Pacific and the Grand Trunk railways.[87] Worried about false impressions many Russian emigrants seemed to have on their arrival in Canada, Passek wrote the Ministry of Trade and Industry in August 1913 asking that all Russians emigrating to Canada be provided with two documents: a copy of "Obligatory Rules, issued by the Canadian Government 22 April/5 May 1913, for the Purpose of the Protection and Defence of Immigrants Who Seek Work or Positions in Canada;" and a piece of his own, "Advice and Instructions for Russian Emigrants Arriving in Canada." He proposed that these documents be passed out to passengers scheduled to embark on the Russian-American Line, the Atlantic branch of the Russian Eastern-Asiatic Steamship Line, which offered the only direct connection between Libau (Lithuania) and Halifax.[88] Steamship service between Vladivostok and Vancouver also opened in 1913, so there was some urgency to Passek's request.

The Consul opened his own two-page document with a warning that reflected the contemporary pogrom-ridden spirit of Russia: "Beware of Jewish-agents. Do not trust them." He cautioned readers not to pay more than once for their places on the ship, to carry the correct documents at all times, especially the *"kvitantsiia,"* or receipt, which was to be shown but not relinguished under any circumstances. Emigrants were told not to "despair" because of their ignorance of Canada's languages, laws or customs: the office of vice-consul in Halifax had been established to help them. Unfortunately, Passek added, the post of vice-consul was still unfilled and the director (Honourary Consul Harry Mathers) was English. On the other hand, the consulate had a full-time Russian officer "who knows English." It was his responsibility to help new arrivals and to make sure that they were not exploited by "Jewish-agents" who operated illegally.[89] The Canada end of the Russian emigration story mirrored the Russian starting point. Kriukov, Struve and Passek all revealed in various ways their personal antagonism against Jews, exposing, one would assume, the prevalent attitude within the Russian government.

The request from Montreal was passed up through the bureaucracy to the Second Department of the Ministry of Foreign Affairs and was approved in February, 1914.[90] The Russian Eastern-Asiatic Steamship Line was ordered to distribute the documents to all passengers journeying to North America. The steamship company replied that it would be delighted to comply and, pointing to several pages in its advertising brochure, insisted that the company already was going to great lengths to counter the "exploitation" of Russian emigrants by "unprincipled and illegal agents." The Managing Director of the passenger line even recommended that Passek's own "Advice and Instruction" be disseminated to the general Russian population as a warning against unscrupulous travel agents. This proposal was accepted by the Ministry and cleared, after a month's delay, with the Department of Police.[91]

Passek still was not to have his way, for Russia's cumbersome bureaucracy had the final word. Senior officials at the Ministry of Trade and Industry were more concerned about another problem. They warned that if the Canadian rules were circulated they might spread the idea that "every newcomer to Canada has an opportunity to get a job and receive income" and the "flow of workers to America, which already has grown on a vast scale recently" would increase still more. More importantly, the ministry's struggle to stem "illegal migration abroad" would be jeopardized. In June 1914, a decision came down that "distribution of these documents among working people of the Empire would not be desirable" because they would promote an increase in emigration to North America.[92] By that time Passek had left Canada, defeated it would seem by the glaring contradictions in St. Petersburg's approach to emigration generally, and to Canada specifically. He was replaced by S.A Likhachev.

---

[1] See J.L. Black, *Canada in the Soviet Mirror. Ideology and Perception in Soviet Foreign Policy, 1917-1991* (Ottawa: Carleton UP, 1998), *passim*.

[2] Engels to Sorge (Montreal, 10 September 1888), *Karl Marx and Frederick Engels. Letters to Americans, 1848-1985. A Selection*. Edited by Alexander Trachtenberg (New York: International Publishers, 1953), pp. 203-04.

[3] Kropotkin, "Some of the Resources of Canada," *Nineteenth Century*, Vol. 43 (March, 1898), pp. 494-514; cited here p. 502. For a general account of Kropotkin and Canada, see G.I. Luzianin, "Kanadskoe puteshestvie P.A. Kropotkina" [The Canadian Travels of P.A. Kropotkin], *Novaia i noveishaia istoriia*, No. 3 (May-June 1994), pp. 235-241.

[4] Kropotkin, "Some of the Resources of Canada," pp. 513, 494-496. On Tobol'sk and Quebec City, see Kropotkin, "Kanada i kanadtsy" [Canada and the Canadians], notes made in Canada, GARF, Fonds 1129, Opis 1, delo 491, p. 92.

5   See especially, GARF, Fonds 1129, Opis 1, delo 491, pp. 116-119, 74-83.

6   Kropotkin, *In Russian and French Prisons* (New York: Schocken, 1976), p. x. On Kropotkin in Canada, see also James Mavor, *My Windows on the Street of the World*, Vol. 2 (Toronto: J.M. Dent, 1923), pp. 91-106.

7   See Kropotkin, *Memoirs of a Revolutionist* (Boston: Houghton-Mifflin, 1930), reprint of 1899 edition; George Woodcock and Ivan Avakumovic, *The Doukhobors* (Toronto: McClelland and Stewart, 1977), p. 131; Caroline Cahm, *Peter Kropotkin and the Rise of Revolutionary Anarchism* (New York: Cambridge UP, 1990); and Jennifer Anderson, *Three Men and a Cause. Lev Tolstoy, James Mavor, Peter Kropotkin and the Doukhobor Migration to Canada, 1899*. MA Thesis, CERAS, Carleton University, 1996.

8   Kropotkin, "Some of the Resources of Canada," *passim*.

9   Kropotkin, "Recent Science," *Nineteenth Century*, Vol. 42 (November 1897), pp. 799-820; cited here pp. 810-815. On the introduction of Russian grains to Canada, see A.I. Sych, "O roli slavianskoi immigratsii v osvoenii Kanadskogo Zapada (1896-1914 gg)" [On the Role of Slavic Immigration in the Development of Western Canada, 1896-1914], *Amerikanskii ezhegodnik, 1989* (Moscow: Nauka, 1990), p. 183. See also the report by N. Struve, 1900, translated below.

10 See, e.g., Kropotkin, "V bytnosti moiu v Kanade" [When I was in Canada], GARF, Fonds 1129, Opis 1, delo 715, pp. 3-5.

11 For a guide to the extensive Mavor collection held in the Thomas Fisher Rare Book Library, University of Toronto, see Dolores A. Signori, compiler, *Guide to the Papers of James Mavor* (Winter, 1989) [Hereafter JMP]. Mavor held the Chair of Political Economy and Constitutional History from 1892 to 1923. See Donald Senese, "James Mavor: Canadian Pioneer of Russian Studies," *International Journal of Canadian Studies*, 9 (Spring 1994), pp. 125-136, and Galina Alekseeva, "James Mavor and the Doukhobors," in *The Doukhobor Centenary in Canada*, edited by Andrew Donskov, et al. (Ottawa: SRG, 2000), pp. 149-157.

12 Mavor, *An Economic History of Russia*, 2 Vols. (London and Toronto: J.M. Dent & Sons, 1914). For a strongly supportive Russian review of Mavor's History, in which his relationship with Kropotkin was noted, see V. Semevskii, "Zamechatel'nyi trud angliiskago uchenago po istorii Rossii" [Noteworthy Work by an English Scholar on the History of Russia], *Golos Minuvshago*, No. 11 (November 1915), pp. 303-309.

13 Mavor, *My Windows on the Street of the World*, Vol. 1, pp. 251-253. Stepniak wrote many articles about Russia for London's *The Times* and several

books which Mavor read carefully. See also D.B. Saunders, "Stepniak and the London Emigration. Letters to Robert Spence Watson, 1887-1890," *Oxford Slavonic Papers*, Vol. 13 (1980), pp. 80-93.

14 Mavor to Kropotkin, 5 July 1905, GARF, Fonds 1129, Opis 2, delo 1826. Kropotkin was still living in London.

15 See a special issue of *Byloe*, Bk. 7 (1919), devoted to Kropotkin.

16 Mabel F. Timlin, "Canada's Immigration Policy, 1896-1910," *The Canadian Journal of Economics and Political Science*, 36: 4 (1960), pp. 517-532, cited here, p. 518. On Sifton and the immigration policy, see also John C. Lehr, "Government Perceptions of Ukrainian Immigrants to Western Canada, 1896-1902," *Canadian Ethnic Studies*, 19:2 (1987), pp. 1-12, and D.J. Hall, *Clifford Sifton*, Vol. 2 (Vancouver: UBC, 1981), pp. 254-269.

17 For much greater detail, see *Sergei Tolstoy and the Doukhobors: A Journey to Canada*, edited by Andrew Donskov (Ottawa: SRG, 2000), and John Woodsworth, *Russian Roots & Canadian Wings. Russian Archival Documents on the Doukhobor Emigration to Canada*, CRCR Canada/Russia Series, Vol. 1 (Ottawa: Penumbra Press, 1999).

18 See Frank H. Epp, *Mennonites in Canada, 1786-1920* (Toronto: Macmillan, 1974), pp. 183-194. Mennonites first came to Canada from Pennsylvania, after the American Revolution, settling mainly in Upper Canada around the Niagara region.

19 Cited in Mary Schaeffer Conroy, *Peter Arkad'evich Stolypin. Practical Politics in Late Tsarist Russia* (Boulder: Westview, 1976), p. 47; see also p. 81.

20 See letter from Russian Minister of Foreign Affairs, Second Department, to A.P. Stolypin (20 October 1907), RGIA, Fonds 1291, Opis 50, delo 23, pp. 51-52. The negotiations had been underway since 1903. For details, see LI-RA-MA, Vol. 20, files 649-650 (1903-1907).

21 GARF, Fonds 1291, Opis 50, delo 23, pp. 72-73.

22 LI-RA-MA, Vol. 20, file 650, see especially letter from Struve to Frank W. Morse, Vice President, Grand Trunk Pacific Railway (6 November 1906).

23 Conroy, *Peter Arkad'evich Stolypin*, pp. 130, 145.

24 David Davies, "The Pre-1917 Roots of Canadian-Soviet Relations," *Canadian Historical Review*, 70: 2 (1989), pp. 191-193.

25 LI-RA-MA, Vol. 3, file 91.

26 "V Pravlenie Severnago Parokhodnago O-va" [To the Management of the
   Northern Steamship Company], (28 November 1907), RGIA, Fonds 111,
   Opis 1, delo 184, pp. 191-194. This directive was issued by the Ministry
   of Trade and Industry, Shipping Division.

27 See, for example, a letter from an official of the Russia-America Line to
   the East Asiatic Co., Ltd (17/30 September 1912), RGIA, Fonds, 104, Opis
   1, delo 265, p. 85.

28 Jewish Colonization Society, *Kanada. Obshchiia svedeniia i ukazaniia dlia
   zhelaiushchikh ekhat' v etu stranu* [Canada. General Information and
   Instructions for Those Who Hope to Go to that Country], (St. Petersburg:
   A.M. Lesman, 1905).

29 Struve, "Torgovlia i promyshlennost' Kanady. — Russkie emigranty v
   Kanade" [Trade and Industry in Canada. Russian Emigrants in Canada],
   Sbornik konsul'skikh donesenii (St. Petersburg, 1909). Issue III, pp. 226-235.

30 The pamphlet about Canada produced by the Jewish Colonization
   Society was, in fact, quite realistic about the climate in Canada, see
   Kanada. Obshchiia svedeniia . . .(1905), p. 3.

31 Louis Kon to Minister of Interior, 23 October 1910, RGAVMF, Fonds 420,
   Opis 1, delo 180, pp. 73-74. Kon was later to be suspected of involvement
   in the Winnipeg General Strike (1919) and was a member of the
   Canadian Economic Commission to Siberia, Vladivostok, in that same
   year. After the Russian Revolution, he became a leading figure in
   Canadian-Soviet Friendship Societies. See J.L. Black, *Canada in the Soviet
   Mirror, passim*. On the search for Railway workers, see Donald Avery,
   "Canadian Immigration Policy and the 'Foreign' Navvy, 1896-1914,"
   Historical Papers, 1972, pp. 135-156.

32 See letter from The Russian America Line to Lord Strathcona, High
   Commissioner for Canada in London (9/22 August 1912), RGIA, Fonds
   104, Opis 1, delo 265, p. 102-108. The term "waste land" was in the
   English-language original, presumably itself a translation from an original Russia-language copy. The money was referred to as a "fee" in the
   letter.

33 Copy of Department of the Interior Circular on Immigration, Ottawa
   (12 March 1913), RGIA, Fonds 104, Opis 1, delo 265, p. 22.

34 RGIA, Fonds 23, Opis 11, delo 354, pp. 1-2. Struve repeated this
   complaint two weeks later.

35 Voloshinov, "Sibirskaia zheleznaia doroga" [Siberian Railway], *Izvestiia Imperatorskago Russkago Geograficheskago Obshchestva*, 27, no. 1 (1891), pp. 11-39, cited here p. 26. See also David N. Collins, "Plans for Railway Deveplopment in Siberia, 1857-1890, and Tsarist Colonialism," *Siberica*, 1:2 (Winter 1990/91), p. 146.

36 For two of them, see "Sibirskaia zheleznaia doroga s ekonomicheskoi i strategichesoi tochki zreniia" [The Siberian Railway From the Economic and Strategic Point of View], *Severnyi Vestnik*, No. 1 (1891), pp. 16-22, 26; A.F. Edziarskii, "Kratkii ocherk Kanadskoi Tikhookeanskoi zheleznoi dorogi" [Short Outline of the CPR], *Izvestiia Sobraniia Inzhenerov Putei Sobshcheniia*, Vol. 10, No.'s 7-8 (1890), p. 106.

37 N.S. Kruglikov, A.I. Imshenik-Kontradovich, "O Kanadskoi tikhookeanskoi zheleznoi doroge. 'Zapiska' inzhenerov" [On the Canadian Pacific Railway. Engineers' "Notes"], *Zheleznodorozhnoe Delo*, No.'s 3-4, 7-8 (St. Petersburg, 1891), pp. 25-44, 77-111. Their reports were also published separately by the Society as a single booklet.

38 See "Spravka ob istoricheskom khod zaseleniia Kanady . . ." [Information About the History of Canadian Settlement], RGIA, Fonds 1566, Opis 1, delo 166, pp. 1-12. The Dominion Lands Act allowed prospective settlers to buy 160 acres (a quarter section) for $10 and an additional 80 acres at $1 each, subject to certain requirements about building a place of residence and planting annual crops.

39 "Osnovy nasazhdeniia zemlevladeniia v Sibiri" [On the Principles of Introducing Private Property to Siberia], RGIA, Fonds 1273, Opis 1, delo 357, pp. 23-35.

40 "Kanadskaia tikho-okeanskaia zheleznaia doroga i ee vliianie, okazannoe eiu na rost' ekonomicheskago blagosostoianiia Kanady" [The Canadian Pacific Railway and the Influence which it has on the Growth of the Economic Well-Being of Canada], *Vestnik Finansov, Promyshlennosti i Torgovli*, No. 45 (1894), pp. 382-385; No. 46 (1894), pp. 525-529. All the sources quoted in the articles were Canadian, British, and German.

   On the CPR's role in opening up Canada, see John A. Eagle, *The Canadian Pacific Railway and the Development of Western Canada, 1896-1914* (Montreal: McGill/Queen's, 1989).

41 *Vestnik, Finansov, Promyshlennosti i Torgovli*, No. 46 (1894), p. 528.

42 On Witte, see especially *The Memoirs of Count Witte*, translated and edited by Sidney Harcave (Armond, NY: M.E. Sharpe, 1990); on Witte as

Minister of Finance, see T.H. von Laue, *Sergei Witte and the Industrialization of Russia* (New York: Columbia, 1963).

[43] See, for example, *Journal de St. Petersbourg* (21 Mars / 2 Avril 1885), p. 1.

[44] On this, see especially Steven G. Marks, *Road to Power. The Trans-Siberian Railway and the Colonization of Asian Russia, 1850-1917* (Ithaca, NY: Cornell UP, 1991). The Chita to Vladivostok line, that is, north of the Amur and Ussuri, was not finished until 1916.

[45] Voloshinov, "Tikhookeanskaia-kanadskaia Sibirskaia zheleznye dorogi," *Zhelesnodorozhnoe Delo*, No. 19 (1887), p. 157, and *Neskol'ko Slov o Sibirskoi Zheleznoi Dorogi* (St. Petersburg, 1890), cited in Marks, *The Road to Power*, p. 33.

[46] Tizengauzen, "Zapiska . . . ," *op. cit.*, RGAVMF, Fonds 417, Opis 1, delo 296, pp. 1-24. See above Chapter 2, endnote 82.

[47] Van Horne cited in John Murray Gibbon, *Steel of Empire. The Romantic History of the Canadian Pacific, the Northwest Passage of Today* (Toronto: McClelland & Stewart, 1935), pp. 311-12.

[48] Whyte to T.G. Shaughnessy, CPR President, 30 August 1901, Canadian Pacific Archives RG2. A.A. 64789. Whyte was given the title "Assistant to the President" for the purpose of this trip. He called Witte, rightly, "the highest and strongest man in Russia." The author is indebted to Judith Nefsky, Corporate Archivist, for her assistance in locating this material in the Canadian Pacific Archives.

[49] On Whyte's report and the results of an interview he gave to the Canadian press about it, see letters from Whyte to Shaughnessy, 10, 16 September 1901, Canadian Pacific Archives, RG2. A.A. 64783; 64789. See also Gibbon, *Steel of Empire*, p. 355. I have not been able to locate the actual report.

[50] See, for example, letter from Canadian Bank of Commerce Head Office, Toronto (12 February 1909) to St Petersburg Discount Bank, RGIA, Fonds 598, Opis 2, delo 585, pp. 1-4.

[51] *Canadian Railway and Business World* (November 1918), p. 492.

[52] See Steven G. Marks, "The Burden of the Far East: The Amur Railway Question in Russia, 1906-1916," *Sibirica*, I:1 (1993/94), pp. 9-28.

[53] Marks, "The Burden of the Far East," p. 18, and *Road to Power*, pp. 179-185.

[54] For a study of attempts by the business community to break out of Russia's "colonial" position in the face of foreign and especially German economic domination, see Ruth Amende Roosa, "Russian Industrialists Look to the Future: Thoughts on Economic Development, 1906-17," in *Essays in Russian and Soviet History in Honor of Geroid Tanquary Robinson* (New York: Columbia UP, 1968), pp. 198-220. For an early picture of Russian/German competition in the Far East, see Albert J. Beveridge, *The Russian Advance* (London: Harper & Brothers, 1904), Chapter 12.

[55] See James Mackintosh Bell, *Side Lights on the Siberian Campaign* (Toronto: Ryerson, 1922). For the Macdonald proposal, see letter of Geo. W. Macdonald to President of the CPR, 15 January 1917; Secretary to President of CPR to Macdonald, 16 January 1917; Memorandum for Mr. Wanklyn [re Bell], 6 September 1917, Canadian Pacific Archives, RG2, A.A. 107558.

[56] Published as Kriukov, *Kanada. Sel'skoe Khoziaistvo v Kanade v Sviazi s Drugimi Otrasliami Promyshlennosti* [Canada. Agriculture in Canada in Connection with Other Branches of Industry], (St. Petersburg: Ministry of Agriculture, 1897). See translations of Foreword and Conclusion below.

[57] Ministry of Agriculture Instruction, No. 2149 (29 January 1897), RGIA, Fonds 398, Opis 69, delo 20141, pp. 3-4. This 200-page file on Kriukov's venture in Canada covers the period January 1897 to October 1902.

[58] *Ibid.*, pp. 7-9.

[59] *Ibid.*, pp. 36-37. This file contains a full list of official recipients.

[60] Kriukov, *Kanada* (1897), pp. v-vi.

[61] *Ibid.*, pp. 213-16. The italics were Kriukov's. He included drawings of Canadian farm machinery, many of which were built by the internationally famous Massey-Harris company.

[62] *Ibid.*, p. 317. The italics were Kriukov's.

[63] *Ibid.*, pp. 206-08.

[64] Rozen, *Postanovka khlebnoi torgovli v Soedinennykh shtatakh i Kanade* [Report on the Grain Trade in the United States and Canada], (Khar'kov: M. Sergeeva, K. Gal'chenka, 1914).

[65] See, on this, Donald W. Treadgold, *The Great Siberian Migration. Government and Peasant in Resettlement from Emancipation to the First World War* (Princeton: Princeton UP, 1957), pp. 153-183.

[66] See, for example, Engineer P.A. Velikhov, *Severnaia Amerika. Tekhnicheskiia vpechatleniia ot poezdki po vostochnoi chasti Severo-Amerikanskikh Soedinennykh Shtatov i Kanady letom 1912 goda* [North America. Technical Impressions from a Trip to the Eastern Parts of the North American United States and Canada in the Summer of 1912], (Moscow: S.P. Yakovlev, 1913); P.I. Stepanov, "Poezdka v Kanadu na XII mezhdunarodnyi geologicheskii kongress" [Trip to Canada for the XII International Geological Congress], (1913); and V. Ya. Generozov, *Promyshlennoe razvedenie Screbristo-Chernykh lisits' i pestsov' v Severnom Amerike. Otchet po osmotru lisovodnykh pitomnikov v Kanade* [Industrial Cultivation of Gray and Black Foxes and White Foxes in North America. Report from a Study of Fox Breeding in Canada], (Petrograd: M. Merkushev, 1916). Kriukov included an annex on Canada's mining industry and Nikolai Struve, Consul General, prepared an entire report on the industry in 1907.

[67] On this, see his father's memoir, N. A. Epanchin, *Na sluzhbe trekh imperatorov* [In the Service of Three Emperors], (Moscow: Nashe nasledie, 1996). The younger Epanchin was born in 1883, emigrated to Berlin in 1923 and then moved to the USA, where he died in 1970.

[68] Epanchin, *Oroshenie i Kolonizatsiia Chernozemnykh Prerii Dal'niago Zapada Kanady Obshchestvom' Kanadskoi Tikhookeanskoi Zheleznoi Dorogi* [Irrigation and Colonization of the Canadian Far Western Prairies by the Canadian Pacific Railway Company], Vol. 1 (St. Petersburg: R Golinke, A. Vil'borg, 1913). For the Hydrological Committee's meetings, see "Gidrologicheskii komiteta" meeting protocols, RGIA, Fonds 426, Opis 9, delo 357, pp. 43-70.

[69] Epanchin, *Kanadskii Zakon o Zerne Izdaniia 1912. Materialu k Elevatornomu Delu v Kanade* [Canadian Law About Grain Published in 1912. Material About Elevators in Canada] (St. Petersburg, 1914).

[70] Sulerzhitskii's *V Ameriku s dukhoborami*, published in 1905, was translated in the 1980s as *To America with the Doukhobors* (Regina: Canadian Plains Research Center, 1982); see also Woodcock and Avakumovic, *The Doukhobors*, pp. 139-140. For Mavor's portrayal of Sulerzhitskii and the debate within the Doukhobor community about retaining "communism" as the guideline for property ownership, see *My Windows on the Street of the World*, Vol. 2, pp. 11-14.

[71] E.W. Laine, *op. cit.*; the term "Russians" included Finns, Poles, Ukrainians, and other peoples who came from the Russian Empire.

[72] RGIA, Fonds 1149, Opis xii-1899, delo 23, pp. 61-63. Struve's report to his ministry included a list of the names of all fifty or so Doukhobors who

were arrested. In fact, at Yorktown women and children were separated from Doukhobor men and sent home; the men continued their walk to Minnesota, Manitoba, where they too were forced into railway cars and sent home; see N.G. Kozachova, "The Doukhobors," in *Russian Canadians. Their Past and Present*, p. 18.

[73] RGIA, Fonds 1149, Opis xii-1899, delo 23, pp. 72-73. Oliver replaced Sifton, who resigned in 1905, and kept the post until 1911.

[74] JMP, Vol. VI, Item 119, box 35-36.

[75] Miliukov, *Political Memoirs, 1905-1917*, edited by Arthur P. Mendel (Ann Arbor: University of Michigan, 1967), p. 419.

[76] On this, see A.N. Yakovlev, "Plakun-Trava, plyvushchaia naprotiv vody" [Fire Weed, Flowing Against the Stream], *Druzhba narodov*, No. 12 (1984), p. 217. Files on this can also be found in RGIA, Fonds 1291, Opis 50, delo 23. See also D. Pavlov, "Dukhobory v Kanade" [Doukhobors in Canada], RGAE, Fonds 478, Opis 7, delo 2940, pp. 30-41, prepared in Montreal, 1924. For even later Doukhobor requests to return to Russia, see Black, *Canada in the Soviet Mirror*, pp. 42-43, 326-327.

[77] See, for example, P.V. Verigin to L.N. Tolstoy (9 March 1907); Tolstoy to Verigin (10 August 1907), in Leo Tolstoy, Peter Verigin, *Correspondence*, edited by Andrew Donskov (Ottawa: Legas, 1995), pp. 82-84.

[78] RGIA, Fonds 382, Opis 8, delo 113, pp. 1-46. For the Ministry's comments on Massey-Harris, pp. 38-40. These files include the instructions for the survey sent out by the ministry, and responses from dozens of the *uezdy*.

[79] RGIA, Fonds 382, Opis 8, delo 113, pp. 15-16.

[80] Merrill Denison, *Harvest Triumphant. The Story of Massey-Harris* (Toronto: McClelland, 1948), pp. 97-98, 174-176.

[81] See correspondence, November 1907-January 1908, RGIA, Fonds 398, Opis 70, delo 24502, pp. 1-11. One of the persons to recommend the North American service was N.A. Kriukov.

[82] RGIA, Fonds 1278, Opis 6, delo 860, pp. 1, 23-24, 52-53.

[83] RGIA, Fonds 23, Opis 23, delo 28, pp. 28-32. The consulate prepared a 25-page report on the resources and growth of British Columbia, 1901-1911, and its potential for trade with Russia.

[84] Passek had been Head of Mission in Australia. His reports from Melbourne can be found in the *Sbornik konsul'skikh donesenii*.

[85] For Goldstein's letters of introduction, see LI-RA-MA, Vol. 18, File 585, Reel M7607. Goldstein was back in Canada in 1919, studying our Railway system for the Russian mission in the United States.

[86] Quoted from the *Borden Papers* by Eva S. Balogh, in "Hesitant Encounters: Episodes from Early Russo-Canadian Trade Relations," *Canadian Slavonic Papers*, VIII (1966), pp. 216-230. See also Davies, *Canada and the Soviet Experiment*, p. 10, who says that Goldstein studied Canada's "use of grain elevators, methods of handling and transporting wheat, of grading and marketing . . . with the apparent purpose of adapting it to Russia."

[87] On this, see Donald Avery, *'Dangerous Foreigners'. European Immigrant Workers and Labour Radicalism in Canada, 1896-1932* (Toronto: McClelland & Stewart, 1980), p. 29.

[88] The Russian-American Line had four ships, the *Tsar, Kursk, Rossiia*, and *Burma*, with the only direct routes from Russia (Libau) to Halifax and New York. The trip took approximately 10 days. Libau, or Liepaia, was annexed to Russia in 1795 as part of Catherine II's share in the partitions of Poland. A 33-page brochure, with pictures of the ships and descriptions of their amenities, can be found in RGIA, Fonds 95, Opis. 18, delo 620, pp. 18-35.

[89] Passek to Ministry of Trade and Industry (30 August 1913), RGIA, Fonds 95, Opis 18, delo 620, pp. 1-4.

[90] S.P. Veselago, Department Director, Ministry of Trade and Industry, to 2nd Department of Ministry of Foreign Affairs (15 October 1913), RGIA, Fonds 95, Opis 18, delo 620, pp. 5-6.

[91] Managing-Director of the Russian Eastern-Asiatic Steamship Line to Veselago (27 February 1914); (12 March 1914); Yu.D. Fillipov, Department Director, Ministry of Trade and Industry, to the Department of Police (31 March 1914), RGIA, Fonds 95, Opis 18, delo 620, pp. 6-13. See also *Russko-Amerikanskaia Liniia* brochure [Russo-American Line], pp. 8, 33.

[92] Letters between Yu.D. Fillipov, Veselago, S.I. Timashev, His Excellency V.F. Dzhunovskii, and His Excellency D. Konovalov (5 May to 23 June 1914), RGIA, Fonds 95, Opis 18, delo 620, pp. 14-17.

Conclusion

Russian Consuls in Canada
During Imperial Russia's Final Decades

By the turn of the twentieth century, a consciousness of Canada as an economic model and competitor, as a drawing card for Russian emigrants (legal and otherwise), and as a platform for policy implementation vis-à-vis Britain and the United States had become fully formed in St. Petersburg's ministries.

The opening of consulates in Montreal and Halifax changed the lenses through which the government in St. Petersburg looked towards Canada. Some details of the official and unofficial post-1900 business between the two countries have been mentioned already. It remains for this concluding chapter to put them in a broader context. The Consul General had lots of diplomatic company in Canada. In fact, Russia was a late comer in locating here. European states had begun to set up consulates in Canada as early as the 1850s and by 1910 thirty-two countries had representatives spread across the country. Many of them, like Mathers, were Canadian residents and none of them had official diplomatic status. Understandably, a few countries — Germany, Japan, France, Italy and the United States — were dealt with by the government in Ottawa as if they had ambassadorial standing. Although senior ministry officials in St. Petersburg had attached some significance to the Russian consulates in Canada, they still must have been surprised at how busy they soon became.[1]

In November 1911, Struve grumbled about his work load in response to a series of requests from St. Petersburg: "the entire Consulate is made up of me and my assistant, a part time secretary — a foreign woman. The Chancellery of the Consulate is located in my quarters in the centre of the city and I am part of it, that is, I am in the Chancellery all day and work in it from morning until late in the evening. Frankly, I have neither the time nor the strength not only to report on, but even to follow up on the interesting questions from the Trade Division."[2] He continued to work under these very difficult conditions, vainly requesting additional staff until he was replaced in early 1912 by Ustinov. Before the end of the year, Nicholas de Passek, formerly head of mission in Australia, was Consul General with funds for one more staff member. He too was soon complaining that the burden was too great.[3]

In addition to the Consul General's regular reports, the office passed on volumes of information, including historical surveys of Canada, notations on daily life, information on specifics of the Canadian economy and, by 1914, detailed reports on the implications for Russia of Canada's loss of trade with Germany.[4] He was responsible as well for arranging meetings between visiting Russian specialists, such as N.N. Epanchin, and appropriate Canadian officials. Long before Epanchin arrived, Struve had been impressed with Canadian agriculture, having both studied Kriukov's book and taking it on himself to call on the Massey-Harris head office in Toronto. His recommendations in this regard fit the pattern of previous, and later, observations by Russians: "As a result of the similarity of terrain and climatological conditions between Canada and Russia, Canadian agricultural machines appear to be ... Best suited for our agricultural needs."[5]

The short-staffed Russian offices provided the same services as the other consulates, with the exception that of their need to report on the activities of the Doukhobors. That religious sect continued to be a bone of contention between Russian and Canadian officials, as Pobedonostsev's intervention in 1901 made obvious, and an object of interest to the Russian public. We have seen that the story of their life in Canada and their squabbles with Canadian authorities between 1901 and 1906 were reported broadly in Russia, as were their successes, and that Nicholas II agreed to allow their resettlement in Russia. Struve's earliest submission to his Ministry in St. Petersburg in 1900 included four full pages on the Doukhobors, some of whom he met first in Winnipeg. Acknowledging that their living conditions were "not enviable," he noted that they had regular work and were not complaining — at least to him. He also visited Doukhobor villagers at Yorkton, where living conditions were "poor" and noted that there was a movement among them to move to California. He did not mention Demens, perhaps unaware of his correspondence with Pobedonostsev or his role in persuading some Doukhobors that their lot would be much better in California, or even back in Russia. In contrast to Demens, in fact, Struve claimed that the Doukhobors were "appreciated [in Canada] as excellent workers, sober and reliable" and that they were unlikely to move.[6]

Reports on Doukhobors passed back and forth between the consulate in Montreal and the Second Department's Bentkovskii in St. Petersburg, and were often relayed directly to, or even originated with, Stolypin. The Ministry of Internal Affairs was involved with Doukhobor matters on a regular basis as well, for the most part processing their requests to return to Russia (for example, from Peter Verigin in 1906), or to secure employment in railway construction in Canada. Struve's conviction that the Doukhobors were prospering and, with few exceptions, living on good terms with the local population, were transmitted directly to Stolypin from the Second Department of the Ministry of Foreign Affairs, and carried the day in the Russian capital.[7]

In some instances the Russian Orthodox Church itself complicated the daily routine of Struve and the successors to his office. Consular files included many missives from the Church hierarchy in Russia, parishioners wanting priests and sites for new churches in Canada, and requests that the Consul serve as mediator, or arrange for mediation, between parties squabbling over church assets and even among claimants for spiritual leadership. In 1904, he arranged for the visit of Tikhon, officially the leader of Orthodoxy in North America, to newly established parishes in Manitoba and the Northwest Territories. At the same time, he had to struggle with the fact that there were competing claimants to the post of spiritual head of Orthodoxy in North America, about which he was flooded with letters and statements from Moscow and St. Petersburg.[8]

The Consul General's despatches about Canada's political scene were often accompanied by clippings from newspapers, news releases from governments in Ottawa and several provincial capitals, statements from business reports, and pronouncements by politicians and church leaders.[9] Conscious that he had been tasked with observing the evolving Canadian-American relationship, Struve informed his superiors in St. Petersburg that Canada more closely resembled the United States than it did Britain, and that its economic and political future lay in association with its southern neighbour. American money and goods flooding into Canada would steadily undermine the British monopoly, he predicted in 1900, implicitly echoing Engels' prediction of 1888.[10] A decade later, with his attention riveted to the new "reciprocity" debate, Struve changed his mind and claimed to have witnessed the formulation of a Canadian national consciousness. The spectre of a tariff war between Canada and the United States in 1910 was the subject of numerous despatches, and reciprocity as an election issue in 1911 proved to Struve's satisfaction that Canada had both the will and the way to stand on its own. Calls by Canadian nationalists for a firm stand against renewed "manifest destiny" urges from south of the border and, in Quebec at least, resentment against

British domination were all duly reported to St. Petersburg. Borden's sweeping victory over Wilfrid Laurier in 1911 was final confirmation for Struve that a Canadian national spirit was now flourishing.[11]

Russia's representatives in Canada had more on their agenda than immigration and surveillance of the United States. In keeping with the practice that saw Russia's foreign and agriculture ministries delegate Kriukov in the 1890s and Epanchin in 1910, Russia's Ministry of Trade and Manufacturing also sought information in Canada. The latter ministry's Mining Department followed suit. Such tasks were greatly helped by the presence of the consulates. Indeed, Struve contributed directly to the latter enterprise by tendering a long accounting of Canada's mining industry himself in 1907, along with copies of Canada's regulations related to mining. Shortly thereafter recommendations from Russian engineers who saw the new Canadian law on the organization of mining as the most suitable guideline for their own country to adopt were submitted to the Chief of the Mining Department, State Councillor S.N. Suchkov.[12] The Canadian law was included as an appendix to a 120-page proposal set forth in September 1908 for the full restructuring of Russian mining.

An overview of the Canadian economy was passed on to St. Petersburg by Struve in 1901, with special attention paid to the great value of shipping facilities on the Great Lakes and the St. Lawrence, and the railroad's inestimable worth in keeping goods moving between Canada, the United States and Europe. The Consul General's presentation treated this enormous complex with almost a sense of awe. A special report on Ontario's Sault Ste. Marie as a case study of economic enterprise confirmed his admiration of Canada as a hot spot of entrepreneurial energy.[13] Nurturing trade links was part of Struve's daily routine, as he processed requests from Canadian firms for information about the Russian market and provided Russian and Canadian business people with copies of regulations, prices, shipping and rail potential, and so on.[14]

The Russian Admiralty's keen interest in Canada remained strong and even intensified after Germany accelerated its shipbuilding programme in 1909. Russia's watchfulness was typified by regular reports from the Russian naval agent in London on the vicissitudes of Canada's official and public attitude toward a national navy. Following the story from the inception of a parliamentary resolution that a Canadian navy be created put forward by the Laurier government in 1909 and approved unanimously in parliament, the agent analysed Canada's relationship with the British navy and the internal politics of the issue. To his surprise the plan remained on the drawing board. Finally, in 1912 the London-based Russian agent forwarded good news to St. Petersburg, announcing that recently-elected Borden had introduced a naval aid bill under which Canada would pay $35,000,000 to have three dreadnaughts built for the British navy. As the agent explained it, in return, Britain would give several cruisers to Canada, welcome a Canadian representative on the Committee of Imperial Defence, and take no important steps in foreign policy decisions without consulting with Ottawa. "Borden's speech was inspired and patriotic and was adopted by the Canadian parliament with enthusiasm. News of the three dreadnaughts was greeted with rejoicing among the English public," he wrote with obvious satisfaction. Russia's ally was now greatly strengthened by Canada's participation in imperial defence and, the agent implied, Germany was weakened.[15] Struve had already informed the Ministry of Foreign Affairs of these developments.

As the 1912 despatches make plain, the decade before the First World War saw the official relationship between Russia and Britain change from long-standing hostility and imperial rivalry to one approximating friendship. Russia's devastating and degrading loss to Japan in their war of 1904-1905 left Britain all-powerful in the North Pacific and enabled it to consolidate its position in Afghanistan. Anglo-Russian negotiations on these areas and on Persia were concluded in 1907. Spheres of influence were carefully mapped out, smoothing the way for a yet another realignment of the powers in Europe.

An exchange of royal visits, King Edward VII to Russia in 1908 and Tsar Nicholas II (accompanied by Stolypin and Foreign Minister Izvolskii) to Britain in 1909, helped generate yet another volte face in British public opinion about the Russian Empire. This diplomatic sea change, sealed by a St. Petersburg-London trade agreement, led to a boost in trade between Russia and Canada of which the Canadian Bank of Commerce association with the St. Petersburg Discount Bank in 1908 was but one by-product.[16] The consulate offices in Montreal, Halifax and, by 1915, Vancouver, grew even busier. Massey-Harris opened up offices in St. Petersburg, Warsaw and Tomsk; the CPR leased office space in Vladivostok. Although Russian and Canadian businesses were still competitors for some of the same British markets, mutual trade expanded exponentially — much to the advantage of Canada in terms of turnover.

As evidence that times had truly changed, the sealing saga had its final hiccup in 1911, with Britain now playing a lesser role than it had in the 1890s. In that later year, Britain, Canada, Russia, the United

States and Japan finally reached an agreement, in Washington, on limited sealing and other fishing rights. During the accompanying debate
between Canada and the United States, Russia consistently supported
the Canadian position.[17]

The semi-diplomatic relationship between Russia and Canada took
on quite new characteristics during the First World War. One problem
was that the bulk of Russian emigration to Canada had been so recent.
According to a report drawn up in 1918 by Consul General S.A.
Likhachev, De Passek's replacement in 1914, 100, 971 "Russians" were
living in Canada by 1911 and their numbers had more than doubled
since that time. In keeping with the long-standing Russian position, he
claimed, the "majority of the emigrants made their way to Canada, not
for the purpose of settlement, but only for temporary work."[18] His
government therefore assumed most emigrants were still subject to the
Tsar, a status that obligated them to serve in the Russian military. For
a variety of reasons, many of the Russian immigrants in Canada preferred to serve with the Canadian armed forces, infuriating the Consul
General, who was responsible for conscripting them to the Russian
army. A compromise of sorts was reached when it was decided by the
Tsar in 1915 that Russian subjects in Canada would be allowed to join
the Canadian Expeditionary Force, but for overseas duties only. They
were issued special identification cards to distinguish them from Slavs
from the Austro-Hungarian Empire who, apparently, often claimed to
be Russian in an attempt to escape internment as enemy aliens. Special
funds were granted by the Russian Ministry of Foreign Affairs to send
an Orthodox monk directly from the Troitskii-Sergiev Monastery at
Radonezh (Zagorsk) to serve with the Russian contingent attached to
the Canadian army in England.[19]

As allies the governments of Russia and Canada avoided presenting each other in a bad light. We have seen that Russian readers were
given glimpses of Canada when several Charles G.D. Roberts' stories
about wildlife and native peoples were translated and in 1915
Mavor's *An Economic History of Russia* was first reviewed in Russia.
Russian youngsters also could read the two little books by Emiliia
Pimenova. The friendly image of Canada being spread in Russia was
not matched in Canada, or so Likhachev thought. The Consul General
pestered the Canadian wartime censorship board with allegations
about anti-Russian characterizations in the press or in theatres, produced mainly by Slavic and Finnish émigré groups. He complained
especially about the contents of Russian, Ukrainian and Ruthenian
newspapers printed in Canada and the United States and widely

circulated among Canada's Slavic community.[20] Whereas the board endeavoured to limit the spread of such material, it explained to a skeptical Likhachev that censorship had to be more flexible in Canada than it was in Russia.[21]

Likhachev had more pressing business to deal with than anti-Russian propaganda, because the war provided unexpected economic opportunity for Russia's allies. As late as 1913 Germany still bought about 30 percent of all Russian exports, chiefly agricultural and forestry products, and supplied Russia with nearly 50 percent of its imports. Britain was a distant second on both counts, taking less than 18 percent of Russia's exports and providing only 13 percent of its imports.[22] Within weeks of the outbreak of war, Russian trading agencies were besieged with offers to fill the void created by Germany's abrupt departure from the tsarist market. In Canada, business representatives inundated the Ministry of Trade and Commerce in Ottawa with requests from members of the Canadian Manufacturers Association to go to Russia to seek out contracts. Canadian business groups applied directly to the Russian consulate offices as well. Overall trade between the two countries grew in value from slightly over one million dollars in 1914 to about six million dollars by 1919.

The Russian government was already well aware that it would have to find other sources of manufactured goods. Likhachev provided St. Petersburg with detailed information on Canada's pre-war trade with Germany and Austria-Hungary, with an eye on how best to turn Russia's and Canada's new needs to their mutual advantage.[23] In the meantime, the Russian Ministry of the Navy purchased an ice-breaker from Canada in September 1914 for service in Archangel'sk. Built in New Sydney, Nova Scotia, it set sail on 24 November. Two more Canadian ice-breakers were ordered later in the fall of 1914, one of them renamed *Kanada*.[24] By 1916 about one half of Russia's entire northern ice-breaking fleet of 13 vessels consisted of former Canadian and Newfoundland ships. Their job was important to the war effort because they kept Russia's northern ports open longer than usual, making it possible to sustain a level of supply.[25] Captains and crews returned by rail across Russia to Vladivostok and then by ship to Vancouver, making their journey a round-the-world adventure. Several of them stayed on temporarily in the service of the Russian Admiralty.

The Canadian government in its turn lobbied the Imperial Munitions Board, a British agency established in Canada in 1915, to obtain Russian contracts for war materials.[26] Even with all this activity, it was only in early 1917 that the Russian Purchasing Commission in

New York, which acted as an agent for the Imperial Munitions Board, agreed to send a purchaser directly to Canada (a Col. Kovaloff). With its long-standing prestige and offices in Russia, Massey-Harris functioned on its own and won a single order in 1916 valued at one million dollars.[27] Other Canadian firms initiated war supply business with Russia before Kovaloff arrived in the country and even before the actual war started. The Canadian Locomotive Company, Kingston, Ontario, for example, had a representative in Russia, Ya. A. Vilenkin (James Wilenkin), who helped negotiate a $1.25 million sale of 50 locomotives and tenders in the spring of 1914. The detailed contract was signed by the Russian Minister of Railways and Communications. Two thousand coach cars were ordered from the Canadian Association of Wagon and Metal Factories in Montreal, May 1915, and in January 1916 large orders were placed with the Eastern Wagon Works in New Glasgow, Nova Scotia.[28] These goods all were to be delivered to Vladivostok, which made the expansion of Russia's consular facilities to Vancouver necessary. The Russian consulates in Canada acknowledged the growing demands for independent business and trade in Canada and regularly put the advantages of trade with Canada to their superiors in Petrograd.[29]

On 31 October 1915, Minister of Foreign Affairs S.D. Sazonov wrote Chairman of the Council of Ministers, I.L. Goremykin, to inform him that the Canadian government was "excited" by the prospects of a full consulate in Vancouver. That city was seen as an important entry point for trade, military supply, and navy repair,[30] but Sazonov's concerns were broader still. The vision of greatly increased war supply might please Canadians, but from the Russian perspective, he said, the interests of some "200,000 Russian subjects" in Canada were paramount. Whatever the accuracy of Sazonov's numbers, one consulate in Montreal was not enough to service their needs and clearly not enough to ensure that they remained loyal to the Russian state. Urged on by Nicholas II, who scribbled on a Goremykin telegram to the Russian ambassador in Washington "it is necessary to set up a consulate in Vancouver at once," the proposal passed quickly through an astonishing number of departments before it was adopted by the Council of Ministers on 2 December 1915.[31]

To manage its own efforts at trade more efficiently, the Canadian government appointed two Trade Commissioners to Russia in 1916. One of them, C.F. Just, a former trade commissioner at Hamburg who in 1915 investigated commercial possibilities in Russia, was posted to Petrograd in April as the Chief Trade Commissioner. The other, twenty-three year-old Dana Wilgress, was sent to Omsk in July, after two months in Petrograd with Just. At the time, agricultural machinery was still the main Canadian export to Russia and it was to the Massey-Harris office in Moscow that Wilgress went first for information. Omsk was by then the second largest distributing point for Canadian products.[32]

In the meantime, the Russian transportation system had proven incapable of delivering troops and supply on a scale necessary to conduct a war, and Russia's industrial sphere was unable to sustain production for a successful war effort. The Russian government was forced to turn to its allies for further help. Agents came to Canada in early 1917 to buy more railroad cars, rails, and agricultural equipment. Enemy military occupation and naval blockades closed Russia's western gates to commerce, leaving open only undeveloped and distant ports such as Vladivostok and Nicolaevsk on the Pacific and Murmansk in the North. But expanding trade connections were disrupted by revolution in October 1917 and ended altogether when the Bolsheviks withdrew Russia from the war five months later. The high hopes of both Canadian Trade Commissioners were dashed by these events. In February 1918, as the Bolsheviks consolidated their hold on power, Just returned to Canada. Wilgress was transferred to Vladivostok, which was still controlled by opponents of Bolshevism.

The Bolshevik government made peace with Germany, sacrificing vast tracts of territory in the West and in the South, over which they had no control anyway. The treaty signed at Brest-Litovsk in March 1918 infuriated Russia's former allies and also ended German military pressure on Russia, enabling the new government to strengthen its position in the Northwest, Siberia and the Far East. Canadian troops were to form parts of a post-war allied intervention against Bolshevik forces in all three of those areas.[33] In October 1918, Wilgress was attached to a special Canadian Economic Commission to Siberia. He was joined in this new endeavour by Just and two others: Colonel J.S. Dennis, who had been Head of the Colonization Department of the Canadian Pacific Railway in Russia and by then liaison officer for the Canadian Expeditionary Force in Siberia, and Ross Owen, representative of the Canadian Pacific Railroad in Vladivostok.[34] A.D. Braithwaite, formerly Assistant General Manager of the Bank of Montreal, caught up to them later, as did Louis Kon. Their haste proved to be unnecessary. Within a matter of months, the last vestiges of Imperial Russia disappeared from Eurasia and the Canadians were home by the end of 1919.

* * *

A few Russian writers — from Karamzin to Pimenova — had drawn a surprisingly consistent picture of Canada: a paradise filled with hard-working, cheerful hewers of wood and drawers of water, living in a society that was multi-national and disciplined, but politically and economically free. They, and others, made it an especially attractive-looking refuge for Russian citizens. Whether they actually believed the image they helped create, or merely exploited it to propagate their vision of a direction Russia should itself follow, is impossible to ascertain. For whatever reason, Canada was portrayed throughout the 19th century by Russian thinkers as a democracy of a different sort, and its vibrant economic development was compared often with the stagnancy of Siberia. Long before Marxist-Leninists perceived Canada as the first major arena of intra-imperialist struggle between Britain and the United States, and as the classic victim of the "general crisis of capitalism" stage in world history, other Russians had described it as a wonderland lusted after by both the British and Americans.

The 19th-century Russian imagination may not have portrayed Canada as Canadians would. That is a matter for someone else's research. Nevertheless, telling our story through the eyes of contemporaries from another large, northern country illuminates our history and theirs from a unique and, it is hoped, constructive perspective.

---

1 Russia first had expanded its consular settings greatly in 1893. For evidence of the global interests of St. Petersburg by the late 1890s, see the collection issued by the Ministry of Foreign Affairs, *Sbornik konsul'skikh donesenii* [Collection of Consular Reports], (St. Petersburg: Nadezhda), the first volume of which appeared in 1898.

2 Struve to Trade Division, Ministry of Foreign Affairs (24 November/ 7 December 1911), RGIA, Fonds 23, Opis 11, delo 354, pp. 1-2.

3 For the added secretarial position, see Ministry of Foreign Affairs report to the State Council and Speaker of the Duma (1 February 1913), RGIA, Fonds 1278, Opis 6, delo 860, pp. 23R-24r, 52-53.

4 See, for example, correspondence between the Consulate and Russia's Ministry of Foreign Affairs, Trade Section, 1913-1915, RGIA, Fonds 23, Opis 11, delo 354, pp. 28-62.

5 Struve, "Ocherk Kanady " [A Sketch of Canada], *Sbornik . . .* (1900),

Issue VI. p. 474. Translated below.

[6] Struve, "Ocherk Kanady," *Sbornik* . . . (1900), Issue VI, pp. 478-479, 481-484.

[7] Struve's opinion was quoted in "Pis'mo ot 2-go Dep-ta Ministerstva Inostrannykh Del k Petru Arkad'evichu Stolypinu" [Letter from the 2nd Department of the Ministry of Foreign Affairs to P.A. Stolypin], (5 December 1906), RGIA, Fonds 1291, Opis 50, delo 23, pp. 5-6. For many more letters, reports, and evaluations of the Doukhobors in Canada, 1906-1913, see RGIA, Fonds 1291, Opis 50, delo 23, pp. 1-78; GARF, Fonds 102, Opis 1910, delo 123, pp. 87G-88; Opis 1902, delo 1498, pp. 1-7. These papers, and many others, have been catalogued for the CRCR by John Woodsworth, *The Doukhobors: 1895-1943. Annotated, Cross-referenced and Summarised.* CRCR Russian Archival Catalogue No. 2 (May 1997).

[8] See LI-RA-MA, Vol. 21, Files 656. The "false" claimant was one Seraphin, about whom the Second Department in St. Petersburg contacted Struve regularly; between 1915-1917 the Consul general was caught up in a bitter fight over control of land purchased in Montreal, on Cartier Street, as a site for an Orthodox Church. *Ibid.*, File 658.

[9] See especially LI-RA-MA, Vol. 21, files 655-678; Vol. 26, file 907; Vol. 27, files 947-952.

[10] Struve, "Ocherk Kanady," *Sbornik* . . . (1900), Issue VI, pp. 493-496. See also AVPRI, II departament, 1-5, Opis 408, delo 867, pp. 2-5.

[11] See, for example, AVPRI, II departament, 1-5, Opis 408, delo 1175, pp. 78-99; delo 1079, p. 30; and Struve, "Ekonomicheskoe polozhenie Kanady" [Economic Situation in Canada], *Sbornik* . . . . (1910), Issue III, pp. 561-564.

[12] For the detailed reports prepared by Yu.R. Butlerov in 1908 and evaluated by K. Robyk in 1909, see RGIA, Fonds 23, Opis 27, delo 17, pp. 1-122. These were general recommendations on the restructuring of Russia's mining industry and not studies of the Canadian mining system. Apparently, Canada's regulations and laws had significant influence on them. According to Butlerov, Russia's mining sector had not been examined seriously since the days of Peter the Great. For Struve's report, "Gornaia promyshlennost' v Kanade" [The Mining Industry in Canada], *Sbornik* . . . (1907), Issue IV, pp. 298-308.

[13] See Struve, "Ekonomicheskoe obozrenie Kanady za 1900 god'" [An Economic Overview of Canada in 1900], *Sbornik* . . . . (1901), Issue V, pp. 349-366; "Promyshlennye tsentry Kanady. Sault Sainte Marie"

[Industrial Centres of Canada. Sault Sainte Marie], *Sbornik . . .* (1902), Issue V, pp. 376-383.

[14] Details can be found throughout the LI-RA-MA collection.

[15] See "Kanada i imperskaia" [Canada and Imperial Defence], a report prepared by the Russian Naval Agent in London (23 November-2 December, 1912), RGAVMF, Fonds 418, Opis 1, delo 2946, pp. 114-120. The agent was quoting directly from Borden's speech, "The Naval Forces of the Empire," delivered on 5 December 1912. These files also included reports from Naval Agents in Germany, France, and Sweden.

[16] See, for example, letter from Canadian Bank of Commerce Head Office, Toronto (12 February 1909) to St Petersburg Discount Bank, RGIA, Fonds 598s, Opis 2, delo 585, pp. 1-4.

[17] DCER, Vol. I (1967), pp. 547-553.

[18] "Kratkaia spravka o Rossiiskoi Kolonii v Kanady" [Short Account on the Russian Colony in Canada], (2 December 1918), LI-RA-MA, Vol. 22, file 712. This information was sent to Serge V. Geiman, New York, who was writing a book on Russian colonists in the United States. The number included a wide cross-section of nationalities from the Russian Empire, 55 percent of whom were said to be Russian or Ukrainian. 10 percent of the 1911 number were Finlanders, the report said, adding that between 1911 and 1917 another 121,242 had emigrated to Canada from Russia.

[19] The request for such funds came from the Ober-Procurator of the Holy Synod in Petrograd, 4 August 1916, see RGIA, Fonds 1276, Opis 12, delo 1773, pp. 1-4.

[20] In 1916, he forwarded copies to St. Petersburg of, for example, *Amerika* [America] a Ukrainian daily published in Philadelphia; *Kanadiiskii Rusin* [Canadian Ruthenian], a weekly published in Winnipeg; *Russkoe slovo* [Russian Word], a daily printed in New York; *Narodna Volia* [People's Will], a Ukrainian-language paper published three times a week in Scranton, Pennsylvania; and the *Kanadiiskii Farmer* [The Canadian Farmer] a Russian and Ruthenian-language weekly from Winnipeg. See LI-RA-MA, Vol. 21, Files 657-658.

[21] For rather extensive files kept by the Russian consulates on war time "anti-Russian" activity in Canada, see LI-RA-MA, Vol. 21, files 698-706 (1915-1917).

[22] See Margaret S. Miller, *Economic Development of Russia, 1905-1914* (London: Cass, 1967).

[23] RGIA, Fonds 23, Opis 11, delo 354, pp. 52-62.

[24] For details, see RGAVMF, Fonds 418, Opis 1, delo 4566, pp. 1-17; delo 5011, pp. 1-25.

[25] On this, see George Bolotenko, "Icebreakers in North Russia, 1914-1920: The Canadian Connection," unpublished ms based on archival materials (Ottawa, 2001).

[26] See DCER, Vol. 1 (1909-18), 72-73, 75, 138, 140.

[27] Dennison, *Harvester Triumphant*, 217.

[28] Details can be found in RGIA, Fonds 266, Opis 1, delo 1672, pp. 1-21, 106; Fonds 273, Opis 1, delo 2987, pp. 8-11.

[29] See, e.g., RGAVMF, Fonds 418, Opis 1, delo 4720, pp. 5-9, 104.

[30] RGIA, Fonds 1276, Opis 11, delo 1277, pp. 1-8.

[31] "Ob uchrezhdenii v porte Vankuvere Imperatorskago Rossiiskago konsul'stva," signed by Goremykin, 10 November 1915, *Ibid.*, 15-17.

[32] Dana Wilgress, *Memoirs* (Toronto: Ryerson 1967), p. 24. H. Gordon Skilling, *Canadian Representatives Abroad. From Agency to Embassy* (Toronto: Ryerson, 1945), p. 57. See LI-RA-MA, Vol. 18, File 601, for Russian Consular correspondence on this Commission, and File 594, where letters between Canadian Minister of Trade and Commerce and Likhachev make it clear that the Russians looked unfavourably on the appointment of Just.

[33] On this, see Roy Maclaren, *Canadians in Russia, 1918-1919* (Toronto: Macmillan, 1976), John Swettenham, *Allied Intervention in Russia, 1918-1919, and the Part Played by Canada* (Toronto: Ryerson, 1967), and J.L. Black, *Canada in the Soviet Mirror*, Chapter 1.

[34] See Robert N. Murby, "Canadian Economic Commission to Siberia, 1918-19," *Canadian Slavonic Papers*, 11:3 (1969), pp. 374-393; Canada, Department of Trade and Commerce, *Report of the Canadian Economic Commission (Siberia)*, (Ottawa, 1919).

"Niagara Falls"

Translations

A. Nikolai Karamzin, "An Englishman's Letter from Quebec" (1803)[1]

I have only just returned from Upper Canada. The land, climate, and success by hard work in this province far exceed the general opinion that we, inhabitants of London, have about it. The number of people is multiplying constantly. Almost every day entire families travel there from the United Provinces [United States] and settle, either by purchasing or leasing land. Unlimited oak forests demonstrate its fertility. Wheat and other grains grow in an astonishing way: each kernel produces forty! In some places it is not necessary to fertilize the fields. Winters are not extended very long; the snow lasts sometimes no longer than two weeks. Chief from among all of its benefits is its benign Government and general freedom from taxes.

When the Governor prepared last year to go the main town of York, settlers from all sides came to him with complaints about the extraordinary abundance of their produce! "Our granaries cannot hold the grain," they said, "and the cattle have no room in the fields. If they do not give us help to transport the grain to Lower Canada, then we cannot harvest the current crop." A few months before that the connection between the two Canadian provinces was finally opened through the dangerous St. Lawrence River. Now the settlers are for the most part sowing hemp. The Government allocated 200 pounds sterling annually to encourage this kind of agriculture. This sum would seem to be a trifle to wealthy Europeans, but it is very large for such provinces, which did not exist twelve years before this.

---

[1] "Pis'mo odnogo Anglichanina iz Kvebeka," *Vestnik Evropy*, Pt. X, No.16 (1803), pp. 272-276. Many of the *Vestnik*'s pieces were extracts or entire items from various European journals, always with reference. This "letter" included neither author, nor source, which suggests that Karamzin himself was its author. Karamzin's status in the late 18th century as Russia's leading pre-romanticist, is reflected clearly in his idealization of nature, hardworking villagers, and heroic native peoples. But his political allusion is more a product of the indecision of Russia's political culture during the post-Paul I era. Translated by Yana Kuzmin.

The homes in Upper Canada are almost all wooden, but are constructed with such taste and are so clean that they are a captivating sight. The settlers are very hardworking and skilful in their business. Their fields are cultivated beautifully. It is true that kind Nature frees them from difficult labour. In Europe it is necessary to push the plough [sokha] deeply into the land, but the fortunate Canadian resident does not plough, rather he only harrows his field and then seeds it!

The roads from settlement to settlement are very good. Mail goes from Niagara to Chippawa every day. There is nothing more pleasant than the road from Niagara to Queen's-Town [Queenston]: one goes along the shore of a great river [Niagara River] and is lost in the gloom of an oak forest, ascends a wild mountain, and suddenly sees the magnificent and frightening view of the greatest waterfall in the world!

Queen's-Town is new and as a result of its location is a very beautiful small town. Here, goods shipped to Upper Canada are unloaded; it is necessary to send them overland to Chippawa, for the terrible current of the river prohibits navigation. During last winter a fairly large merchant ship, which arrived at Chippawa from Lake Erie, was shipped from there to Queen's-Town overland! It was placed on many planks, bound together, and then hauled, with its sails and rigging, by oxen through hills and dales . . . a sight without parallel[2] . . . and in Queen's-Town it was launched on the water again.

I will say nothing about Niagara Falls: this miracle has been described by others; but no one has yet been able to adequately describe its magnificence.

The Town of York was constructed in a valley, surrounded by oak groves, and is very pleasant for the eyes. Six years ago there was no sign of human hands there: the town, as if by an act of magic, appeared suddenly in the midst of impassable forests! The inhabitants brought the art of cutting trees to the highest level of perfection. I was told that one Englishman, who had recently come to York, agreed to pay a day-labourer 20 kopeks for any tree cut down, and thought that he hired him not expensively. But the York worker, beginning early in the morning had succeeded by the evening to earn 70 rubles! The Englishman paid him right away, so that he would not be ruined by him in a few days.

---

2   Here Karamzin added a footnote of his own, "And we do not wish to believe that Oleg could pull his fleet by chariot to Tsargrad!," referring to the first historical ruler of Kiev whom the Russian chronicles say led a successful campaign against Constantinople (Tsargrad) in 907.

Nikolai Karamzin, "A Letter of a Young Frenchman from Montreal" (1803)[3]

I was travelling in a canoe with two Abenaki from Lower Canada. We already had left behind us the so-called waterfall of St. Lawrence, when suddenly our boat hit a stone and smashed. The first snow had already fallen; we had neither an axe nor any means to set fire. All our stores consisted of frozen fish. We decided to go south along the river, so as not to get lost. We suffered from cold and hunger and on the third day, with indescribable joy, saw smoke which brought us to a village of Mohawks. My comrades sat under a tree and as usual began to howl. The villagers ran out of their houses and proudly told us: *Stand up!* We stood up. *Follow us!* We followed them. We were given three huts. My host, the *Sachem* or chief of the village, told me; "Whoever you might be, wherever you came from, welcome! Do you hear me? Sit down on the bear's skin, get warm and eat. . . " I told him that I was going from Katavaki [Kahnawake] to Montreal. "The land is white and hard; the river is covered with ice; you can not go to Montreal until the sun comes back. Take off your clothes; dress as we do; you will be more dear to Mohawks." . . . I shook his hand as a sign of agreement. Two women cut my hair and painted my eyebrows; the third brought some clothes. Soon I came to like my hosts, caught fish with them and was happy when I could feed them with the fruits of my art and happiness. Besides we had enough potatoes and millet because the villagers, having taken the Christian faith, became more hardworking than others. I made a book from the white tree bark and wrote down different words of their language. They liked it very much. At last they easily understood me. The old man also spoke a little French. Time passed imperceptibly and without boredom. In January a giant man appeared and brought many animal skins and frozen meat. This giant was my host's son-in-law and the husband of the young woman who had cut my hair. I noticed that he spoke Mohawk no better than I and I also learned that he had been taken prisoner. By cruel tradition of the savages he was to have become a

---

3   "Pis'mo odnogo molodago Frantsuza iz Monrealia," *Vestnik Evropy*, Pt. XI, No. 20 (1803), pp. 279-283. This essay was chosen and translated by Karamzin from what he called a "German journal." Translated by Yana Kuzmin. Thanks to Prof. Kerry Abel, a specialist on the history of native peoples, History Department, Carleton University, for checking the names as they were transliterated from the Russian.

victim of death. The Sachem's daughter, a young widow, had taken
pity upon him and married him. He was very skilful trapper. This
young stranger had lived several years in the Mohawk family when
his first wife appeared. She had walked over 100 miles, found out at
last his whereabouts and demanded her husband back from the
elders. "There had never been anything like this before," one of the
elders said, "We answered with words to words. The winter was coming to an end. The missionaries took up the case. At last we decided
to settle the problem at the general meeting and Nizuassu, the chief of
the Miskinon [possibly Muskegon] people set the fire of the council.
All the elders and the Sachem sat around it. The decision of the council was as follows; on the day when Penampa (my son-in-law) became
a prisoner, according to ancient custom he had to die, but Kippogisha
(my daughter) having married him granted him a new life; but he
remained dead for this first wife. The unhappy woman was in
despair. At last a brave warrior of the Oviskan [possibly Ojibwa] people consoled her with his tenderness. She lives with him happily. But
her generous love which made her undertake such a dangerous and
difficult journey surprised many colonists. They showered her with
gifts. This woman was the first among the natives who had a cow,
milk, bread, and feather-bed." ... I wanted to know her name to enter
it in the book and in my heart: it was Neion-Vega.

B. Pavel Svinin, "Fishing On the Grand Banks of New [Found] Land" (1811)[1]

The banks of the New Land, which are usually called the Newfoundland Banks (terre neuve), are very famous for cod fishing, considered the richest in the world. The Banks represent one of the greatest underwater mountains, 160 miles in length, and 90 miles in width. On the other hand, two of its ends stretch so far into the sea that its size can not be determined with accuracy. In the middle, on the European side of it, there is some kind of a bay or trench. It is located at 51 degrees western latitude and 50 degrees longitude. The distance from St. Petersburg to it, measured in a straight line, is over 5000 versts, and from the mainland of America in the closest place — about 700. The shallowest spot is 20 Russian fathoms [1 Russian fathom = 1.83 meters] deep, and the deepest spot — up to 90 Russian fathoms. Sun rarely comes out of the black clouds here; damp and cold air produces fogs which are almost always predominant.

On 29 September (old style) 1811, after a happy 24-day long voyage from Kronstadt, we arrived at these banks. The depth turned out to be 82 fathoms. But suddenly the head wind carried us again into the ocean, and it took us three days to get back, tacking through constant fog and through a terribly wild sea.

On October 1 (13) at 7 in the morning the thermometer we dipped into the sea showed 9 degrees difference in temperature between the atmosphere and water, which confirmed that we had arrived at the banks, and the plummet showed that we were at 32 fathoms depth. This is the best depth for fishing and we immediately heaved to. The morning was unusually nice, not a single cloud overshadowed the sun, a light breeze was waving the sea slightly, and our sails were flapping a little. We breathed in the cleanest light air. Do we ever have such mornings in Petersburg in June?! We cast 10 fishing rods, each of us had two rods, and in no more than 5 minutes we pulled out 6 big fish. One can not describe the joy, the happiness one experiences during lucky fishing. In three hours we caught over 200 fish; some of them weighing about 45 pounds and only 6 or 7 weighed 10 pounds. As soon as we cast the fishing rods we pulled out the catch, sometimes two fish at a time.

---

[1] Svinin, *Opyt' zhivopisnago puteshestviia po Severnoi Amerike* (St. Petersburg: F. Drekhsler, 1815), pp. 205-219. The remainder of the footnotes are Svinin's. Translated by Yana Kuzmin.

The cod scale is light blue in colour with green spots, and the belly is absolutely white; the eyes are big, blue, the jaws are huge, especially big are the lips. The amount of cod caught at this bank every year surprises everybody; maybe the home ground of this fish is located here, or perhaps the qualities of local soil are especially nutritious, drawing them to this place; and maybe all the sea depths are full of these fish, because they usually either lie on the sea floor or swim on it. Fishermen coming here always have luck and are certain to return with a catch. Having chosen a convenient spot they heave to, and do not leave until they fill their ships with fish. At night they light up several lanterns and constantly ring the bells to warn the passing ships which, because of the constant fogs, could run into them easily.[2]

During our fishing, the whales, huge tsars of the sea, swam around our ship noisily and entertained us with their rainbow fountains, which they shoot into the air from their nostrils while whistling. It seemed they were about to wage war against us in revenge for ravaging their kingdom, and they approached the ship so closely that we could see their terrifying jaws: two of them were extremely big. Flocks of sea birds were flying in the air over our heads; some of them were so daring that they attacked the whales from the air and pecked their backs: but this hardly bothered the sea creatures. There were also many birds flying over our ship, screaming as they seized from one another the food we threw for them. Finally they all focused on the same object, all rushed after the fish that, having taken our fishing rods were swimming almost on the surface of the water. At this point an internecine fight started up among them: sometimes they landed on water and went up and down with the waves. Their bright whiteness mixing with the blue sea presented a striking contrast. Sometimes they dove for fish and then soared into the air. After about thirty days of seeing nothing but the endlessness and monotony of the sea our eyes were hungry for anything new, any change. That is why we very much enjoyed their fight, as we could not see anything else in the sea.

New land, as well as this bank, was discovered by a French sailor Ivan Kabot [John Cabot] in 1497. Quite soon after that the English government acknowledged the importance of fishing, and Queen Elizabeth in 1582 sent Cavalier Hampshire [Sir Humphrey Gilbert, June 1583]

---

2   The very fog of this bank is praised by many. Having a lot of oxygen in it, it is very beneficial for people with tuberculosis. I knew two women in America who were cured from tuberculosis after two trips to this place.

with 5 ships to set up permanent settlements for the fishermen and to encourage this trade. In 1615 over 250 ships came here to get fish, which corresponds to 10,000 tonnes of barrels. Cod fishing goes on here year round. In taste local cod is superior to any other caught in the seas of Northern Europe. Unfortunately because of its delicacy it can not be delivered anywhere fresh, but has to be salted and dried.

England, France and Spain tried to capture this trade, and each of them interchangeably owned it to a smaller or larger degree. But they were never satisfied with their share, and always tried secretly, and sometimes openly, to gain the upper hand in this competition.

Now this trade branch belongs solely to Englishmen and Americans. It is known from the Parliamentary reports that this fishing brings England in an average year about 400 thousand pounds sterling, and could bring even more. Currently it is not as flourishing as it used to in the past, when France and other states participated in it equally.[3] Barely 1000 ships are now involved in this trade, out of which 600 belong to Americans who come here from the shores of [Nova] Scotia and from Boston, and the rest are Englishmen. But the English ships are twice as big as the American ones and that is why Americans do not have advantage over the Englishmen. One can suggest that no more than 12,000 people are occupied in this trade. After supplying Southern Europe with fish, it is usually taken to Africa for sale.

At three o'clock in the afternoon a favourable wind started blowing and we were sailing at a speed of 9 knots an hour for over 15 versts without feeling it; it seemed that our ship was not moving — this is the pleasure and advantages of sailing! The invention of the ship was in fact the most useful creation of the human brain; and perfection achieved by modern sailing can impress the bravest imagination! Abandon a sailor in the middle of an unknown sea, he will look at the sun or star and a sextant will tell him where he is. Let the winds blow and the storm rage —

But the brave ship flies,
Having spread its huge wings,
Into the far away countries.
Vainly are the abysses yawning below it —
Vainly are the waves rising in it way!. . . . . .

---

[3] Probably, now that France and Holland are at peace, they will soon demand their rights!

Here a man triumphs over the laws of nature; he conquers, he, so to say, shackles the very winds themselves.

By the evening we entered the Mexican Gulf stream, which comes here from the Mexican shores without mixing with the sea, so that it even preserves the warmth it absorbs while passing the volcanoes on the seabed between the shores of Florida and Cuba. Constantly expanding in the shape of a crescent it spreads for over three thousand versts into the ocean with almost unchanged force, and only then mixes with the sea. In its outset it is so strong that without a strong wind ships are forced backward.

This evening and night were more wonderful than the morning. The silence was not disturbed by anything except the quite noise of the waves caused by the moving ship. On the one side the crescent was peeking from behind the dark clouds, on the other — a comet blinded with its shine.[4] Can one look at these heralds of the unknown without admiration? Circling around the universe they undoubtedly perform in each world some role determined by the Creator! If there is a moment when the sea voyager can experience true pleasure from the sea, forget all dangers, all the troubles of sea life, forget that only one board separates him from imminent death — then this is the moment. And then there is a new, most wonderful view: spirits and foam created by the ship digging into the sea waves; they spread like a fire; it is strange to see these splashes, as they fall on the deck in a fire rain! The trace of the steering wheel looks like a winding fire dragon chasing the ship. Wonderful! Astonishing!

---

[4]   This was written in 1811.

C. Aleksandr Borisovich Lakier's Travels Through Central Canada, 1857[1]

It was quite surprising for me that on the ship there were more passengers speaking French than any other language; there were many
Catholic abbots, whom I haven't seen for awhile, mixed with the
Americans; among the servants and even sailors there were
Frenchmen or, as they call them here, Canadians [Kanadtsy].[2] In the
evening on the deck they started singing a song, the tune of which
clearly testified to its French origin. I asked the oldest singer how long
he had been there, and he answered that he had been born in Canada
and his parents had not spoken a word of English. He does, of course,
though he would like to be more fluent. Here, the same as everywhere
else, a Frenchman studies a foreign language very reluctantly, perhaps because his native tongue is spread everywhere in the world or,
on the other hand, the language is spread everywhere because it is
necessary to speak it. I don't know which is true: the former or the latter. But a Frenchman never renounces his nationality and in this
respect sharply differs from a German who changes his nationality
each time he goes to a new place. In America the German will call
himself an American, in Russia — a Russian. He will modify his language, he will notice all the favourite expressions of an American and
the second generation will completely forget the native tongue and

---

[1] Lakier, *Puteshestvie po Severo-Amerikanskim Shtatam, Kanade i Ostrovu
     Kube*, Vol. 1 (St. Petersburg: K. Vul'f, 1859). The material on Canada
     begins on page 304, Pt. II, and continues to the end of the volume,
     page 374, Pt. III. Lakier's two volumes were translated into English and
     published by an American publishing house in 1979. Inexplicably, the
     lengthy sections on Canada and Cuba (Vol. II, Pt. VIII, 268-335) were
     omitted from the American translation. See *A Russian Looks at America.
     The Journey of Aleksandr Borisovich Lakier in 1857*. Translated and edited by
     A. Schrier and Joyce Story (Chicago, 1979).
        Bracketed and italicized materials are reprinted as they appeared in
     the original. Punctuation also follows mostly from the original. Unless
     otherwise stated, or in italics, footnotes are J.L. Black's. Translated by
     Marina Sabanadze and Yana Kuzmin.

[2] Lakier used the Russian *Kanadtsy* for both English and French
     Canadians/ canadiens throughout. No attempt to differentiate them will
     be made here.

probably will be insulted if someone mentions old Brownschweig or any other principality where his forefathers were born and lived.

The voyage on Lake Champlain was particularly successful. Having started it in Whitehall [NY], when the sun was still fairly high, we arrived at the other end of the lake late at night when the moon was pouring its lustreless light on the mountains of the State of Vermont on one side and New York on the other.

Generally speaking the banks of the lake are extremely intricate and diverse. If one were to be carried away in his thoughts to the earliest centuries he would imagine a sea strait, taking its beginning from the St. Lawrence River and ending near New York. There is a reason why the states of New England were for a long time assumed to be an island. A skeleton of a whale, dwelling in these waters long ago, serves to confirm this assumption. It was dug up recently on the bank of Lake Champlain. Even now they are still catching seals in the lake. There, as well as in all the neighbouring areas, we find historical evidence of wild Indians, who maintained their independence for a long time, unwilling to become slaves to white people. They did not become accustomed to work and, having better lands, left them uncultivated and harvested animals in the primary forests. Frenchmen were always more gentle and more indulgent to the native people than Englishmen: a simple fact is that one has to go to Niagara in order to see a couple of ragged Indians in the State of New York while in Canada Indian settlements can be seen even next to Montreal. However, the natives were pacified most of all thanks to heroic deeds undertaken against them by geographer [Samuel de] Champlain [1570-1635], former governor of Canada at the beginning of the 17th century. The lake was named after him. The places our ship passed witnessed conflict between Frenchmen and Englishmen for a long time and later between Englishmen and North-Americans. One can still see the remnants of fortresses, once strong but now in ruins. They hoped to accomplish by means of weapons and victories what now is being done in the same places by ships and locomotives; that is, by mutual benefit, a conviction that the common good generally does not accrue from holding vast parcels of land, but follows from proper organization of relations between the citizens themselves, as well as between citizens and their government. Moreover, striving for prosperity on the part of settlers made nations became more tractable for mutual benefits. Both sides would have profited by that.

A battle on Lake Champlain in 1814 was supposed to settle the question of boundaries between English and American possessions in North America. The border starts now at the mouth of the lake, at

Rouse's [Rouses] Point. There I bid farewell to the United States and the charming lake, which made me think of Switzerland, such as Lakes Thun or Lucerne.

If it were not for boulders and rapids in the St. John's [sic] and Richelieu rivers, which connect Lake Champlain to the St. Lawrence, it would be possible to sail as far as the latter river. Now they have built a railway to provide a detour. Our baggage was looked at only briefly in the English customs house; the examination was limited to a single question, "Do you have anything forbidden?," to which, of course, everyone answered "No!" It would be surprising if the process between the two trading partners, who understand the disadvantages to trade that any type of delay and break may cause, was conducted in a different way. Communications are frequent and uninterrupted, the origin of water flowing onto the territory of the [United] States is located in English hands, and the border is just a straight conditional line.

III

Once again people around us started talking about pounds and shillings, the shape of a train ticket became different, no more American checks and stamps which Americans neatly fixed into the hat band in order to avoid annoying questions from a conductor. The majority spoke French. Strangely enough, we covered only one mile and have noticed no natural boundaries, but we were surrounded now by a different people, a different language, a different attitude: the company seemed happier, polite and attentive. Their faces did not express the eternal thought of Americans about dollars and cents, ladies sat next to gentlemen, something against etiquette in the United States; mixed with them also were priests and *soeurs grises* [Grey Nuns], who were on some kind of mission and reading their prayer-books, as well as Canadian farmers who were speaking in French.

Passing the villages consisting almost exclusively of wooden huts, I was startled by the fact that there was a fence between narrow, but very long, pieces of land, which probably were owned by different proprietors. I could not find a better person to ask to give me an explanation of this phenomenon than my neighbour — an old planter or as he called himself *habitant* who had already managed to declare that he had been born in Canada and owned a piece of land by the St. Lawrence River. He asked me questions about modern France. He knew something about Napoleon and said that, if it had not been for the worthless Norman accent which was brought here by the first settlers, the Canadian dialect would have been more pure than the modern Parisian dialect; but in the meanwhile in the word "Canada" alone he repeated the letter "o" three times. Indeed, my neighbour explained to me that from the time of the first French settlement, the kings gave the so-called *seigneuries* huge parcels of land, granted in eternal possession with the obligation to pay annual rents (*cens et rentes*), to seigneurs for their services or for spreading colonization. Since the best lands, meadows (*prairies*) were on both sides of the St. Lawrence River, and further to the mountains the climate was cooler, soil less productive and very rocky, everyone wished to have at least a small piece of land by the river. Then the land was divided between heirs, which contributed to the formation of those strips of land which puzzled me so much. And it was clear why there were so many fences, they had so much wood that they didn't know what to do with it, though they used it as a fuel for ships and locomotives and as a material for construction.

I knew that rents for land, introduced by the first Dutch patrons in New York and paid by vassals to land owners, existed in democratic America until 1847. I was not surprised by the fact that ancient seigneuries existed in the New World; but in the United States the disadvantages of an institution that blocked free improvements and prosperity was soon recognized, voices were raised against it until in the long run the party of *anti-renters* had won. In Canada farmers pay an insignificant rent for land; they generally are neither productive nor rich and therefore are not seeking the right to invest capital in the land along with the annual rent. Thus, feudal relations which were abolished in France during the revolution of 1789 continued to exist on the new continent.

Although in 1854 the Canadian Parliament decided to change the relations between land owners, new rules are being implemented somehow very slowly. The landholders are accustomed to the old routine and, because they are treated well, the rent doesn't rise; in the meantime the value of land grows in proportion to the population and it is impossible to do without an intermediary institution, a bank established by a company or the government. Incidentally, I later had an opportunity to read charters of the French kings in which they presented their retinues with 4.5 and more square leagues of land and indicated that their rights over the land was completely feudal.[3] In

---

[3] Here Lakier cited as follows, "*Documentary History of the State New York,*" by *Hon. Christopher Morgan, Albany. Vol. 1, p. 539.*

addition to the right to collect rent from the so-called tenants the landowners had the right of high, medium and low jurisdiction and each appeal to a seigneurial court was brought to the *cour royale de Montreal*. Furthermore, the landowners had the exclusive right to cut the forest, to hunt, to trade with Indians, to build mills and to have a share of the fee when sections were transferred from one owner to another (the so-called *lods et ventes*) and so on. I think that this small estate owning is good for Canadian landowners on the banks of the St. Lawrence River because the French like to live in villages, "chacun veut entendre la cloche du village" [everyone wishes to hear the village clock], and for newcomers from England, Ireland and Germany there remain entire realms on the Ottawa River and its tributaries. Only the banks of the St. Lawrence and the Great Lakes which make up the border between the United States and Canada are significantly populated. The seigneurial right was spread only up to Lake Champlain, areas close to modern Montreal, and banks of the St. Lawrence River up to Quebec.

The rails on which we traveled were laid on the picturesque, so-called *prairie*, perfectly cultivated and well populated. In the distance, I noticed a hill, which was not very high by itself but stood as a giant in the middle of the plain. Soon I saw the outskirts of the city and, pulled up by the shore of the St. Lawrence, a steam boat already smoking. I could clearly distinguish the buildings, the churches, and a fleet of ships on the opposite bank. Within two or three years a tubular bridge, surpassing by its size the Royal Britannia tubular bridge, will be built across the wide river at that point. I was told that while constructing this bridge for the so-called *grand trunk railroad* (this means that the rail bed will cross the main body of Canada) they spent three million pounds sterling on stones alone, that is, approximately 18.5 million silver rubles. The material was certainly nearby, but a huge amount of stone was required to retain the current, consisting of waters of all the five lakes of the North America and their tributaries.

The ship let us off at the stone embarkment, in which, like a cup, the waters of magnificent St. Lawrence were becalmed. Remembering the way the hotels were run in France and England I was very surprised by the fact that in Montreal they were maintained in the American manner: the same *office* in the hall, the same register book, the same parlours scattered on all the floors and a buffet for everyone with multitude of dishes from different kitchens, the same two and a half dollars a day, the same separation of ladies from gentlemen as in America. Though it's easy to explain: the overwhelming majority of travellers to Canada are Americans and they are unwilling to change their habits. Besides, the owners of the hotels are Americans, just as are a great many of the mechanics, engineers, and merchants who have their small businesses in Canada. American citizens enjoy the same privileges here as Englishmen. The inhabitants of New England feel at home here.

Having become acquainted with several French-Canadian families, for whom I had letters, I asked them the same question: "Will the increased settling here by Americans harm the interests of the English government?"; "Would they not sometime wish to add to their States the English possessions in North America?" I wondered also if the large garrisons in the English fortresses in Halifax, Nova Scotia and Quebec were evidence of the fact that the Englishmen are worried about American intrusion. An almost unanimous answer was that in the case of Canada, England had nothing to fear. An American party, though existing, is small and insignificant, and the majority of both French and English have the same understanding of things, especially since 1837, when municipal rights were extended and equal rights were granted to both peoples. Before, quite naturally, the relations were different and the sympathies of Canadians were on the American side, believing that union with which would improve their circumstances. Now it is different: not because the Americans represent, by means of their institutions and ideas, fewer guarantees for the independence and well-being of Canada. But because the English government, remembering the consequences of its obstinacy and lack of foresight in relation to their former colonies, current North-American States [United States], took a different approach to requests and demands of the country, inhabited by people who are civilized enough to understand their needs and necessities.

The honour of discovery and initial occupation of Canada belongs to the French. It was discovered in 1497 by Sebastian Cabot,[4] but the first settlement for trade with Indians and harvesting furs came half a century later, in 1541, also by a Frenchman, Jacques Cartier, who sailed on the St. Lawrence River and gave it its present name. It was no earlier than 1608 that another settlement was founded on the same spot where

---

[4]   Lakier was confused here. Presumably, he meant Sebastian Cabot's
     father, John Cabot (1449-1498 approx), a Genoan whose expedition
     in 1497 was on behalf of England's Henry VII. Sebastian and his two
     brothers were members of the expedition.

Quebec now stands, a perfect strategical fortress by dint of its geographic features. Only the banks of the St. Lawrence River were, properly speaking, populated and cultivated; the rest lay fallow. The French, with their aristocratic and feudal institutions, were as incapable of colonization on the banks of St. Lawrence as they were in North Africa or South America. They could not attract peaceful settlers even by force of arms, and in the entire present-day Canada, which was then called New France, there were no more than 60 thousand people who, certainly, had sacrificed a lot to reach the new land and make the place suitable for settling. The colony was not particularly productive and suffered from restless neighbours, — wild Indians and Englishmen.

The French at first were somehow able to coexist: trading with them, pacifying them by force of arms. But the English could not forgive Frenchmen for the fact that they owned such huge parts of the continent which they hoped to settle in the name of the Anglo-Saxon race. Ultimately, Canada fell under the authority of Great Britain in 1759 and now the country already has been under the sceptre of English kings for a century.

Accustomed to considering the English as their enemies in Europe, the French could not help but bring their hatred to America and when the war for independence of the American colonies was launched, the French in Canada, as well as their compatriots in Europe, sided with the Americans. Therefore, the mutual relations between Frenchmen and Englishmen suffered; the garrison at the Quebec fort threatened to suppress the least popular movement, the government held the reins of power and the king's advisers tried to govern the remote colony from London. Eastern, former French, Catholic Canada was in law made subservient to the other half — Western or Upper — populated mostly by English descendants.

Clashes occurred often; they became more and more dangerous as the communication between the Old and New World grew and, with the expansion of railroads, as the number of settlers from all countries of Europe increased. Canadians began to compare themselves with their neighbour on the other side of the St. Lawrence River and were dissatisfied with what was left to them — as if out of mercy — by an envious parent state. In 1837 Canada finally rebelled. Order was restored by means of a new administrative structure for both halves of Canada, which were amalgamated [1841]. Now there is no doubt that Canada, with her population of two million, will be reluctant to join Americans who are as alien to the Frenchmen as are the English. But the English promised to leave untouched and unaltered French beliefs and traditions.

While England keeps her promise the population of Canada will grow and vital forces will flow there from Europe into Canada. When talking to newcomers, I often heard the same explanation of why they preferred Canada: the lands are fertile, they said, the forests are virgin but nevertheless they were safe from Indians because they were close to the St. Lawrence and its tributaries. The railroads cross wild areas and so far, because of the small population, land is cheap — from a shilling to one shilling and a half per acre. The Englishmen on their part established shipping companies providing links between the harbours of Great Britain and the mouth of the St. Lawrence River. Industry and trade expands into a new frontier every year. Raw materials, grain, logs and lumber are being exported to England, which provides manufactured goods in return.

The management of Canada is the same as that introduced by England everywhere in her colonies. The executive and legislative powers are completely separate from each other. The former is in the hands of the Governor General who exercises control over the other possessions of Great Britain in North America, that is, New Brunswick, Nova Scotia and Prince Edward Island. Each province has a council with executive powers, composed in Canada of directors of separate ministries: the attorney general, the postmaster general, the chairman [speaker] of the legislative assembly, commissioner of public lands, and other officials appointed by the higher authorities of the province.

The English Parliament does not interfere in the legislative orders of the province, leaving it to the Provincial Parliament which, like the parliament of the metropolis [London], consists of two assemblies: an upper chamber, the members of which are selected by the King, and a lower chamber — whose members are elected by the people. The Governor General has the same influence on matters passing through the *legislatif council* [sic] and *legislative assembly* as the King does on parliamentary bills. Only when the issue concerns more than Canada, that is, its relations to the metropolis or other authorities, does the provincial parliament have to send it for approval by the King and his ministers.

The English and French have equal rights in both chambers of the Parliament. The legislative assembly held its meetings by turn in Montreal and Quebec, the main cities of Eastern or Lower Canada, and in Toronto, the capital of Western or Upper Canada. But recently, when the building in Montreal was destroyed by fire, the Parliament conducted its meetings in Toronto, but only in the last month of last year [December 1857], Bytown, or Ottawa-City, situated on the river with the same name, was chosen as the capital city of the Canadian government. Besides the satisfactory circumstances of this town, the government hoped to move the official capital away from the border of the North American States and chose a central location. Neither half of Canada is satisfied with the decision of executive authorities; the provincial parliaments, as representatives of the people, did not approve the Governor General's recommendation, and his ministers thought that they had lost the confidence of the population. The Canadian cabinet witnessed the repetition of what very often happens in London.

As far as the judicial power is concerned the administration of justice is different in Upper, purely English, and Lower, mostly French, Canada. In the former, the English courts have been maintained: Besides the appellant court (*Court of Error and Appeal*) and the *Court of King's Bench*, there is the *Court of Chancery* with its chancellor and vice-chancellor, the compensation for losses (*equity*) court and the court for common citizens' affairs (*common pleas*). There are many other special courts for different matters: to test wills (*court of probate*), to hear arguments about land and boundaries (*heir and devise court*), and so on. Counties have their own courts (county courts), and for criminal cases there are assizes (*courts of quarter sessions*).

In Eastern Canada, with a predominantly French structure, local customs (*coutumes*) are taken into consideration. For civil and criminal cases, however, a barrister is required, and many lines of the French administration of justice have been improved by touches of English court procedures: for example the question of whether to start a preliminary investigation or not is decided by the *grand jury*. This eliminates the arbitrary influence of bureaucrats and gives lawyers more control over questioning witnesses. These innovations can prove useful for the French administration of justice. Lawyers appear in the courts without wigs, which, it is true, makes them different from those in England; but the judge sits alone in wide, flowing robes, conducting the legal proceedings in English or in French, depending on the nationality of the litigant or defendant; in conformity also with those who are selected as jurors. Judges speak both languages, English and French, and this is necessary. The lawyers are also educated and are capable of conducting the defence equally well in both languages.

Generally speaking the higher classes now consider these two languages both natural and indispensable. And only the lower layers of the population in Eastern Canada achieve little success in English — there French predominates along with the old traditions and the old way of life brought from France. If one visits a townhouse of a Canadian who leads a traditional way of life, one would think that this was a family of a French bourgeois with his small pretensions, with casual gaiety and the same kitchen which still can be found in a remote corner of Paris and in every provincial city of France. Naturally, there are exceptions and some Canadians who have done business with the American States and England, lose their natural French type and adopt an alien one. But this happens only in social life and in trade while in his private life a French Canadian does not forget his language or his traditions. At least the exceptions are very rare. There exists an opinion that the Catholic faith is one of the reasons for the lower class ignorance in Eastern Canada. Even if that were so, the schools maintained by Catholic priests, the divine service and preaching, unite French society: of course, the English government of Canada leaves the Catholic institutions as well as other religious institutions unaltered.

However, we must give credit to French clergy: when people like Cartier and Champlain went on to discover new lands or clear them of savages, the religious monastic orders followed them to teach the word of God. Frenchmen were the first to bring enlightenment to these places. The zeal of missionaries was vitalized by the wildness of the areas and the danger to which the preachers subjected themselves. The schools opened by monks and sisters of charity from different orders and callings facilitated European influence to a degree they would never have had otherwise. It is clear why clerical monastic orders own vast estates here, granted them soon after the foundation of the city. Montreal has always been and continues to be a centre from which missionary activity is spread to the most remote parts of Canada. The Montreal seminary supplies the wild frontiers of Canada with preachers of the word of God and teachers.

Many of the Catholic orders have their educational institutions and hospitals in Montreal: Jesuits devote themselves to educating young people and maintain the large St. Marie gymnasium. The so-called *frères des écoles chretiennes* also have their schools in which they provide education to 2000 boys. But the model school is said to be the *séminaire de St. Sulpice*, which has a great deal of money and exercises control over schools and educational establishments in most cities of Canada. Womens' convents, scattered like the monasteries in all the parts of the city, also devote their labour and life to the great mission; the so-called *soeurs grises*, the *filles de Providence*, and finally the *soeurs de charité* brought their schools and hospitals to every corner of Canada. Their influence here is as beneficial in the sense of enlightenment by the Word of God and upbringing as it is in the East, in the distant cities of Asia Minor and in Africa: everywhere the same gentleness of service. In all the schools established by French "soeurs de charité" which I had a chance to visit, I observed the same system of education, the same courtesy, the same condescending kindness to children whom they encourage to love themselves and come to love goodness. But the labour of Catholic preachers goes far beyond the boundaries of Canada — to the American States. Many schools in the western states are indebted for their existence to Canadian preachers. I do not know if the Americans are right when they look with fear at the rising power of Catholic clergy and the Pope in states with predominantly Catholic populations. In fact, this is no more than a fear that an aristocratic element of hierarchy will destroy the democratic equality of the people: neither the Irish nor the German population can enter into a struggle with the Anglo-Saxon race, which has its strength and superiority in productive capacity and labour.

Be that as it may, Montreal is a purely Catholic city and churches, with which it is littered, give it a beautiful appearance. Although there are so many of them, new ones are still being built. At present, the best church is the *Eglise de la paroise*, or *l'Eglise de la Notre Dame*, built in 1829. The city itself is devoted to Holy Virgin Mary. Before its founder *Mr. de Maisonneuve*[5] came here in 1642 the city had an Indian name — Hochelaga. It was renamed *Ville-Marie* by *Mr. de Maisonneuve*. *Mont-royal* [Montreal] was in fact the name of a mountain that rises in the city, and only at a later time was the name given to the city. The population of the city is from 60 to 70 thousand people and the Church *de la paroise* can accommodate 10 or even 12 thousand people. Its wide gallery is big enough to be a separate church. The architecture is medieval Gothic: two high quadrangular towers along the edges of the facade. There are spires on the tops of towers; the walls are toothed; the facade is like a wall of a fortress; entrances and windows are Gothic. In order to acquire a true and precise concept of Montreal's location, one should climb one of the towers of this church on a sunny day, and if your eyes are not blinded by the reflection of rays you will see a view which will stay in your memory for ever.

Montreal is situated on an island. On one side the wide branch of the St. Lawrence River is easy to see. The mouth of the Ottawa River lies on the other side, forming many small islands at the confluence with the St. Lawrence River. If it were not for the mountain which

---

[5] Paul de Chomeday, Sieur de Maisonneuve (1612-1676), first governor of the island of Montreal. Lakier spelled it "Maissonneure."

rises over the city there is no doubt that the island would not be able to stand the pressure of waves on both sides. Montreal is located on this very island and, on a sunny day, can be seen from the church tower. On the opposite bank of the powerful river one can see a number of houses of Canadian farmers and further on there is a limitless plain, the treasure of all Canadians.

The city is intersected by straight and broad streets, almost all of them carrying the names of Saints. The main street, *rue Notre-Dame*, with many stores and sparkling exhibitions, which the French can so brilliantly organize, draws people to its cafés and restaurants. In the evening there is a big crowd on the street, which, reminiscent of far away France with its songs, merry jokes and inborn ease, comes to life.

And should you decide to visit a theatre there is the same impatient stamping as in any theatre in Paris except that here it is more harsh and frank. No one here is afraid of a commissaire or gendarme. And if the French preserved their natural character even in small things, they certainly did not change it in the more important and significant sides of their life. The substantial trade and industry, which require large investment, risk and sacrifices, can be found in the hands of the English or Americans. The French were left with businesses that do not need major expenditure and therefore do not provide hope for much profit, that is, small shops, stores and barbers' saloons. Americans and the English occupied and purchased the best districts in the city, while French families settled in the outskirts: here one passes low wooden houses and cross over wooden bridges. Pigs swarm in the streets and children run around unsupervised and unrestrained, just as they do in France. The same thing happens in other countries and cities when Frenchmen come to live close to the English and Americans. The predominance of the latter is as striking in New Orleans as it is in Montreal, though in both of them the population is French in both numbers of residents and in the character of the country. It is this inherent distinction between the characters of the two races which makes me think that they will never fuse. Nevertheless, living closely and mutually influencing each other, the two races will nurture that side of practical activity which they like most. Neither of them will have any reason to complain about the law, which remains, so to speak, neutral and patronizes each race equally.

Montreal has had its own university since 1821. There are also secondary, elementary, parish and Sunday schools. Generally speaking the city can boast of its public institutions, buildings of various kinds, markets, water pipelines, gas illumination, and a monument to

Nelson. The rapidity and success of the growth of its population, trade and industry, also is praiseworthy.

Every day on the Mars Field (*champs de Mars*) a changing of the guard takes place, inside the city and accompanied by music. During my stay there, several Russian guns were shipped from England. These guns were taken in Crimea and granted to the English colonies in America for the support they gave to their parent state. Curious people crowded around our eagles, which came to earth so far from their native land . . . .

The most pleasant of all the tours around the suburbs of Montreal is the so-called Mount Royal (*Mont-royal*).[6] The road winds along remote streets, past gardens and market gardens. To the side, on rising ground, lie the water basins that supply the city and houses with water. A little bit further on there is a church farm (*Priestfarm*, as it is called locally), which has its own school for clerics and previously was a monastery, with two embrasures in the gate. I mention them because they still carry their old name, *les forts des messieurs du seminaire*, in memory of a seigneury which once belonged to clerics. According to local legend these turrets contain the remains of two savages who turned to Christianity and spent saintly lives here. The old building of the seminary is completely hidden behind the huge wings of a new one which grows very fast. One of those wings will be used as a Gothic-style church.

The ascent to Mount Royal starts right here, that is, from the seminary. The higher one climbs the more striking is the view of the St. Lawrence River, flowing between flat green banks. Finally you see waves of the Ottawa River sparkling in the sun. *Mont-royal* rises alone in the middle of the plain and that is why it seems so high. The slopes of the mountain are covered by dense forest. The autumn did its usual job: some leaves on the trees, touched by frost, turned red and yellow, while other leaves, less sensitive to cold weather, were still green. It seems as if a vast forest was painted by a gigantic brush, without sparing the purple in all its re-arrangements. The mountain is supposed to be used as a cemetery, but there still are not many monuments and these are scattered throughout the dense forest.

The overflow of the Ottawa River on the flat land forms numerous islands near Montreal. The largest of them is called *Ile Jesus*. Spits of sand under the water could impede navigation up from Montreal, preventing sea trade from proceeding further than this point. To eliminate this inconvenience, canals were built, and big vessels now use

---

6   The literal Russian was "Royal Mountain."

them as sea routes from Lake Ontario sometimes directly to Europe; some ships even risk passing through the rapids. Someone tried to assure me that those ships, drawn by current power, develop speeds of 25 to 30 instead of the usual 10 miles an hour. The canal starts at Montreal and ends at a place called *Lachine*. A railroad covers the same 10 miles. I went there to see a truly ancient French village with its *bons-vieux*.

This trip was particularly pleasant because the area we saw from the train was very well cultivated and extremely fruitful. We saw plenty of fruit trees in orchards. Canadian apples are brought from here to Quebec and further on. The oddness that the place was named China (*la Chine*), situated so far from the real China, would have surprised me if the inhabitants of that same place had not born another name of little respect — Indians [*Indiitsy*]. Whether Cartier and his companions thought they had discovered a way to China, and exclaimed with joy — *la Chine!*, which is difficult to believe, or it was cruel joke by someone who wanted to laugh at the word "Indians," we don't know.[7] It is known only that the name has existed since Cartier's time. Until now this place was a central post of the Hudson Bay Company which occupies entire limitless kingdoms north of the large American lakes. The company's main office is in London, but it is from here that it sends the so-called *voyageurs* to different Indian tribes who live on the company's land and conduct an exclusive trade in furs with the company. From Lachine they carry gifts, blankets, clothing, gun powder and fire-arms, to exchange for fur coats and pelts, from which the company makes its living.

On the opposite shore of the St. Lawrence there still remains an Iroquois settlement — the village of *Caunawaga* [Kahnawake], where savages are frightening only in name, and now do not differ from French farmers or *habitants*. Canadian-Iroquois are Catholic; they have their own schools, churches and fields. They dress like everyone else and call themselves, as all the other Canadian Indians — savage (*sauvage*). They earn their living building light boats, hollowed out from thick tree trunks, fishing and hunting, with which they trade in

---

7 Lakier used here the Russian words, *Indiets, indiiskii,* which referred specifically to North America's "Indian." But this was rare. In almost every other reference to Canada's native peoples, he used *dikar'*, or the adjective *dikii*, that is, "savage" or "wild man." He may have been translating the commonly-used (then and now) Quebec term, "sauvage" into Russian. Sometimes he used *Tuzemets*, which usually means native, or indigenous person.

Montreal. In the winter they manufacture moccasins, soft shoes and skis. It is impossible to say whether the Iroquois appear contented, or if their homes are particularly neat. But the signs of their origin are maintained only in their black coarse hair and the dark-copper skin of their faces.

It was interesting for me to see the so-called *Thousand Islands* scattered in the St. Lawrence River at its juncture with Lake Ontario. Generally, this river — the final source of the North American lakes [Great Lakes] — is extremely diverse and capricious: it is sometimes narrow, sometimes three or four miles wide, forming sand bars and islands; sometimes it flows quietly, sometimes it forms rapids. On the way from Montreal to Kingston, for example, one can see Lakes St. Louis and St. Francis, which are precursors to those huge lakes from which the river flows.

Our ship had to change its course every now and then in order not to find itself on an island. But the problem became much more serious when we got to the Thousand Islands, scattered in the St. Lawrence's river bed in the most various shapes and groups. Only the largest of them have their own names and are populated: those closer to Lake Ontario. Others were in fact small spots, overgrown with forest. On a sunny day they sparkled like emeralds on the light blue surface of the St. Lawrence. Our trip past these beautiful islands ended at Kingston, the ship docked, and I took a train back to Montreal. From there I travelled further north. I had to hurry up. Autumn in Canada is as cold as in Russia. It was the time of what they call here *Indian Summer*, something like our Ladies' Summer [*bab'e leto*] with cool weather in the mornings and warm sunny days. The trees were covered by purple foliage. So as not to spend the winter in the cold North, when Cuba was so alluring, and not stay over again in Montreal, on the day of my arrival I bought a ticket for a ship going to Quebec.

Chapter VIII
From Quebec to Niagara Falls.

I could have taken a train on the *Grand Trunk Railway* from Montreal to Quebec, but I preferred to go by ship, so as to become better acquainted with the further flow of the St. Lawrence. The price of tickets for a *state* room (a sleeping room for two) with a big window for air and light, plus service and meals during the whole trip is insignificant in comparison with prices at European ships: three dollars (approximately four silver rubles) includes transportation fare and meals during the trip, which takes 16 hours if there is no fog or wind. Several ships with goods and passengers leave at the same time and each of them tries to load as much cargo as possible and keep ahead of all the other ships. I admit that, though I was accustomed to the fast American ride, I could never remain calmly seated while it was trying to pass another ship. The captain of the ship that comes up from behind forgets all precaution and good sense and travels at maximum speed. To be passed by another ship means loss of reputation as a good captain, especially if the ships are of the same model, the same size and carry the same cargo. This time the captain of our ship was an Englishman and he strongly criticized the rashness of Americans. To illustrate the consequences of American *avos'*, that is, *go-ahead*,[8] he told us a story of a collision of a ship carrying passengers to Quebec last year. A fire started from over-heating machinery and the passengers, afraid of danger, demanded that the ship quickly head for the shore. They tried to stop the fire but the high speed of the ship only fanned it. As a result the ship was smashed on a rock. Our captain saved more than 100 survivors. No one knows how many people died, and it is such a shame that courts treat this type of awful mistake or carelessness much too mildly.

Our captain, however, was not of the rash type. He was stopped in the morning by fog and blew his horn every minute so that no one would run into him.

The banks of the St. Lawrence are dotted with small farms with their wooden houses, fences and noisy life, for almost its entire course from Montreal. In some places there were larger buildings, *manoirs* (grand country houses, family estate[9]), or dachas of wealthy Canadians. Everything on the shores was bustling; the fields were covered by rye, oats, barley, less often by wheat and still more rarely by maize. Beyond the fields, the area was black with forest and quarries could be seen. There is no shortage of anything, everything is harvested from the soil by a merry Canadian, who is happy and delighted when someone calls him *l'heureux Canadien*, whether or not the term is used in jest or seriously.

Almost in the middle of the road between Montreal and Quebec the St. Lawrence River widens and forms Lake St. Peter with several small islands in the middle of it. The further we go, the higher and

---

[8] Lakier translated the Russian *avos'* (his italics) as "go-ahead," though "risk-taking" is more accurate in the context.

[9] Lakier used the Russian word *pomestie*, in brackets, which referred in Russia to an estate granted on conditions of service, during the Muscovy period.

more wooded the banks of the river become; its slightest curves form natural harbours, where ships gather in order to get loaded with timber and planks to go to Quebec and from there into Europe, to English wharfs.

Early in the morning we saw the upper parts of Quebec fortress and rays from the rising sun started playing on the spires of Quebec's Cathedral. The city is divided into upper, governmental, and lower, trade districts. I had to select a hotel in one of them. I chose the upper city in order to be closer to the esplanade and the fortifications, from which there is a beautiful view of all the surroundings, ships, the cathedral and other places of interest for travellers. From my hotel window I could see the picturesque flow of the St. Lawrence and its opposite bank, so I could enjoy it without leaving my room. After settling in, I went to have a close look at the rock on which the intimidating fortress of Quebec, the key to English holdings in North America, looms. This fortress is astonishing not so much by its height, as by the fact that it stands alone in the middle of a plain as if it were dropped there on purpose to serve as a stronghold against enemy attacks and as a strategic point.

The rock descends almost vertically to the sea, leaving only a narrow strip of land for the streets of its coastal neighbourhood. At the bottom of the rock there is a beautiful harbour in which is concentrated all of the trade between Canada and Europe, because big sea vessels can reach Quebec without any obstacles. That is why the geographer [explorer] Champlain who founded a city here in 1608 called it a cape, formed by this rock, *Cap aux diamants* or, as the English say, *Cape Diamond*. The English understood very well that to hold Canada they had to possess this diamond-shaped rock and, whenever the opportunity arose, attacked it in an effort to conquer the fortress. In 1619 Quebec was in the hands of the English, but later it was given to the French.[10] In 1759 England began to rule Quebec again, and with it all of Canada. Now the English government attaches the same importance to this fortress as it does to Gibraltar or to fortified Malta. The forts have guns, there are hidden batteries in the mountain, and anyone who determined to invade the city now would meet the same fate as the American General [Richard] Montgomery in 1775 when, during the War of Independence, hoping to drive the English from their last

---

[10] Lakier probably refers here to the capture of Quebec City in 1629 (not 1619) by a force led by adventurer Captain David Kirke and his brothers; they were ordered to return it to the French as a result of the Treaty of St. Germaine in 1632.

den, he paid with his life. This kind of misfortune could have been foreseen. When the English took Quebec in 1759 General [James] Wolf had acted differently: he was able to go around the rock with the powerful fortress on it and drew the French to battle on the plain behind the fortress, the so-called *Plaine d'Abraham*. The French General [Marquis Louis de] Montcalm, who was charged with the fortress defence, lost the battle and, like the equally brave General Wolf, was destined not to see the surrender of Canada to the English. A monument has been erected on the place where Wolf fell. Moreover, there is another monument in a small garden under the Citadel[11] in memory of both heroes and was built by money collected from both French and English.

A place for promenades was built on the esplanade. One can only regret that it is too small, and there are no trees to protect walking people from the rays of the sun. To complete the enjoyment of the view, which could not help but move even the coldest and the most prosaic traveller, one should climb the top of the citadel where the English flag is flying. From here you can have a look at the broad St. Lawrence, at the Orleans Island (*l'Ile d'Orléans*) lying in the middle of it, at the Louis rock behind it and at the mountains covered with forest! Below, people are bustling around like ants, ships are being loaded, timber is being brought in from everywhere; in the city everyone hurries to do his business and it seems that the observer is lifted above all those worries of everyday life as if by magic. I often climbed to my favourite place and always came back absolutely enchanted.

The prevailing language in Quebec is French. There are slightly more Frenchmen here than in Montreal. Landowners here preserve the same old provincial type one finds in Montreal: he is dressed in a grey coat in the winter time, on his head a hat in the form of a cap and, generally speaking, his clothing depends on the climate. Approaching a building occupied by courts, I saw a large number of Canadians evidently waiting for their turn to enter the meeting hall. Policemen, dressed like English police, were running to and fro, as if trying to find someone. In the court I discovered a crowd of people. Barristers were called from a list. A hot-headed barrister, very carefully agreeing to the selection of this or another person to a jury, rejected many until

---

[11] The Citadel was built between 1820 and 1831 by the English to strengthen the existing fortifications.

finally there were enough people chosen.[12] Those who were chosen in this manner, were sworn in as jurors and a case of a somewhat insignificant robbery began. The witnesses were interrogated one after the other. The barrister, in whom it would seem no English blood flowed, lost his patience every time a witness's answer was not to the advantage of his client. He screamed as much as he could, but nevertheless the jury found his client guilty. The trial did not stop in the courtroom: having left it, the jurors had to defend their verdict in front of their compatriots who crowded around them. There is no doubt that this custom provides a greater guarantee of justice. It is a pity that the courtroom is small, especially when there's an unceasing movement of the curious and those who are taking part in the case. The warning shouts of a gentleman in black uniform, incessantly crying, *silence!* in English and French failed to have any effect.

There are translators in the court. Previously the British government wanted to introduce an exclusive use of English, but this did not go far and now even the laws are printed in both languages. Lawyers use either one or the other language, depending on the case. It may happen that one of the jurors does not understand the language in which the case is conducted, and if either the person who is participating in the case or his lawyer is not willing to switch to another language, all the court proceedings will have to be translated for that one person.

In Quebec's cathedral, which is distinguished by its huge size, I found nothing extraordinary. But it is one of the oldest buildings of the city and was consecrated in 1666. Next to the cathedral there is one of the oldest educational establishments not only in Canada but in the entire North America: this is the Quebec seminary which has existed since 1663, both for training clerics and for people of other estates. Funds for this institution are as high as those for the Montreal seminary. For a long time it has been maintained by the collection of one thirteenth of everything produced by labour and land. Although recently this portion was reduced by half, the institution nevertheless remains rich: it owns a huge house and educates up to 500 boys, not only from Quebec but from England and the United States as well.

---

[12] There were no juries in Russia and Lakier clearly hoped that a provision for juries might be the result of juridical reform then being under discussion. Very limited trial by jury was introduced to Russia in the sweeping juridical reforms of 1864.

Having never seen Niagara Falls, I was curious to see Montmorency Falls, one of the largest next to Niagara, and hoped to visit the indian village Lorette on the same day. I left the city early in the morning. The fortress prevented proper planning in the lower, commercial city, lying at the foot of the mountain: its streets were crooked and narrow, the city was built as the population grew, the roadways are extremely bad and our light carriage was shaken mercilessly until across the bridge and the *Saint-Charles* River we came to the open field. From the first words of my coachman, who spoke excellent French, and from his extremely polite manners I knew I was not dealing with an ordinary driver. It was true. He told me that his father was a notary and he himself had studied at the seminary. Then had been taught in some kind of a collegium, owned a farm, and now, because of his love for horses, works on weekdays as a coachman. On Sundays he sings in a parish church. To the story about his past my coachman added that he is absolutely satisfied with his life and promised to introduce his wife and children to me in the village on our way. Naturally, I did not refuse and was very glad to have a chance to see the life of Canadian farmers more closely. My interlocutor was as happy as I was: the sun was not warm and the strong autumn wind was piercing to the morrow. The village was called *Beau-Port* [Beauport]. We stopped at one of its squat houses. The family of my driver was busy doing some kind of work and I was introduced to the family members just as one might introduce a guest. With a sort of regret, which I shared with him, the host declared that he belonged to the sober society and that except for *soupe à l'ognon* [sic] quickly prepared by his hospitable wife, he could offer me nothing. I did not want to lose time, but had no choice but to wait. And I was compensated for that with an onion boiled in water with pieces of bread in it. But the best spicing of this unpretentious meal was the pleasure with which the Canadian hostess offered me this soup. She had a cow, a garden, and a house of her own, and like her husband was delighted with her life. Giving me an idea of other Beau-Port residents' lives my driver told me that each of these grey coated and capped farmers had their own farmstead, a house and common fields. The fields here are excellent, but are expensive and very rarely for sale. Further inside the country there are still unoccupied lands and many newcomers from Europe, especially the Irish, come to settle there. Here as everywhere else they remain poor and are well-known, unfavourably, for their short tempered and careless character.

From the village, we were not far from Montmorency Falls. It is located on the territory of a private estate and there is an entrance fee of 1 shilling. Although I did not like the idea that it was possible to shut off the view of the waterfall by a key, I was struck by the beauty of its white foaming water, which falls from the rock 250 feet high and later enters the St. Charles River as a very calm streamlet, bearing no trace of its wild origins. Before getting to the falls there was once a bridge on the rock from which the water drops; now only its posts remain. Below Montmorency there appears to be some kind of a giant in a white robe, angry and smoky, surrounded by dark rocks and trees. I was told that in the winter the view is not that conspicuous and solemn but nevertheless water splashes, frozen on the rocks, and their strange shapes draw many people here on warm winter days. In the old days, though, this waterfall was incomparably more picturesque: now part of its water is used by a sawmill, which has damaged it significantly.

Throughout its course the St. Lawrence's generally abounds in waterfalls, several of them situated above Quebec. If Niagara were not so close and nature shared its beauties between different countries, each of these waterfalls would evoke equal amazement. Now one automatically compares Montmorency with the giant-waterfall, and this comparison is, of course, not to its advantage.

From Montmorency I went to the Indian village of *Saint Lorette* [Lorette]. There I expected to find savages in their original condition, that is, with painted, tattooed faces, shells and beads in their ears and nostrils, feathers on their heads, and blankets instead of clothes on their shoulders. Having arrived at the place I did not want to believe that I was already in an Indian village. An Indian can be hardly distinguished from a Frenchman living in Canada: he has adopted French clothing and housing. And if it were not for his dark strong Indian hair and dark complexion it would be impossible to tell one from the other. Living so close to Indians for centuries the French, or more accurately the Canadians, have in their turn borrowed something from the Indians. For example, they have adopted a dish called sagamité, corn and milk porridge. Though, of course, the French influence on Indians was much stronger. Suffice it to mention only the schools built for the offspring of wild Hurons. The teacher was also a Huron and consequently belonged to this formerly terrifying tribe. Now he is educated and brings the benefits of education to his tribesmen, who will be occupied not only with hunting and fishing but also farming. Nevertheless, here, as in the United States, the copper race runs away and dies out as the white race approaches; and it is not in vain that Indians wear amulets, and know grasses and stones that save them from a dangerous contact with white men. This does not mean, however, that the French were cruel to Indians. It was not their fault, but rather it is to the natural course of events that one can attribute the fact that only small villages with a hundred residents remain of entire tribes that once so intimidated Europeans.

Outside Quebec, a chain of French settlements line the St. Lawrence. The way of life in these places is still simpler than it is in the vicinity of big cities: Canadian houses are never locked; they are open to everyone, even for Indians. All the savages here are Catholic. There is much space for hunting, and Indians can live very well without even changing their habits and old way of life. Other times will come, of course, when villages like St. Lorette and Lachine, will be built there, but the savages are already prepared for this change, and the transmission will be easy and painless for them.

II

I took a train back to Montreal and stayed there no longer than necessary to make inquiries about ships departing up the Ottawa River. However, all my inquiries turned out to be superfluous. The ships departed every morning and in Montreal itself one could buy a ticket for the voyage on the Ottawa River. Even though it was autumn, traffic on this route had not diminished; in fact, they were hurrying to raft timber to Quebec in time, before winter arrived.

Having arrived at Lachine by a familiar road, we found a ship already waiting for us. This ship was of the same model as those that plied the St. Lawrence River. Most of its passengers were migrants to Upper Canada, the area between Ottawa and the North American [Great] Lakes.

There were Irishmen and Frenchmen who are still more willing to settle in Canada than in the United States. There also were Germans. The goal of many of them was to settle either on the banks of Ottawa River itself or somewhere close to the railroad, which connected the Ottawa and St. Lawrence Rivers. Land here is plentiful, and all those not taken yet are divided into lots, each with a statistical description of its location and advantages, so that a person willing to buy it knows in advance the best place for him to settle. Besides that, detailed information about the land can be obtained from special agents who have land maps and descriptions and are able to answer all the questions in the most positive way.

The main enemy of all settlers in this region is the forest, which must be cut or burned beforehand. Irish settlers explained their preference for Canada because of the dominance of Catholicism in this area and because of the love which they have for trees and rivers. But perhaps the main and more prosaic reason lies in the fact that the forest does not require one's constant care and such patient labour as is necessary for arable fields; the forest can be felled according to need. Surrounding the Ottawa River and its tributaries are the most wooded areas in all of Canada, making the region the main source of timber for the Quebec and European markets. Now the movement to settle this side is stronger than ever before because the links between it and remote parts of Upper Canada is easy and inexpensive by ship. There was a time not so long ago when only boats [canoes] made of birch bark and saturated with oily substances were able to navigate the Ottawa River and its rapids.

The birch bark is stretched on light wooden ribs. The hard outer birch cover passes easily over rock outcrops and are easy to carry from one place to another when it is necessary to bypass the waterway. On such fragile boats, among wild savages, came the first enlighteners of this country, Jesuits, who feared neither hardships nor even death while serving the word of God. The same boats were used and are still being used by enterprising agents of the Hudson's Bay Company for fur trade with Indians in remote places. The fur is exchanged for fabrics, wool clothing, weapons, utensils and trinkets for the savages, their wives and daughters.

Now things have changed: we sailed on a large luxurious ship. Its light parlours on the deck had soft divans. Breakfasts, dinners and tea were served in special hours. Sitting in this cosy home, chatting with a neighbour or reading a newspaper, one could easily forget that he was sailing on a river which could be quite inhospitable.

Passing by Lake *St-Louis*, formed by the St. Lawrence River south of Montreal Island, our ship rounded the island and entered the Ottawa River. Soon we saw the place where its muddy waters, which had not mixed with the St. Lawrence's light waters, flowed together for some time until they finally converged for their further course to the north. Meanwhile, I noticed a large train rushing at full speed on the suspension bridge across the Ottawa River. The question why, for whom and for what millions of dollars are being spent in this sparsely populated country would be impossible to answer if one were to examine the situation only from the point of view of the present. On the other hand, the achievement of permanence or at least a long existence, is being built for the future, to be used by future generations. Now, in fact, the road goes through deserted, uninhabited places and ancient forests, but it is for these rails and by these rails, that the contemporary population will grow. Besides, at present the cost of railroads is relatively low in these thick forests; there are no settlements of any kind to prevent the construction of direct lines. Owners of farms lying on the roadbed willingly sell the lands needed by the railroad company. The company receives a strip of land on both sides of the rails. Thus, both the company and the province as a whole benefit from the construction of the railroad: the prices for land rises and the population craves rail lines because of their accessibility. The calculation proves to be correct and in North America they have for a long time built no roads, rather they construct only railroads to serve as the first bearers of civilization to deserted frontiers awaiting a population.

The Ottawa River is as capricious and diverse as the St. Lawrence. As soon as it flows over a lowland it forms a lake with small islands covered with trees. Then the river-bed becomes narrow again. Sand banks and rapids are common and they provide obstacles to navigation. In such places canals are built for safer navigation. It is difficult to count all the lakes formed by the Ottawa River, for there are too many of them. One of the largest and most beautiful is called the Lake of the Two Mountains. Indeed, on entering it from the narrow river-bed, one is surprised to see two mountains in its further corner and an Indian village on the picturesque shore. The houses on the shore face the Ottawa River, and their residents are as little like their savage ancestors as the people of other Indian villages along the banks of the St. Lawrence and its tributaries.

At Carillon the Ottawa River is interrupted by rapids; ships cannot pass through them. The passengers descend in wagons and both their luggage and freight are placed on rails. The train rushes through the forest. We discover places where huts have been knocked together hastily; a parcel of land has been cleared of forest; a fence surrounds the dwelling and provides temporary defence for cattle from wild animals. The fields are dotted with piles of stones on fields which had to be dug out in order to clear the place to form arable land. But how long will it be before the axe will fell the entire ancient forest where a variety of animals had roamed and savages chased them! They don't spare the forest here, they burn wood for locomotives and burn brush to fertilize the fields. Everywhere huge piles of logs lie, doing no good for anyone.

Carillon Place is a French settlement, and one of the oldest. Further on there are other locations which gained importance only recently. In Grenville where the railroad ended, there was another ship waiting for us. The view of the banks of the Ottawa remained the same: the same dark strip of forest, the same occasional settlement.

The cold and damp brought all the passengers to the common room and, while drinking tea, I started up a conversation with my neighbour, a young Catholic priest who had been visiting not far from Grenville and now was returning home.

The conversation started with a complaint that in Upper Canada Catholicism is being pushed out by Protestantism, that American and English missionaries, especially methodists, advance deep into the forests, and that the achievements of the region's first enlighteners, French missionaries, are preserved only in Lower Canada. The greater part of the people in Upper Canada belongs to the Episcopal Church. The words of my interlocutor were proven by the following official facts: At that time, 84 percent of the entire population in Lower Canada was Catholic, only 5 percent was Protestant, 3 percent was Presbyterian and the Episcopal Church did not exist; in Upper Canada the opposite was the case: Catholics were 18 percent, Protestants 24 percent and Episcopalians were 48 percent. Nevertheless, new Catholic communities are formed in Upper Canada by newcomers from France and Ireland, and they are provided with priests from Canadian seminaries. My new friend was on his way to one such community, and he invited me to be his companion in the forest where he had been living. I readily agreed because of his promise to show me the life of lumbermen and wild Indian tribes. We had to spend one day in By-Town or as they have started to call it now, Ottawa-City, where we arrived very late in the evening.

The name By-Town was given to the place in honour and memory of the English Colonel By who founded a settlement here. Barely a quarter century has passed since they began to clear the forest here, but the title "town" no longer applies to this settlement, which, thanks to its geographical location has attracted more than 10 thousand people. It covers a vast territory, has broad though still unpaved streets, lit by gas, and has good hotels. In addition to being nourished by government, it tries hard to become the capital of all of Canada. Apparently the name "town" was not enough for such a place and it was renamed "city" with municipal rights and city authorities. There is no doubt that, in time and perhaps soon, this new city will play the same role in the lumber trade as Chicago, in the western American States, does in wheat; or New Orleans, on the southern Mississippi, does in the cotton trade. But at present this place is waiting, as the Americans say, for different types of *improvements*, to be completed.

In fact there still is no city. There are rows of big buildings and beside them vacant lots or wooden huts of the first settlers who earned their living working at logging and hunting. The advantage of the location selected for the city consists in its central position between Upper and the Lower Canada and the fact that it is on the route of the timber trade, which comes here at the juncture of the Ottawa River's tributaries. From here timber can be rafted either down the Ottawa River to Montreal or up the so-called Rideau Canal to Lake Ontario. In this way, ancient (if only such a word was applicable here) By-Town will become a centre of trade relations for a new area, which is waiting for its own fresh population.

Within the limits of a future city and not far from its present boundaries there can be found its most interesting place, the Ottawa waterfalls or, as the Jesuits called them, *la chaudière*, a hollow [sic].[13] This name reveals the nature of the place as clearly as possible. Rushing over rocks, which even the powerful water could not move, the river divides into several arms, foaming into numerous rapids, swirling and frothing, it crashes over cliffs into a cauldron, where spray boils and splashes. Dark cliffs, which rise above the white froth of the falls, are mute witnesses to this wild scene of nature. But humans have used these waterfalls for their own purposes. One branch of the Ottawa River sets a sawmill in motion. The power of the waterfall is said to have been weakened because of it, but people gained a lot instead. However, the waterfall is beautiful even now, especially if one looks at the Chaudière from the foot bridge thrown across it. In general, Canadian nature is rich in waterfalls, and in many places there are facts and phenomena still not explained by science. In Chaudière, for example, a powerful branch of the Ottawa River falls into a rocky precipice, and it is unknown whether it comes out on the surface or if it disappears into the earth.

Further on up the Ottawa River ships are replaced by trains and then the trains again by ships. Ships finally give way to carriages and not very safe boats. Nonetheless, I decided to travel with the Catholic priest in order to see his forest dwelling and the people among whom he lives and works. The first few miles we had to travel on the highway past the cataracts and rapids of the Ottawa River. After that the river becomes calmer, and a small white ship of the same structure and comfort as its larger version navigates it. From the village of *Aylmer* one can easily cover 30 miles to *Chats Lake* [Lac des Chats], the entrance of which is blocked by stones. Here we took a train for 2 miles and later a ship to *Portage du Fort*. There we again took a train for short distance, and then a ship. Another transfer and we were able to continue still

---

13 Lakier used the Russian word *kotlovina*, which means "hollow." *Chaudière* actually means "boiler," probably in reference to water 'boiling' up from the waterfall.

further in a birch bark canoe. The rapids don't allow us to measure the upper flow of the Ottawa River precisely. Meanwhile, because of its tributaries, it provides the shortest route to Lake Huron and from there to the Western States. Hudson's Bay Company agents have their own maps, but they are not quite accurate.

At *Portage du Fort* we left the Ottawa River. We had to travel ten more miles in order to reach my companion's settlement. A carriage with one small and quick Canadian horse was waiting for him. In this carriage we continued our journey on a road through the forest, from time to time bumping against tree-stumps and stones. But how could we pay attention to such conditions when on both sides of the road there rose huge platens, maple trees, oaks, sycamores, endless birch trees, fir and pine, still untouched by human beings. I love the forest, and always in the most remote countries its poetic rustle turns my thoughts and imagination to our own northern woods. However, I couldn't help but ask my companion if he was not bored here, especially during the long winters when snow interrupts communications even with many members of his parish who live in the same forest. But the priest, it seems, became accustomed to the woods just as had the Jesuits who spent entire years in it, seeing no one but wild Indians. Now, at least, Christians who sympathize with their priest, live there: it is possible to converse with them. Besides that, groups of wood-cutters frequent such places and they sometimes bring news, sometimes a newspaper and sometimes a letter. New settlements are no longer isolated from the rest of the world. In winter and in autumn, it is true, nature sleeps. The Indians come from remote places to hunt, the inhabitants cut wood and prepare it for rafting. But the real feast comes in April when a warm sun ray strikes the trees, when a maple tree awakes from its sleep and starts giving its sweet juices to people. Everyone is involved in gathering maple sap: old and young carry baskets and pails made of birch bark. They come back with the sugary sap which they boil after and turn into syrup.

As the snow melts wild animals leave the edge of a forest and go into the thicket. Birds arrive and flowers start blooming. Wild plums, cherries and grapes promise a rich harvest in autumn. Berries of different names and descriptions bloom and ripen. Among them I recognized, sometimes, our blackberries, cloudberries, cranberries, sometimes raspberries and black currants. And if you love these endless forests with the love of a wood-cutter, you will be able to understand the language of the poplars and oaks and you will feel an immense respect for the labour of those *gens de chantier* or *lumbermen*, as Americans call them!

I shared the young priest's rapture in his story about the virgin forest where he lived and toiled, though I didn't manage to see a lot of what he was talking about. Near the settlement the forest became very thin. Finally the cabins of residents and the wooden church with a cross on its top became visible. Here one cannot say that the village hears the church bells: there were no bells, but there is hope that the population would grow and in the new village other churches would be built. The settlements already are growing: not much further on there is another church, a Protestant one, it seems, because there were several dissidents. In the poor dwelling of the priest there was hardly enough room for two, but I don't know what I would have done without him! The farmers, in general, are very hospitable; nearness to nature makes people kind and compassionate. But one has to have before it is possible to give. On this occasion, however, I was secure and went for a walk around the village. I heard the tap of a hammer and saw several dozens of people working hard near a hut or a fence. No one was giving orders, and everyone worked hard as if for oneself. One of them, an Irishman who was glad to use the chance to talk, explained to me that they were helping a compatriot who had just arrived from the *old country* to build his first dwelling in one day. He added that everyone needed help here and should the necessity arise the neighbours helped each other. And, in fact, the hut was ready by evening. True, it was very primitive but sufficient to serve as a shelter from bad weather or wild animals. At first the newcomer also is helped with livestock and utensils, and after that he lives as best he knows how.

During my stay in Lower Canada in villages near Montreal I often heard from residents that their sons had been living somewhere in remote forests for several years already, that they were safe and sound and were not going to return home soon. I would always like to know what made those people leave their places and spend years and years in wild forests, cutting trees. Once, when alone with my host, I started talking about it, he stopped me at my first word "abnégation" [self-sacrifice] which I used in reference to such woodsmen. He wouldn't allow this word to be used in respect to American "lumbermen" or French "gents de chantier" (from which the English settlers called them *shantymen*). He insisted that the teams of lumbermen were organized perfectly well and their business was one of the most profitable.

He began his story with an observation that more than 175 billion acres of land remained still unsettled and was in the hands of the government. Almost all this land is covered with dense, still untouched forest, where timbers for masts and wood construction grow, not controlled by anyone. Among the population, who would be very glad to see land not covered by forest, industrial dealers cut the woods and pay an established rent to the Government. An agent of the government, the so-called *crown timber agent*, has charts and maps of his own where he marks all the woods that are leased and which are still free. Any woodsman can choose a spot and buy a *license* for the right to fell timber. In order to make sure the forest is used by the person who has a license there is a requirement that he sell a certain amount of timber in the market. Otherwise the rent will be doubled and license taken back. The first industrial dealers felling the woods were Frenchmen, and their workers called them *bourgeois*, from which Englishmen derived their *boorshaw*. These industrialists, having chosen a convenient place for felling near a river for the purpose of rafting the logs, sent groups of 10 or 12 men led by a *conducteur* or *foreman* who was stronger and cleverer than the others.

These pioneers, even if they are scattered several hundred miles from any source of the light of enlightenment because there was still nothing to educate, at least brought daylight into impassable forests and thickets, building blockhouses close to streams. These are, for the most part, poor dwellings in which smoke and light pass through an opening in the roof. The cots of workers are spread along the walls of the dwellings. A gun and a hammer are inseparable companions of these enterprising people who spend their whole summer at work felling trees. In the winter-time they haul the cut logs across the snow to the river in order to make it easier to float them when the water rises in the Ottawa River. They get so accustomed to their dwellings that they leave them only after having felled all the trees on the piece of licensed land. The foremen are almost always from Scotland: the Scots are known for their temperance, love of order, strength, hard work and the ease with which they endure hardship. These personal qualities are indispensable for a man who, by his example and word must, alone in the woods, without any help, direct the work and an entire group of people, every one of which consider himself fully independent and free. Making up their minds to work as a single association, the party works closely together, with confidence in their associates, and one does not hear of discord or arguments between them.

Sometimes these groups would run up against savages with whom they try to live in peace by exchanging gun powder or some trifles for footwear or game. To communicate with Indians the Scotsmen learned several of the most important words and they mix them with their dialect. That is why Indians believe that the European language closest to their own is Scottish.

At the end of all this work, the wood cutters divide up a general sum; they usually earn, after all expenses, 250-300 dollars a year. Of course, they are deprived of many modern conveniences, but they live freely, and in the end become accustomed to the forests and are very friendly with nature. In fact, it is more difficult to find labourers for any other kind of work than cutting trees.

This, of course, is not the end of the forest industry: the cut logs must be rafted on small rivers falling to the Ottawa and then by the Ottawa River to Quebec. From Quebec they are shipped to the Old World. If the Ottawa was a calm river, without chutes and rapids, rafting would be much easier. But at present the frames of the rafts are weak and not connected strength-on-strength, completed with squared timbers, boards, or couplings between them. They must be manoeuvred through rapids, broken into sections when the entire raft cannot make it through a chute, and with great skill are guided between thousands of islands, from which the routes can only barely be seen from under the water. Frenchmen are known for their bravery at wood rafting, and Americans don't lag far behind them.

I was very glad to hear this detailed account of the general working of the lumber industry in Canada from a man who was familiar with the forest. But I wanted to get acquainted with Indians, and actually on the next day I saw wigwams, i.e. dwellings of itinerant Indians who came here to hunt. They were covered with branches, wood bark and rags to protect their poor inhabitants from dampness and bad weather. In the wigwams there were only wives (*sqwaws*) [sic] and children, as the husbands and fathers had gone hunting. Everyone thinks that these people are quiet and even courteous, but very proud and intolerant of alien rule; Indian tribes more quickly become friends with white people, than with each other.

One tribe will not enter into kindred relationships with others. This is why the savages, before the arrival here of white people, always considered it necessary to wear trophies captured in battle from dead enemies as the best attribute of their costume and its best decoration. Their wives are ugly, squat, dirty and poor. Pride and belief that an Indian is the best person in the world, that he is free and independent prevents them from bad behaviour. But killing men in battle or robbing on the highway, subjecting themselves in that way to danger, not only are not considered a sin but are treated instead as a form of valour. In the west of North America, where the savages are still found in their original circumstances, one can readily meet a savage who will take you by the arm, not unlike a real gentleman, and having wrapped himself up in a blanket will tell you the story of his adventures, the captured trophies he is wearing and his hunting, but he will not say a word about his needs.

I could not continue further up the Ottawa River alone, and I didn't have a companion. Besides, as people who visited the estuary of the river assured me, neither the river itself nor its banks represented anything special: there were virgin woods on both banks; rapids prevented access by decent ships, allowing only wooden (*canoes*) made of birch bark.

I took the same route, i.e. by ship and railroad, and returned to Ottawa City. From there I had to go down to Lake Ontario and cross into the United States. I had two possibilities for getting there: the first by the Rideau Canal, the other by railroad. I chose the second route, and my God! what a remote area surrounded that railroad! Train stations were nothing but wooden, quickly built huts. In some places, however, the sound of hammers are already heard, trees are cut down for dwellings, and the future promises much life.

The town of Prescott, on the St. Lawrence River, where the train brought us, also represented nothing of interest. Since there was no possibility to leave it on the same night, I decided to cross the St. Lawrence River on a steam ferry and spend a night in Ogdensburg, in New York State.

In spite of the fact that the border between two countries lies on a line drawn in the middle of the St. Lawrence River, there is neither a customs office with its boring officials, nor police, nor passports. One can do everything and go everywhere he wishes, until the violation of law is clearly demonstrated: then a trial begins. That is the way in which Americans understand freedom: do as you please, *help yourself*, but don't disturb your neighbour, don't violate his interests! This completely free application of one's own power and abilities is far from being self-indulgent, which is considered to be an abuse and is persecuted everywhere. And in the meanwhile in Europe many people think of American freedom as a matter of fists and guns. To be sure, that freedom is flourishing without guardians and guardianship, but it creates many great and good phenomena.

And if sometimes this freedom abuses a person who, besides his passport and old aristocratic privileges, happened to bring from Europe pretensions for total respect to his armorial bearings (family emblem) and nobleness, then that's neither America's fault nor its inhabitants; but rather a fault of those who hoped to find in the New World what is not there. And if one looks closely, it is thanks to this freedom that American well-being grows and huge cities arise suddenly in places where man appeared to have arrived only recently. Take, for example, the same Ogdensburg, where now several rail lines come together, a town that holds a population of more than ten thousand people. One hundred years ago it was little more than a tiny fortress built by Jesuits as defence against savages. As one of Jesuits wrote, the route from New York to Niagara was impassable because of forest and swamps. Now it is luxuriously cultivated land. The route passes through towns, all with the same design. Each one is gas lit, there is fresh and healthy running water in all the private houses; there are streets, schools, and a municipal government. The towns manage themselves, tend to their own interests and find means to implement them. Every town usually has more than one newspaper, and also several different parties and factions. Thanks to these local organs of openness [glasnost], every American knows what is happening in the most remote areas of his country, and gets acquainted with the needs of his compatriots and the opinion of their society on events either in the entire world or in the United States.

From Prescott I took a train to Kingston, connected by means of the Rideau Canal to the city of Ottawa. During the French period, when fortresses were built everywhere for defence against the savages, a small fort was constructed here called Frontenac or Kataraki [Cataraqui] (this was the name of the St. Lawrence River in the area from Lake Ontario to Montreal). Now the English have erected a fortress against a more dangerous neighbour, the North-Americans [United States].

Kingston is one of the towns that asked to be designated the capital of all of Canada, mainly because of its fortunate position between Montreal and Toronto. It built large government buildings and churches; it has started a university, but what interested me most here was its prison for criminals who are sentenced to long-terms for terrible crimes. In each county there is a prison (jail) for people convicted of minor crimes, but just as in each American state, every Canadian province has at least one state prison, and I stayed in this town mainly to familiarize myself with conditions in that prison.

Like Sing-Sing prison on the Hudson, the Kingston prison is built of grey, hard stone, which is prominent throughout the local area. It is enclosed behind strong walls with towers at the corners, and the noteworthy thing is that here the prisoners built for themselves, and for their successors, strongholds behind which they are no danger to their co-citizens. Seven hundred men and fifty women from among the convicts work in a special building; they are paid by manufacturers, who provide them with all the necessary materials. There are furniture makers, metal workers, boot makers, shoemakers, and if it is possible to regret anything here it is that children are not separated from adults. Although strict silence is ordered about the work, the lack of prisons for youth is explained only by the lack of means, for no one denies their necessity.

At night everyone is locked up in special cells: they are oblong and narrow. If it were not for the draught, one could not help but praise the structure of the barred windows which face a corridor lighted during the day by the rays of the sun, and in the evening by gas. These windows must be very useful for refreshing the air in the small cells. But since they also made it difficult for the guards to go unnoticed as they observe the prisoners entrusted to them, a special wall was built for them to walk behind. Through openings in this wall the guards may see if the convicts are asleep or not. I have not encountered this type of secret patrol in the other prisons which I have been taken to see, and I note this peculiarity mainly because in America every new prison differs somewhat from earlier ones.

In the evening a ship was leaving for Lake Ontario. I did not want to miss it and so took leave of the shiny metallic cupolas of Kingston's public buildings. Once again a white ship, a large model, took me on the lake to the town of Toronto. At first the ship travelled beside islands and peninsulas, in narrow and tight bays, and only at night did we lose sight of the shore. The weather was calm, the lake was like glass, and it was a pleasure to watch like a swan out rocking on the water. The passengers conversed at a common meal or strolled on the deck. I said to an American from Kingston with whom I had waited for the arrival of the ship, which was delayed a bit by the fog, that I wouldn't want to be in this flat-bottomed boat during a storm. *Nevermind!* he exclaimed: it is true that sometimes the ship rolls strongly, but if accidents happen on the lake, if the ship, baggage and people are lost, this is not from storms but from collisions with other ships, because in the middle the lake is as deep and as safe for navigation as is the sea. Besides, in the worst case there are several *life-preservers* for each passenger, always ready when they are needed. Hollow tin boats, which won't sink even when they are filled with water, are attached to the sides of the ship; there are cork preservers ["circles"] and even the cabin chairs are made so that one can cling to them in case of an emergency. They are tin and filled with air; therefore it is possible to swim with their help, as long as one is strong enough, and even then one can survive motionless on the water. This perspective, I admit, was not attractive. I knew from earlier conversations with Americans that it was impossible to convince them of the need to swim calmly; they insist that it is impossible to control a person who cannot control himself.

However, in the present circumstances such apprehension was superfluous. The night was beautiful, the moon was out, and passing ships exchanged whistles and went on their way. Most of the passengers were on deck late into the evening, until evening dampness drove everyone into his *state-room*, where everything was arranged in comfortable compartments. How pleased I would be if ships like this one could be found in our rivers, and how strange it is that such flat-bottomed palaces, which float so softly on the water, are not used everywhere that ships sail.

Although it is quiet on the ship, everyone gets up early in this small kingdom. The sun barely lights up the *state-room*, so one must leave it to enjoy the morning, and to find out what is happening on deck. When I arrived on deck, the Americans already had been greeting each other in their customary manner: *very fine, beautiful day*, and, in fact, the day was worthy of such recommendation: the morning freshness yielded to the rays of the sun and my American friend of the previous day from Kingston predicted a sight which, he said, would astound a European. He pointed to the horizon, where one could see a rosy stripe just like the dawn; but the dawn was already long gone. Is this not a forest fire, I asked the American, don't they glow like that? Not at all, this is the American *"pink-haze,"* a really rosy mist which happens in the so-called Indian summer, when the mornings are fresh and the days are as warm as summer, from the broiling rays of the sun.

Indeed, the horizon was flaring up more and more and the pink beams were concentrated in the centre; in the middle of all this pink light expanse, in all its brilliance, was the sun. Such a picture was new to me and I was no less delighted with it than when I had seen the northern lights under the moon for the first time in another part of the world. Neither phenomenon is very well explained, but both catch the fancy and the eyes of those who see them for the first time. The Americans are not enthusiastic over this pink radiance, for they are accustomed to it. But I was struck not only by the sky, but also by the water in which the sky was reflected. The lake seemed to be on fire. Only by noon did the horizon begin to fade and take on its usual colour.

In the evening we disembarked from the ship in Toronto, the residence for the time being of the governor-general and the provincial parliament of both Canadas. It is strange to see how many cities in Canada compete with each other for the honour to be the central place of government: in the light of history, Montreal and Quebec have the right to such an advantage because of their antiquity; Ottawa and Kingston claim this right because of their more central location. Toronto claims it on the basis of its absolutely British character and absence of French citizens. In Canada, the chief administrative city of a province is looked upon quite differently than in the United States.

Things that cannot be appropriately argued in the United States are debated in Canada. To be designated the leading city in a state means to be condemned to a very insignificant role; it means to lie far away from the trade routes, and to be located as much as possible in the centre of the state, while at the same time some other city flourishes in wealth and population because of its proximity to trade on a large river or sea. In its turn, the capital city must house a senate, a legislative assembly, a governor and his ministers, and be subordinated to the influence of parties and their horrors. Large cities, such as New York, are delighted that the official capitals are distant from them; for that reason, their municipal administrations have greater independence. They govern themselves and most of the money, taxes collected from their citizens, are spent on their own needs and, being wealthy, they do not begrudge the honour which falls to the capital. In Canada different understandings and aspirations prevail because their needs and interests differ from their American counterparts.

Toronto has for some years benefitted from the advantages of serving as the capital of Canada. After the houses where parliament met in Montreal and Quebec were burned down, meetings were held in Toronto. During the period when parliament gathers, Toronto is as noisy as Washington in the United States. Generally, it gives the impression of a government city: there are many large buildings, constructed for public purpose, wide streets, and many stores. I was led to believe that if this town was not a government centre, it would still be the small York, as it was for 20 years, and would never have reached the heights it has attained now. It is true that a lake splashes on the small city, but it is off to the side; it cannot be an important trading centre, for behind it, to the West towards Lakes Huron and Simcoe, the population is still too small. It would be wise, therefore, for Toronto to hold on to its present status.

Toronto is a completely English city; like almost all of Upper Canada, it shows evidence of influence from the metropolis [London]. Institutions here are English without exception, the English language is dominant and French is seldom heard; the law also is English, whereas in Lower Canada the French Civil Code remains in force (criminal and commercial laws are English). They are changed when necessary by statutes of the provincial parliament. *Attorney general, solicitor general* and representatives of the treasury have greater significance in Lower Canada, under the influence of French bureaucracy, than in Upper Canada. Judges are not elected as they are in the American States, but are appointed by the crown and their term of office has no time limit. Representatives of the people are chosen by election only to the *legislative assembly.* The right to vote is held only by those who own real estate with a value of at least fifty pounds sterling, or with an income from it no less than five pounds sterling. During Canadian elections there are the same arguments between parties, which resort to tricks and ruses to overcome each other, as there are in the United States. In addition, in Canada there are conflicts between faiths and peoples, Irish Catholic and English protestants, whereas in America arguments are dominated by political opinions and principles.

Religious conflict in Canada, dividing the people into political parties, has a pernicious influence on that side of the national life which should be kept outside the influence of parties so as to spread enlightenment successfully and evenly. I speak about education (*vospitanie*).[14] Even though at the present time the benefits of education are great and plentiful, and although partisan arguments do not undermine the fundamental convictions of the people, who see in education an indispensable good and guarantee of general happiness and tranquility, it is true nonetheless that when forces are divided and resources that are needed for schools are needlessly broken up and, above all, the bonds that necessarily exist between citizens are cut, then such conditions make it impossible to achieve the purposes for which education exists. That is why in Toronto there is such a vast array of colleges of different denominations, diverse *separate schools,* as distinct from *mixed schools.* But, setting aside all the disadvantages, which are inevitable when education is in the hands of the people, I must dwell on the institutions which deserve general emulation, especially since they do not require great expense. There is a *public library book-depository* in Toronto which holds more than 100,000 copies of books of different content, on all branches of human endeav-

---

[14] The Russian word used here was "vospitanie," which has a broader meaning than "education." It translates best as "upbringing," that is, the total training of young people — including their behaviour. Schools, what few there were, in Imperial Russia were classic in loco parentis institutions, training students in the 3-R's plus inculcating proper political, religious and social beliefs.

our, the arts, sciences, and so on. The library is an essential companion of learning, and upbringing, and that is why libraries are needed as soon as schools are established in new and growing communities: but where, why and who will purchase it even if there are sufficient funds? Who will make the final selection? Subscriptions are issued quickly, and money is raised even more quickly, usually sooner than there are opportunities to acquire the necessary books. The Toronto book depot came into being to deal with this problem: lists of books are sent to it from various schools, along with sums of money collected by them. The depot, having large sums of money decreed to it by the government, sends the requested books at a price 25 percent cheaper than the cost to it from the bookseller; moreover, it forwards books free, valued at the sum of money collected locally. But in this case the depot selects the books. Thus, there are libraries everywhere, even in the smallest schools. There also are museums of natural and local history. According to accounts in Canadian almanac for 1857 it would appear that at the beginning of the year there were 300 libraries in Upper Canada, holding 124,184 volumes.

The surroundings of Toronto are not unusual. Vast forests begin just outside the city; further on there is Lake Simcoe, where the Chippewa Indian tribe lives.

My route lay in the other direction, to the south from Toronto to Niagara. Here I hoped to conclude my wandering around Canada by viewing the famous waterfall. This time my trip was short: it was necessary to cross one corner of Lake Ontario to arrive, after 2-3 hours, at the mouth of the Niagara River, which flows into Lake Ontario from the south, almost opposite Toronto, which lies on the north shore of the lake. Once again the American ship was filled with a large crowd and we were not able to see the pictures hanging in the main saloon very well; nor were we able to read the morning newspaper, sold for a cent (1.25 silver kopeks) by noisy *newboys* [sic], before we left, when a whistle told us that we had entered the Niagara. Here, and all along the Niagara, English and American territories are very close together. Fortifications stand on both sides. They are now silent, but not long ago witnessed considerable fire and bloodshed.

Our steamship, however, did not stop at the mouth of the Niagara. It moved further up river until the rapids made necessary the transfer of passengers to a locomotive waiting for us. The banks of the Niagara, as they rolled past us, were high and sheer, and the water was so calm that it was difficult to believe that we were so close to the waterfalls. Because the river channel was so straight, one would think that it had been dug by men; it had neither sands banks, nor islets.

The isthmus between Lakes Erie and Ontario, joined by the Niagara, stretching for nearly 30 miles, had quite different levels in different places. For a stretch of 8-10 miles there is high rock, which, while almost at the level of Lake Erie, is 300-400 feet higher than Lake Ontario and ends in a precipice over which water cascades. Did this cliff originally have the same even height? Did the Niagara run from the cliff straight into Lake Ontario? Did the stream dig a bed in the cliff while falling down? Can one assume that the cliff, dug in at the base, from which the flood rushes downwards, formed the rapids several miles below the waterfall? Nothing is impossible here, if one considers the mass of water which has had to flow down the Niagara from four lakes above Lake Ontario, and how huge that flow must be. When the water level is average in Lake Erie, 170,156 tons of water falls from the Niagara waterfall every minute; or 102, 073, 730 tons in an hour. Famous American and English geologists, Hall, Leielle, Gitkok, Agassis[15] and others devoted their research to these subjects and the latest conclusion is that the current is of such force that it dug a bed in the cliff and, consequently, the waterfall gradually retreats from Lake Ontario to Lake Erie, and its shape is constantly changing. The scholar Leielle even calculated that the waterfall recedes no less than a foot per year. This generally accepted theory of explanation for the Niagara Falls is not only true, but is undoubted, because it is demonstrably proven by the changes in the waterfall since its first description by the missionary [Louis] Hennepin in the second half of the XVII century, around 1678. Even recently the crumbling at the cliffs is changing the face of the waterfall.

What was here before, when the wild Iroquois, praying to the god of thunder and miracles, chased buffalo, and when the shrill, wild cries of warriors in tribal warfare rang through the pristine forest? Did the Indians worship this unique phenomenon? The impenetrability of this area, its wild population, and the forests that stretch along the southern shore of Lake Ontario, meant that Niagara and its banks were for a long time unknown to whites and, probably, the wild[16] people counted on their inaccessibility behind the noisy currents and so kept it secret from the Europeans. Perhaps, indeed it is very likely, that missionaries before Hennepin knew about the waterfalls but,

---

[15] These names are translated phonetically from the Russian and may not resemble the actual names of the individuals very closely. "Agassis" appears to be Louis Agassiz (1807-1873).

[16] Here Lakier again used *dikii*, i.e., wild or savage.

having reached the mouth of the Niagara, explored no further. It is difficult even to believe that Champlain, who was in these countries in the early 17th century, did not pay attention to this common source of the American lakes. In any case, the waterfall was described for the first time by Hennepin and to him, as far as we known, goes the honour of discovery.

Now, naturally, a trip to Niagara Falls means less. Every train, from either the American or Canadian side, and every ship brings hundreds of curious people here daily. They express, each in their own way, awe at the miracle, the like of which can be found nowhere else in the world. Now one need not be afraid of the wild Iroquois, who come here not as warriors to defend their freedom, but as poor manufacturers who long since have stopped shedding tears over their former greatness and power. Two or three centuries ago everything was different, and no one who heard of the waterfalls would have dared marvel at them. In this lies the great merit of Hennepin. Even after him the Europeans did not rush into these dense forests to see the waterfall and it was necessary to improve the means of transportation to their current accessible and inexpensive state so that one could travel even from New York, some 500 miles away. Can one criticize a Franciscan monk because he was so taken by the grandeur that he described it in such glowing phrases and made it thrice the size it is? Much later, in our enlightened age, did not a poet describe the great forces of nature precisely this way in his *Atala*? Can we reproach Chateaubriand[17] because, unable to paint what could not be painted with a brush or a pen, he used poetical pictures, hoping to transport our imaginations to unknown frontiers, among beauty and the original populations? I came to read *Atala* on the so-called *Goat Island*, where I felt the beauty of the book more strongly than I had in Europe. But this is not a description that can be measured exactly; indeed, can we expect anything from poetry but moral satisfaction? It seems to me that attempts to depict Niagara are likely to be as unsatisfactory as taking photographs of it. Close to the waterfall there are several mobile workshops for picture taking, but the cloud of water rising to the sun and sprinkling the world beneath shows up on the paper as a white, lifeless spot.

Approaching the waterfall in a railway car from the Canadian side,

---

[17] François-René de Chateaubriand (1768-1848), founder of the Romantic School in French literature, author of *Atala*, 1798, an idyll based on the loves of two young "sauvages."

the noise of the train causes one to see the cloud of mist which stands like a pillar over Niagara before one hears the sound of falling water. But, moving a little further, to applause and whistles, you wonder if this is the Niagara of which you have heard since birth as a miracle, the waterfall that has inspired your imagination? There is a sense that it is a shame that the previous charm has disappeared. I did not think of comparisons, but visions of distant Switzerland came to mind and, strangely, even the Schaffhausen and Reichenbach waterfalls seemed more beautiful. Niagara seems to want to strike one dumb; from the cliffs, which cannot be seen under the wall of water, there is a great deal of water, that is true, but that seems to be all there is. This unfavourable impression does not last long. After you drop your bag, settle into a room, and then move to a window in the Clifton House, situated close to the waterfall, where you can see the semi-circle of waterfall facing Canada, and all the rapids below it. What's this? Quite a different picture? Yes, this Niagara exceeds anything I had ever dreamed of, and I was prepared to exalt it no less than Father Hennepin or the poet Chateaubriand. The matter, indeed, was very simple: when one stands at the same level as the waterfall, it can't really be seen. The eyes are confronted with a mass of grey-green water, staggering the viewer by its immensity, and that is all. But when one stands above it, when you see hell boiling below, when you see the waves breaking up into droplets and rising skyward, or when you go down below into the trees of the Table Rock and stare upwards, you are annoyed with yourself for doubting, even for a minute, the grandeur of Niagara. And in whatever weather one goes to admire this behemoth shaking both sky and earth, no matter if there is a dark cloud looming behind it, and a white column of steam drops down on it, if the sun is shining and a thousand rainbows are mirrored in it, or if the moon is rising — if it is dark, cold, or warm — the waterfall strikes you with something special every time. The week I spent here was hardly enough to get well acquainted with both sides of the waterfalls, Canadian and American; to walk along all the steep paths near the rapids, to sail almost into the giant on the ship *Maid of the Mist*, to swing out on the lively waters of the rapids, to be splashed with spray, and in the end learn nothing about the phenomenon: it allows you to draw near only to entice you, no more.

But mankind was not satisfied with this. He penetrated the falls, wanting to see what was happening on the other side of this immeasurable mass of water. To be frank, there was even less to see here. Covered from head to foot in rubber clothes and under the supervision and protection of a negro, he ventured between the arch of the waterfall and the cliff from which it was cascading. The English pic-turesquely call this trip a "walk under the sheet." This sheet is transparent and dark-green. If one managed to enjoy the picture of sun rays reflected in the massive liquid curtain while passing beneath it, one could consider the further walk through wind and water rewarding. There is an abyss on both sides; looking for a foothold, in vain; pressed to the wall, aware that death lies beneath your feet, you call out to the negro for help. But he is deaf and mute, raging waters splash over you. There is no turning back, your eyeballs stop work-ing; you stop breathing.

The relief you feel as you emerge on the American side can be understood only by someone buried alive who suddenly hears the tap of a hammer and the voice of a friend opening up the gloomy dun-geon. God's light is an enormous blessing. When you rise from hell and remove the Eskimo clothing, you enthusiastically enter your name in a book beside those of other brave souls who have made the same voyage under the curtain of water. Among these were ladies as well. When later I saw an American or English woman on top of an Egyptian pyramid or on a camel in the Sahara desert, I often smiled and tried to recognize in her the woman wrapped in rubber Eskimo clothing walking under the wet curtain of the Niagara.

The shape of the cliff over which the main current rushes is concave and it is from this that the falls gets its name, the *horse-shoe falls*. Its for-mation is explained easily enough by the enormous pressure of the water mass on the middle, rather than on the edges of the cliff. Naturally, it is impossible to measure the depth of the water in this place, but a deep-water ship launched from Lake Erie passed close to the cliff and was sunk into eternity and was flung into the lower rapids as a mere mass of chips. The calmness of the water a few hun-dred feet above the waterfall lulls one into forgetting its proximity. I saw sleepy ducks swimming on the deceptive waves in flocks right up to the brink, ducking below the surface only to pay for their trust-fulness with their lives. The waters of Niagara, incidentally, have a magnetic aura, a mermaid draws you to them and, walking around Niagara, one often hears local place names explained in stories of lovers who lost faith in the strength of love on earth and buried it in the rushing waves, or of a beautiful woman who tired of loneliness and gave herself up to the water. On the edge of Niagara now it would be possible to sing ballads the equal of those produced at Schwarzwald if only people here were as poetically inclined as the men from that blessed region of Germany.

The Canadian side, where I lived, has many conveniences. Here on the shores of Niagara there is an entire range of cafés, different panoramas, and photograph studios. In the evening there are illuminations. The climate is cool in the summer, and in the winter it is warmer than in the surrounding region. In general, the Horse-Shoe Falls belongs more to Canada than to the States even though the border runs down its middle. On the American side the waterfall presents beauties that cannot be seen from the opposite shore. I went almost every morning to the American side, either in a boat or a small steam ship, or over a suspended bridge which finally was completed after many attempts and failures. The town of *Niagara Falls* already spreads out on this side. Two railroads already run across it and foreigners like to stay in its hotels because there are more diverse walkways over there.

I was especially interested in the bridge, one of the wonders of the new art, not because it is long — on the contrary, the cliffs of the opposing banks are closer here than along the rest of the Niagara, about 100 feet — but because of its strength. Entire trains go along this bridge, which has no support from below and everything is held up only by rods from above. Hundreds of experiments were conducted, but gusty winds blowing through the deep Niagara valley destroyed in a single night what had taken many months to construct. Meanwhile, the bridge was necessary to connect railway lines extending in several directions along the banks of the restless river. In the place selected as the most suitable for the ridge one could not cross by boat. To carry the first wire it was necessary to rely on the wind and fly it with a kite, and people were as just as delighted to witness the first connection as they recently had been to greet the first underwater Atlantic telegraph. Once the two sides were connected by a wire, the bridge was assured. And, indeed, this thin wire has become a stable link to send messages; one can even send a basket across with a person in it. Machines, managed by private entrepreneurs, were placed on the banks to move a mobile carriage back and forth, establishing regular communications across the abyss. Goods were sent across in the same manner and a pedestrian bridge was built. But that was blown away by a strong wind, and the work was begun anew. All that was gained was experience. Construction was re-started and the current bridge is one of the best in the world in strength, lightness and beauty. It rises 250 feet above the surface of the water where it is quite windy. Iron rods, thick as masts, descending from poles to the middle of the bridge, hold it at this height. There is an upper level for railway trains, and a lower gallery for pedestrians and carriages. Steel cables are fixed to the cliffs close to the bridge, making the joint effort of the

English and the Americans, which cost half a million dollars, capable of withstanding any storm and bad weather.

The most beautiful view is from the bridge, where one can see the full mass of the Niagara Falls from the first fall to the rapids. The picture is complete, and the company that built the bridge did well when it decided to take 25 cents from everyone who crossed the bridge; otherwise only curious people would congregate here. However, even now the fee keeps few people away. No wonder: one could admire this view for hours without getting tired. The traveller wishes to take away a deep impression and hopes to implant upon his memory something that he could not see more of. Americans, it is true, sometimes sit with their backs to the miracle, but they either have become accustomed to it, as one can get used to anything, or they want to enjoy only the noise and the cracking which in the long run is turned into a form of music.

The North American States [United States] own, besides half of the Horse-Shoe Falls, several islands and part of the rapids, making it possible to construct the bridge and a tower, those essentials, as everyone knows, of every picture of Niagara. After paying 25 cents for the right to walk across the bridge and during one's stay there to walk around *Goat Island*, one can take an involuntary thrill to the bridge under which raging waves boil, smashing against black stones. Logs are thrown up on the boulders. One can see a steep slope down into the main pool; as if anticipating its imminent fall into the abyss, the water foams here in a convulsive rage, flying towards its unhappy fate. Looking at the waterfall for any length of time, one unwittingly grants it a soul and a consciousness, resuscitating it in the imagination. One has an urge to attribute every curve of the waterfall, and each tense moment, with human feelings and desires. The imagination involuntarily follows the stream, which for centuries has been struggling with adversity, overcoming them or, on the contrary, breaking against them, boiling angrily. The more practical human, however, took advantage of the ability of the water to set the wheels of a pulp and paper mill in motion, and constructed warm and cold baths to cater to public demand. But on watching the same human as he walks the bridge across the rapids, one realizes how small and powerless he is! A single misstep and he is gone!

One more small bridge and you are on Goat Island. It is not in vain that this place is called *Indian Emporium*, for the signs depict entire groups and stories from the life of the wild Iroquois who lived here before the arrival of white people. One finds on the canvases the savage faces of rival tribes and if the American artists did not spare paint to give the aura of wildness to his Indians, then owners of the stores on which the signs were hung expected you to be drawn inside, to admire the paintings, which are tasteful and are made from a multi-coloured bristle on bark. On seeing this, one naturally wonders: how did such an industry come to the wild forests of North America, for one will not find anything like it anywhere else?

The paintings are taken directly from nature: fruits, berries, birds, flowers, animals, and sometimes groups.To represent forms in relief, especially berries, beads acquired by savages from the whites are skilfully used. The painted threads of bristle can barely be distinguished by sparkle and delicacy from silk. How difficult it must be to embroider this mixed design in Indian wigwams, among the dirt, cold and dampness, by women who are condemned to do all the housework, and handle all the housekeeping and children while their warlike husbands are chasing wild animals or fighting for their freedom! Sometimes the Indians offer their goods themselves, but the greater part of their products are purchased and sold from the stores for a somewhat higher price.

On Goat Island, surrounded by raging rapids and waterfalls, there are special wonders. Just as on the Canadian side, it is possible to go down to the river and gape at the mass of water rushing into the abyss; here one can enter the *cave of the winds* and gaze at the waterfall and the rainbows formed by it. The sensations felt under the curtain are repeated. Every step brings a new, unexpected view: then a new descent, then a new rise, a new tower on the steep bank, and from all points the waterfall reveals different beautiful vistas. I repeat, one more time, that I do not know if one can get bored contemplating the source of such varied impressions. I liked to be alone to converse better with nature; most often the goal of the lonely stroll was the tower situated between all the horrors and rapids of the American waterfalls. By calling this tower, built on the fragment of the cliff, *prospect-tower*, the Americans wanted it to be known that from here one could see the Canadian side, the Horse-Shoe Falls, the distant rapids and the famous *whirlpool*, which spews out uprooted trees and beams torn from the shore. Standing by the balustrade at the top of this tower, I felt sympathy for the Indians who had called this place Ongakarra, a powerful and roaring current. The white people replaced this picture-like name with Niagara, but it is good that they substituted one Indian name with another, newer one.

I am glad to bid goodbye to Canada near the Niagara Falls: I took pleasant memories with me to the United States, including awe in the face of the wonders of nature. And, moreover, to marvel at the wisdom and activity of the men who managed to subjugate mighty nature and turn its destructive powers into a useful implement.

D. N.A. Kriukov, *Canada. Agricultural Economy in Canada . . .* **(1897)**[1]

FOREWORD

In terms of exports, the foreign trade of Russia is concentrated mainly in products from the agricultural sector; what we obtain from our agriculture, beginning with grains and ending with eggs, make up the most important part of our export trade. But in the international markets and above all the English one, we are faced with very strong competitors who deliver goods similar to ours. The United States, Canada, Argentina, Australia and India also trade mainly in agricultural products. Therefore the most important consumer of agricultural goods, England, is able to choose both the best and the cheapest from among a large volume of transported items. The demands of the world wide market can be expressed by a certain formula:

Good products + at a reasonable price = guaranteed sale.

Keeping this formula in mind our competitors have exerted all their energies to deliver goods of the finest quality to the market and reduce their cost of production. They closely monitor the trade operations of their own markets, and just as carefully study their so-called peaceful enemies.

In this regard, Russia stands completely alone. We not only do not know and do not follow the international markets, but we also ignore our competitors. England is our chief consumer, the English are the wealthiest, the most efficient and the wisest buyers; therefore, it is in our own interests, our own well-being, that we become better acquainted with this customer. In the meantime, articles about England that appear in our periodical literature are notable for their extraordinary shallowness. The majority of them are written by people who do not know the language and have seen the country only through the window of a train coach. Therefore it is no wonder that incorrect judgements about England and Englishmen are spread throughout Russian society. If that were the case for Portugal or Brazil, countries which have almost no significance for us, then it

---

[1] Kriukov, *Kanada. Sel'skoe khoziaistvo v Kanade v sviazi s drugimi otrasliami promyshlennosti. S kartoiu i 30 risunkami* [Canada. The Agricultural Economy in Connection with Other Branches of Industry. With a map and 30 Drawings], (St. Petersburg: Ministry of Land and State Authority. Department of Land Holding, 1897). Only the Foreword (pp. v-vii) and Conclusion (pp. 215-218) of this 235-page book are translated here, by J.L. Black. Italics are in the original.

would be to a certain degree excusable to have inconsistent and incorrect information; but about countries which conduct world wide trade, about a people who have achieved the highest industrial and marketing strength, one cannot be content with casual and poorly thought-out articles.

What do we have as a consequence: not knowing our principal clients well we are incapable of organizing our export trade and must turn to Germans and Jews for help. These unwanted middlemen became sort of a wall between Russian producers and English consumers; over the course of many years they have built up impediments that have the nature of a yoke; at the same time they hinder the dissemination of correct information, filtering it through their own hands. The day when the Russian producer offers his hand directly to his main customer, an Englishman, is still far away. There are too many obstacles to be overcome. But sooner or later that moment will arrive and will be a death sentence for useless commissioners. Aware that change will not happen soon, but that the moment will come, the middlemen attempt to preserve their current significance with all their strength, extracting millions from both countries for their mediation.

It is obvious that our knowledge of our competitors is quite weak: while it is true that we know something about the United States, especially because of the Chicago exhibition, our cognition of Argentina, India, Australia and Canada is next to nothing. We must recognize that this is a very serious matter. Hoping to do what I could, I undertook to study Canada during the past winter and spring [1897] and the present work is the result of that trip. Owing to insufficient means, the work is not perfect and not finished. Unfortunately, in the circumstances under which I had to operate I could not do everything I wanted to do. It is hoped that this first attempt will be followed by other, more complete and serious ones! Generally it is very desirable that the business of studying our competitors on the international markets is not left undone and, on the contrary, that the study take on a constant and systematic character so that the Russian government and Russian society may have reliable and full information about the resources of those countries with which we are engaged in a battle for trade.

* * *

CONCLUSION

Having completed this short overview of the agricultural industries in Canada in connection with certain other fields, this is the place to draw some conclusions and, if possible, pick out which of them are the most useful for us. Everything that has been said above can be divided into two groups, which can facilitate representations about this country as our competitor on the world market. In the first place, it is interesting to characterize Canada in a few words: that it presents itself as our competitor; in the second place, it is desirable to formulate what one can expect from this country in the future. Having presented all that in, so to speak, large strokes, we will attempt in the conclusions to note what would be best for us to adopt from Canada.

Having a population of more than 5 million spread across a territory of 5,500 versts east to west, Canada would appear to have very weak unity if it were not for the creation of an astonishing iron link in the form of the Pacific railroad. This line not only connects the entire country into a single whole but it unites the population, giving it the means to enlarge its vital resources. The line is an artery of life, the pulse of the entire country. Trunk lines run north and south from the CPR, making it possible for the population to participate in new ventures where they live, and in areas where not long ago bison roamed and Indians galloped farms are appearing, dotting the country in an ever increasing dense network.

The Pacific railroad had an important influence on the agricultural industries of the country. Before the construction of this line central Canada [the Prairies] was completely empty and the main product of eastern Canada [Upper and Lower] was wheat. But since only farmers gained the right to work the black earths steppes of Manitoba and the Northwest territories, they began to produce huge quantities of wheat and in the eastern provinces a cattle industry arose and rapidly developed and, connected to it, a dairy industry. Now wheat plays the primary role in central Canada and in the east cheese and butter is produced. With the development of the cattle industry there arose the possibility of exporting surplus cattle to England, and more recently the question of organizing the export of meat, a question with which Canada will probably cope with successfully as it has with many other matters.

Horticulture has only recently come into its own. Much time and effort was spent on finding fruit suitable to Canada's climate. But when they were found, cultivation spread quickly and Canada not only has a mass of fruits for domestic needs, but they also play a significant role in export. Parallel with the agricultural industries other industries, especially machine building and mining, are also advancing rapidly. Currently, Canada manufactures every possible agriculture machine for its own farmers, and has begun to export them to Australia, South America and Africa. The magnificent harvesters made by Massey-Harris have opened the way even into South Russia. The fishing industry has been very successful and the quantity of fish and fish preserves exported from both oceans is growing.

The energetic and industrious population, its practicality, efficiency and skill in trade has created a faith in Canada on the part of English capitalists. Any industrial enterprise in Canada attracts the attention of London's banks, any trade problem or an embarrassment in a credit operation will find support in London along with a willingness to offer assistance. It is difficult to earn the confidence of London, but once that has been achieved no enterprise will go short of funds. Canada has just such a reputation, which has vast significance for the economic life of the entire country.

Industry, which has been firmly established in Canada and expands and develops on an hourly basis, has a reliable ally in developed trade. Going hand in hand, these two branches of the national economy display the strength of the country on both flanks: on the Atlantic Ocean and especially on the Pacific, the industrial and trade significance of Canada moves irrepressibly along the path of rapid progress and increased commercial prestige.

The administration, both central and provincial, deals tactfully with all the needs of the country, turning its attention most particularly to the development of agriculture as Canada's main resource. The organization of agricultural experimental farms and the construction of special schools create an entire army of instructors in cheese-making, butter—manufacturing, horticulture and other specialties, inspections of agricultural products, the creation of an entire network of refrigerators and the organization of speedy and convenient transportation of everything that a farm produces, the development of interest in agricultural methods by arranging public lectures and funding agricultural societies, attracting new settlers to the country, and so on — all make up the agricultural policy of the country. One cannot help but notice three features: 1) Each agricultural question is granted the closest attention in the government sphere and even parliament participation fully in all agricultural measures. 2) There is a certain continuity in all these measures. Every time one was approved or decided upon by Parliament, it had to be supported and scrutinized carefully by Ministers, independently of changes in the Ministers themselves or of other prominent people. Therefore, many of the measures are likely to meet with success from the earliest, most difficult stage and can, so to speak, become full fledged and inspired from the beginning. 3) Any agricultural measure demands especially trained people. Therefore the government tries hard to increase its army of specialists, considering this to be the main guarantee of success. To maintain the   specialists, because of their value, their material circumstances are steadily improved so that the government will not lose the specialists trained by them and on which they have spent so much time and resources.

But the main cause of the material progress of Canada lies not in the development of industry and trade, and not in government measures. No, the industry and trade and the general economic growth of the country are the result of two central circumstances: *the private ownership of land* and *the high moral quality of the population*. Here are the foundations of the current and future prosperity of Canada. Families of farmers who live on their own land, are religious, hard working, and frugal are the first line of defence of the state's ramparts and of the industrial forces of the country. A simple life of labour and tireless activity is part of a man's environment here from his first appearance on earth. A general prayer is said by the father with his entire family in the morning, evening and before each meal. A life of work from dawn to sunset for both father and the mother, and the fact that on Sundays when the entire family gathers, there is an absence of falsehood and hypocrisy, are conditions that influence the children strongly, as they anyone in a similar situation. Thus, it is little wonder that people with strong health and strong spirit, whose given word is considered more reliable than any document, come from the farm families. Such people do not know how it is possible to lie around all day in bed, or to turn the night into day, or to work only by using their tongues, not reinforcing by personal example.

And they do not give up under such conditions, nor become a burden to others. If the son of a Canadian farmer decided to try some other field of endeavour, he would not fail. He would work six days a week tirelessly and in all of his efforts and actions full confidence in his identity and an unshakable respect for religion, inherited from his birth family, would win through. Therefore, it is not surprising that a young Canadian, no matter where he is, tries at the first opportunity to acquire his own house; have his own family, where he is able to discover for himself the joy and comfort which children can bring. And this is a healthy attempt to increase imperceptibly the quality of the front line on which the strength and power of the state are based. There is no place for idlers in Canada. Concerns about the general welfare which are not matched by one's own example are not met with much sympathy there, and Canada can be considered a very fortunate land in that there is not a crowd of parasites in its healthy organism like those that have exhausted and weakened certain of the older European countries.

In what ways can Canada be instructive for us? What should we hope to adopt from there?

Above all, we turn our attention to the assistance the government gives to the development of different branches of agriculture and industry. All those measures practiced in Canada are desirable as well in our fatherland. It is true that many of us have already or are moving in this direction, but unfortunately not to a sufficient degree, for we are cautious and often without sufficient means. The absence of sufficient means at any given time frequently kills many government measures. One need not forget that if, even in a developed country like Canada, it is considered necessary to provide any help needed by agriculture, then it is more necessary to do so in a raw country like Russia. This, however, is such a simple truth that we need say nothing more about it.

But it goes without saying that all government measures can only help or contribute to the development of the economy. The basic cause and guarantee of the success of agriculture is due in Canada to private ownership and the spiritual quality of the population. According to my deepest conviction these two basic factors can set agriculture in our own country on the path to solid progress as well. Certainly, uplifting the personal quality of a population, its wisdom and its moral growth is a very difficult task. It can be achieved only through an entire series of government measures, as part of an entire system of internal policies. Consequently, the main causes of growth in agriculture lies in those areas which appear to go beyond the boundaries of labour. But in conclusion, I must repeat my deepest conviction, based on personal and widely extended study of the economies in different countries that the *basic cause of success in agriculture is neither money nor machinery, rather it is the people themselves.*

E. N. Struve, "A Sketch of Canada," Report to Ministry of Foreign Affairs (1900)[1]

This sketch is based on the reports of the Consul in Montreal, N. Struve, after his journey through parts of Canada following the establishment of the first Russian government consulate in the present year. Mr. Struve begins the reports of his journey with a description of his visit to the city of Toronto (in the province of Ontario).

First of all I travelled through Toronto, the main city in the province of Ontario and the second after Montreal in its trade significance throughout all of Canada. After getting acquainted with some of the representatives of the local administration I busied myself with an inspection of the city, and became convinced of the extraordinary liveliness of its trade, and especially of its manufacturing activity. Toronto lies on the northern shore of Lake Ontario and represents a trade centre, linking the whole Western half of Canada with the North-American United States, located only two hours travel from the border and from such large commercial centres as Buffalo, Cleveland, Niagara and other cities. Another most favourable reason for the trade-commercial development of Toronto is the fact that it is located on a great water route, consisting of the largest lakes in the world: Superior, Michigan, Huron, Erie and Ontario, which have egress into the Atlantic Ocean through the St. Lawrence River. When the project of deepening and widening the canals linking all these lakes is completed, and when Chicago and Fort William become accessible to sea-going ships, the importance of Toronto will increase to even more, possibly, than that of Montreal. At present Toronto is the largest interior port of Canada. In manufacturing the city occupies first place in all of Canada, which it supplies, in large part, with agricultural machinery and implements necessary to utilize work all of [the country's] numberless and endless fields. Companies such as Massey, Harris and Co. are world renowned, and are not unknown to Russian farmers. As a result of the similarity of terrain and climatological conditions between Canada and Russia, Canadian agricultural machinery appear to be, I maintain, the best suited for our agricultural needs also. Mr. Kriukov, in his book on agriculture in Canada, provides a sufficiently comprehensive description of local machines, probably for the same reason.

---

[1] N. Struve, "Ocherk Kanady," *Sbornik Konsul'skikh Donesennii* (St. Petersburg: Ministry of Foreign Affairs, 1900), Issue VI, pp 473-496. Translated by George Bolotenko.

Regarding the geographical features of the land along the railroad from Montreal to Toronto, it is most uninviting and most unfit for agriculture, covered wholly by sparse conifer forest intermixed with birches, and covered by small and large rocks. The scenery over the duration of approximately 300 English miles reminds one very much of the Finnish lowlands. The territory is very sparsely populated and along its whole length there are almost no settlements, as well as no farms. The population here is concentrated largely along the shores of the St. Lawrence River, its tributaries and lakes. The railway line which I took, namely the Canadian Pacific Railway, runs a substantial distance away from the river and reaches the lake only in Toronto itself.

From here I continued to the city of Winnipeg — the centre of the black earth region of Canada, whence I intended to visit the numerous colonies of Russian settlers, German Mennonites from Tavria and Ekaterinoslav provinces, and the Doukhobors.

Winnipeg is a most interesting city. Up to the 1870s on its place stood only a small fort, at first the property of the North-West Company, and later the Hudson`s Bay Company. The founding of the city is generally held to have occurred in 1870 [incorporated 1873, ed.], when it (the fort) was still called Fort Garry, having only 240 inhabitants. In 1881 it was renamed Winnipeg, with a population then of already about 8,000 inhabitants. After the Canadian Pacific Railway went through the city began to grow extraordinarily quickly; at present its population is in the neighbourhood of 50,000 persons. Winnipeg is the main trade centre not only of the province of Manitoba, but of all of the North-West Territories. Its bank transactions in 1898 amounted to more than 90,000,000 dollars, behind only Montreal and Toronto in the value of transactions.

Regarding the province of Manitoba, I think it appropriate to provide some information as a supplement to that which we have in the above-mentioned book by Mr. Kriukov. I have now visited the southern part of the province, the so-called Red River valley and its tributary, the Assiniboine. This is wholly our Russian steppe, level as a canvas, with endless fields of wheat, with farms sheltered under copses of trees scattered here and there. The surface of the steppe consists of a thick layer of black earth, where the best wheat in all of Canada grows, producing in times of good harvest up to 35 bushels and more per acre. In this current year the harvest, contrary to the usual, is very poor, and in places will result in not more than 5-7 bushels per acre.

The province of Manitoba is covered with numerous large and small lakes, which constitute a good half of her surface territory. There

exists the idea that this southern portion in pre-historical times consisted of a massive gradually-drying lake, whose organic deposits
account for its most-rich black earth, which in certain places reaches a
depth of 8 feet. The drying up of lakes and rivers in this part of
Canada is a phenomenon constantly visible even up to today. Thanks
to the great expanse of the lakes, this does not at all affect the harvests.
True, this year spring and summer droughts have reduced the harvest
to an unheard-of minimum; this, however, has been an exception,
unseen in the last 20-25 years. In southern Manitoba the winters are
exceedingly fierce, and the summer extremely hot; everything grows
and ripens unusually quickly; there is no winter planting; the land is
so fertile that on some farms they plant wheat on the same field for
two years running, each time bringing in bountiful harvests. In 1898
Manitoba alone exported more than 19,000,000 bushels of grain.

From Winnipeg I travelled south to the border with the United
States of America, part of the way by railroad, part by horse. In the
region between Emerson to the east and Morden to the west, only
Germans are settled there, which one can see from the names of the
towns here: Altona, Gretna, Rosenfeld, Reinland, Winkler, etc. These
are all Mennonites, resettled here from Russia in 1874 and 1875, who
attracted their brethren to follow here steadily after the very first
migration. The initiator of the Mennonite migration from Russia to
Canada was the Baden-born Hespeler, presently a deputy from the
riding of Rosenfeld and speaker of the provincial parliament of
Manitoba. His right hand man is the Mennonite Klaas Peters, one the
first Mennonites resettled here from Russia, a very wealthy and very
energetic man. He supports ongoing contact with Russia and with his
co-brothers residing there. The German farmers in Canada live as ver-
itable gentry and are superb farmers. The richest own land of 600
acres and more in extent. They work their land themselves, with their
children and with the assistance of one or several hands hired for the
whole year or for the summer. "We prefer to live in small houses and
to have big money," one such farmer told me. One should, however,
note that their homes are not at all small and are fully and fairly richly
furnished: farm buildings, machinery and livestock are of exemplary
model.   They are all characterized by hospitality, and remember
Russia with fondness. In the home of one of them I found a portrait of
the "Emperor Alexander III in God's Repose". In Gretna I met a
German pastor of Russian ancestry, having no connection, truth to
say, with the Mennonites. He is responsible for German Protestant
colonists, living in these same areas and intermixed with Mennonites
from Russia, who came largely from the provinces of Kherson,

Volynia and Podol'. It`s an interesting fact that the Canadian federal government has over the last little while to concern itself over the exclusiveness and particularism of German, and especially the Mennonite, colonists. Being well off, they maintain their own personal schools and make do without English ones. If the latter are found somewhere amongst them, the Mennonites try to find teachers for them who speak and teach in German. The situation is forcing the ruling circles in Canada to compare the Mennonites to the Doukhobors, also characterized by extreme separateness. Neither one nor the other, it seems, surrender to assimilation into the surrounding population, at a time when the system of sporadic re-settlement of the colonists, an objective to which the federal government holds and continues to hold as its chief aim. It would seem that the somewhat communistic spirit, especially amongst the Doukhobors, flies in the face, of the colonization policy of Canada.

In Winnipeg, as in other more significant centres of Canada, there is a so-called Immigration house, serving as a place of assembly for arriving settlers. The office of the Immigration Agent, a servitor of the federal Department of the Interior who manages the settlement of immigrants, is located here. Immigrants come here for required documents and information; work is found for them here, if they do not have the means to develop their own farm economy on land assigned to them. I went into this building several times and had discussions with settler-labourers. In large part they were Austrian Slavs: Galicians, Slovaks, Rusyns and so on, and also Doukhobors. Of the latter there were 150 men, waiting for promised work. Soon thereafter they were sent as day-labourers into the south-west part of the Province of Manitoba. The women work in Winnipeg itself, washing linen, receiving 10 cents an hour or one dollar a day; even so, not everyone finds work every day. Because the Doukhobors, having received land here and being in their second year in Canada still find it necessary to go off in large numbers during summer to find day labour, one can conclude that their situation is not at all one of the best. True, the harvest this year is wholly unsatisfactory, but they, according to their own words, are always in need of day labour. The Austrian Slavs also pointed out their difficult situation.

From Winnipeg I directed myself to Brandon, a lively little town in western Manitoba with 5,500 inhabitants, two or three bank branches, several elevators with a capacity of 300,000 bushels and a very significant grain trade. On the outskirts of town there is a large hospital for the mentally ill and a government model farm. This latter was the chief objective of my visit. Such farms exist in other areas of Canada also, for example in Ottawa, in Guelph (province of Ontario) and in Agassiz (British Columbia). The aim of the Brandon farm is to serve as a model for agriculture in the province of Manitoba.

The word "farm" should not be understood as we are given to understand this term. This is a small, model holding, managed by a knowledgeable and experienced farmer. Mr. Bratford, the managers of the Brandon farm, with great willingness dedicated an entire day to viewing the whole holding with me, an extent of approximately 600 acres. He showed me diverse ways of working fields, some of which served as models worth repeating, others as models of how not to farm. This manner of demonstration seems to me to be most demonstrative and practical. The methods of dealing with weeds, everywhere an evil for farmers, are demonstrated most plainly in a number of fields lying next to each other. Much attention is paid to the planting of trees, a most important matter, in my opinion, in deforested or never-forested regions of Canada. There are nurseries here of various species of trees and bushes, most adapted to the climatic and soil conditions of Manitoba and other northwestern regions. It was with great satisfaction that I saw here species of poplar and spruce from Russia, sent from the St. Petersburg Botanical Gardens, then various sorts of maple, brought from the Priamur Region, various sorts of acacias (yellow) and, finally, bushes known under the name artemisia arborensis, also brought here from Russia, specifically from Siberia. According to Mr. Bratford, the Siberian bush has great advantages over others; after only three years it is growing into a large bush and serves as a wonderful natural hedge and wind- and snow-break. The livestock also receive much attention; model livestock and horses are bred and cared for, and work the model farm. Of course, the full absence of fruit trees (at this farm) is most notable; a nursery of apple tress, again brought from Russia, is in a most lamentable state. This is explained by the extremely fierce climate here, and a very short summer. The Mennonites also explained this to me, those living in the very south of Manitoba; only among few of them did I find apple trees which had been nurtured with the greatest of care.

Because of the absence of convenient rail communication, I went by horse (about 50 miles) from Brandon to the little town of Minnedosa, with about 500 inhabitants, beautifully located on the little Saskatchewan river. Here I awaited a train, which came through only three times a week from Winnipeg to Yorkton, and in this manner reached this small town located in the province of Assiniboine. In the area around Yorkton there are 34 villages of Russian Doukhobors, and it was thence that I was headed. Around Minnedosa there dwell many

German farmers, in large part re-settled from Russia, and also Galicians, Rusyns and Slovaks. The life of these settlers is not easy, since most of them reached this country at the cost of their last pennies and, even though land was granted them freely, they still find themselves in fairly difficult conditions. The land they received was not particularly good and they complained to me about the spring and autumn frosts. Unlike Manitoba, the locale here is hilly, overgrown in places with sparse forest and bushes. In its features it presents many advantages for livestock rearing on a large scale; but to undertake it one requires much capital, which the poor settlers, of course, do not command. Hence one comes across many abandoned farms here; it is evident that people tried their luck here, and moved on.

I reached Yorkton late in the evening. At the railway station itself I was powerfully struck by the fact that, all about me, one could hear nothing but the Russian language; a whole crowd of Doukhobors awaited the train. The following morning I occupied myself with getting to know the town. In truth, it is a hamlet which is designated as a town; it has been in existence no more than 7-8 years, but already numbers about 500 inhabitants. There is a Russian quarter here with houses and yards for Doukhobors who come here on their business. The apothecary has a large sign in Russian; in the shops the vendors are beginning to speak in Russian. I was present at purchases made by Doukhobors; they count in Russian and in rubles and kopeks, in place of dollars and cents. The Canadian government maintains a Russian translator in its local land office.

Presently Doukhobors number around 7,200 in Canada. They are settled throughout 60 villages, of which 34, as I have already mentioned above, are located all about Yorkton, 13 are found on Swan River a little to the north of Yorkton, and the remaining 13 near the city of Prince Albert, in the province of Saskatchewan. I dedicated two days to visiting the villages located 30 to 40 versts distant from Yorkton, in the area of Chertova [Devil's] Lake, now renamed Ozero Dobrogo Dukha [Lake of the Holy Spirit]; the Doukhobors call it simply 'the marsh'. The following six villages are located here one next to the other; Blogosklonovka, Novogorelskoe, Novoselovka, Uteshenie, Novotroitskoe and Gorelovka. Between the third and the fourth of these villages the Quakers have set up a camp, establishing here in tents an elementary school for the children of the Doukhobors, where they instruct them in the English language, grammar and arithmetic. The children attend the school eagerly, astonishing the teachers with their abilities and receptivity [to learning]. As we know, the

Quakers, having given the Doukhobors the possibility of re-settling in Canada, do not desert them even here; they constantly visit their villages and read sermons to them, recognizing them as "brethren". Just before my arrival they were visited by the well-known and wealthy Philadelphia Quaker Joseph Elkington, who gave the government agent up to 12,000 dollars for the purchase of sheep for the Doukhobors, to which they have grown very accustomed and in which they experience a want.

In Yorkton I met a young Quaker teacher, who had come here from Cambridge with the express purpose of determining under what conditions it would be possible to establish yet another number of new schools in Doukhobor villages. Far less a desirable element, in the opinion of the Canadian government, are those Russian Stundists [sectarian group similar to Baptists] who are active among the Doukhobors. I met two of them in Yorkton. One of them continues to live with the Doukhobors in one of their villages; the other also lived amongst them earlier, but then left for California, from where he has recently returned with the aim of inciting the Doukhobors to go there for day-labour. Eighteen Doukhobors have already left for California, and I later met another group of 20-30 at the railroad preparing to leave. They are departing for an offer of two dollars per day without board, on the stipulation that they work off the cost of their journey and return, a total sum of 90 dollars. Some time earlier there were, amongst the Doukhobors, yet another two Russian Stundists, as people told me, who afterwards left for California. Canadian authorities and the Quakers are very displeased with the activities of these Russian "seekers of virtue," but are not yet in a position to undertake any measures against them.

From the Lake of the Holy Spirit I travelled to the villages lying north-east of Yorkton, including the village of Poterpevsheie, where the Doukhobor "grandmother," the elder Anastasia Vasilevna Verigin, lives; at present she is over 90 years old.

In material terms, the condition of all the villages is not enviable. A portion of them have been established on communal principles. Everything in them is communal: land and horses and cows and flour. The men, departed for day labour, send their money into a communal treasury, and in such a manner the village feeds itself. Such villages manage relatively better, even though they lack livestock, and ploughed fields and planted fields are extraordinarily few in number. One finds vegetable gardens, but they also have suffered greatly from spring frosts, which have killed even potatoes. Even more disheartening are those villages in which each family must manage its own farm with its own resources. Such families, of course do not manage any farms at all, and are in no position to do so because of the lack of necessary means to do so. Someone has a horse, another a cow, one has a plough while another has nothing. Sown in the gardens are a little wheat and oats for experimental purposes and for seed; the land was often dug by shovel, and sometimes women were harnessed to the plough and the land was so turned.

The government, in keeping with the general law, set aside 160 acres for the Doukhobors, for every labourer who had reached the age of 18; but no one has yet started to exercise ownership over this land. One meets almost no males in the villages; they have all gone away to do day labour. I do not think that they'll manage to plough their land and get on their feet soon. The Canadian government treats the Doukhobors with extraordinary equality; an exclusive right to settle in villages was extended to them, supplied them upon their arrival with the most necessary seed and special barracks were built for the first arriving party, which appeared in winter. They are now abandoned. The best which the Doukhobors have are cottages built by themselves, constructed of logs, smeared on the inside and out with clay, with large Russian stoves, about which no one in cold Canada had any idea until now.

The Doukhobors are valued here as wonderful workers, as sober and honest men and, as I have some basis to contend, people would not like to see them migrate to California, into which various types of agents whom I have described above are trying to trick them. The Premier [sic], Laurier, during discussions about the Doukhobors with me some time ago in Ottawa, expressed the opinion, with which I wholly concur, that they should not even think of California since one can farm there only with a large amount of working capital required for necessary irrigation works, which is a constant feature of all forms of Californian agricultural activity.

From Yorkton I travelled to Regina, the location of the Governor of the four western territories: Assiniboia, Saskatchewan, Alberta and Athabaska, united into one administrative unit under the name of North-West Territories. At present these regions are members of the federation on a basis absolutely analogous to the province of Manitoba and the old provinces. The territories have their own parliament and ministries which control all local matters. The city of Regina presents itself, in fact, as a village scattered in a disorganized fashion, with a population of 2,000 and some, without paved roads and street lighting, and with buildings of wood. There is, however, the fairly attractive building of the Bank of Montreal, which is held to be, as we know, the third most capitalized bank in the world. The buildings housing the Parliament and the ministries, part of them wooden, are located outside the town, while the residence of the Governor, a large but unattractive stone structure, stands alone in an open field, about two versts distant from town.

As regards the region itself, doubtlessly a grand future awaits it. The guarantee of this future are the fertile soils, marvellous grazing lands, a surfeit in the northern reaches of the region of excellent forests, as well as the certain existence in the bowels of the earth of very significant mineral wealth. Presently the region is most sparsely settled; according to the last census, the three districts of Assiniboia, Saskatchewan and Alberta, 304,304 square miles in extent, had a population of not more than 67,000. The population of Athabaska is so inconsequential that the numbers are not even counted. The scenery of the North-West Territories is very unique. The railway passes through wholly empty lands; only here and there solitary little homes appear, with their surrounding corrals for livestock and with long ricks of hay stored for winter. Across this whole expanse there is neither bush nor tree, however small. In this entire area, rising extraordinarily high above sea level (Calgary is located at a height of 3,390 feet), the population works exclusively at cattle and horse raising, which graze here in whole herds. Only further north, as the land begins to dip away from the plateau on which Calgary stands, does the character of the area begin to change gradually about mid-way to Edmonton. Again there appear fields sown in wheat, forests appear and, the further north one goes, grow thicker and thicker

The first settlers in Edmonton appeared only 10-12 years ago; before this the region was an area exclusively of furred animals and nomadic Indians, from whom the Hudson's Bay Company bought up animal pelts. Presently there are relatively many settlers here, having pushed the former masters of the land, the Indians, deeper into the region or into the north. The settlers are, in the main, Germans who resettled here from the United States of America, Galicians and Rusyns. Of the latter there are 14,000 in the territories; a significant number of these settlers live mainly in the Edmonton area. I had long discussions with many of them. They are all Orthodox and speak in a language closely approximating Maloross [Ukrainian]. In general they are happy with their situation in Canada, and regretted only the lack of priests among them; their children, in their words, remain unchristened, while the dead are buried without memorial services. This year they were visited by a Russian priest who came from the United States. To the west of Edmonton, about 50 versts distant, the

Rusyns have built themselves a little church in an open field, but it is not yet completed, and they are not certain whether or not they will be able to decorate it and to furnish it with the necessary church plate.

Returning to the matter of this area's future, one should remember that presently there are plans to build a long railway line to link the town of Prince Albert with Edmonton, and Edmonton with the shore of the Pacific Ocean. For the present Edmonton's only market is British Columbia, and especially its mining region. With the extension of a railroad along the shortest route to the sea shore, the North-West Territories will assume a most prominent position in Pacific Ocean trade. With a abundance of coal and kerosene, they could in time develop into a very serious competitor for our trade activity on the shores of the Pacific Ocean and in Siberia.

In Regina I met with the already-mentioned Mennonite, Klaas Peters from Gretna. As it turned out, he had come here with scouts from Molokans [sect similar to the Doukhobors] residing in Russia, intending on migrating to Canada, and searching in this country for suitable unoccupied land.

British Columbia, next on my journey, is a part of Canada lying between the watershed of the Rocky Mountains to the east, the Pacific Ocean to the west, the 49th parallel to the south, that is, the border with the United States of America, and the 60th parallel north latitude to the north, where is borders on Alaska which cuts it off from the Pacific Ocean here, and the district of the Yukon, recently separated into a distinct administrative unit by the Canadian federal government from the general composition of the North-West Territories. To the west islands lying along the length of its shore are also a part of the province, the main ones being Vancouver and the Queen Charlotte group. In truth, one should see British Columbia as consisting of two separate parts, southern and northern. The former is very sparsely peopled, presenting most unfavourable conditions for settlement because of the lack of arable land, a very severe climate and the general nature of the soil. Its chief advantages are, nonetheless, the certain existence of gold, and the plentitude of furred animals. The southern part, a sweeping level highland, bounded to the east and west by mountainous ridges, is richer and at the same time more accessible.

The Rocky Mountains which pass through here, comprising the backbone of the whole continent, so-to-speak, stretch the entire length of its western shore and only between the 56th and 57th degrees of north latitude lose their uniquely fierce character, changing gradually into low highlands and hills. Near the border with the United States of America the elevation of the mountains is 10,000 feet. The highest point of the whole divide, the peak of Mount Murchison, from whose ravines the Saskatchewan River has its source, reaches a height of 13,500 feet. There are a number of passes through the divide, numbering close to twenty. Parallel to the main chain of the Rocky Mountains there run two others — the Selkirk and the Coastal ranges. Between these ranges there are plateaus and mountain valleys, presenting broad and wonderful grazing lands and arable lands extraordinarily easy to work. According to the opinion of experts, all of British Columbia south of 52 degrees north latitude is usable either as grazing land, where not above 3,500 feet above sea level, or for grain growing in places lying below 2,500 feet and which also permit of artificial irrigation. Independent of this, all of British Columbia's mountains are filled with precious and other metals. Gold was first discovered here in 1848 on the Queen Charlotte Islands, and afterwards in 1858 in the gold-bearing river, the Fraser. Currently the presence of gold has been noted almost everywhere. Along with gold, silver, copper, iron, lead and coal are also mined.

In sum in British Columbia in 1896 there was mined:

	(in millions of dollars)
gold	58,882,724
silver	4,028,224
lead	1,606,427
copper	254,802
coal	33,934,427
building stone	1,200,000
other minerals	25,000

The value of furred animals taken between 1890 and 1896 can be represented as follows:

Year	Value in Dollars
1890	2,608,608
1891	3,546,702
1892	3,017,971
1893	3,588,413
1894	4,225,717
1895	5,655,302
1896	7,146,425

Great deposits of rock coal are found on Vancouver Island where, according to official statistics, the area of the mine pits in Nanaimo is 200 square miles; the pits in Comox are almost 300 square miles, with a square mile producing, on average, up to 16,000 tons. In Crow's Nest, in the Rocky Mountains, a vein of coal from 132 to 148 feet in width has been found. The coal mined everywhere is of the highest quality, and is located in the main in areas with notable advantages, not only for the mining, but also for the transport of the coal.

The rivers of British Columbia are also very significant sources of its wealth; some are gold-bearing, and all are so teeming with remarkable amounts of fish that fishing constitutes one of the main forms of local commerce. Of the rivers, the main ones are: the Columbia, flowing through a whole series of the so-called Columbian Lakes and draining an area of 195,000 square miles; the Fraser, teeming, regardless of the presence of gold, with colossal numbers of fish and draining large expanse of land which offer up the best of conditions for farming; the Skeena, about 300 miles in length; the Stikine, serving as the main artery of an extensive region of several thousands of square miles north of the 57th degree of latitude. Doctor [George Mercer] Dawson, when presenting before the Royal Colonial Society the report on his journeys throughout British Columbia, undertaken at the direction of the Canadian government, says that the [British Columbia], in its agriculture, can be compared most readily to Vologda province [in Russia]. One has, however, to keep in mind the notable mineral wealth [of British Columbia]. At the present time the region has virtually no permanent inhabitants and is visited from time to time only by seekers of gold and hunters of fur.

Of the districts which comprise British Columbia the wealthiest is the mining district of Kootenay, 16,500,000 acres in extent, drained by the river Columbia, having interior steamboat communication and served by several railroads. To the north it is crossed by the Canadian Pacific Railway, whence visitors to this region leave for it from the town of Revelstoke. Out of the towns which have arisen here, the most important is Nelson. The district of Westminster, 36,000,000 acres in extent, is blessed with a surfeit of very rich forest expanses and land fir for agricultural endeavour, especially in the areas lying near the delta of the Fraser river. Fishing in the river is one of the most important branches of local industry. There are close to 50 fish processing plants, working, in the main, in the taking and processing of salmon. The development of this branch of industry began in 1876, when only 10,000 cases of salmon were processed, 48 pounds each in weight. In 1897 the overall production of the fish plants amounted to approximately 1,000,000 cases, with a value of 4,000,000 dollars.

The main trade port of the Pacific Ocean is located in British Columbia. Vancouver is the terminal point of the Canadian Pacific Railway, to which it owes its existence and ever-increasing development, which began in 1885. In 1886 Vancouver had only 600 inhabitants; at present it has a population of 25,000. The city is located on the shore of a wondrous natural bay and has direct sea-communications with Japan, China, Australia and the ports of the United States of America throughout the whole year. The main city of British Columbia, Victoria, is in second place as a port, and competes with Vancouver. In 1897 this port, in extent and value of goods shipped, was still substantially ahead of its rival, but over the last while, given the extraordinarily rapid development of [Vancouver], [Victoria] has lagged behind noticeably. The history of the development of Pacific trade, which in truth is but of short duration, has very many examples of an unexpected rise [to prominence], such as happened with Vancouver. Not too long ago California, which has now become a sort of promised land of North America, was almost unknown. Washington and Oregon before our eyes became wealthy and very populous states, with ports such as Seattle and Tacoma, while the very empty expanses of British Columbia, where only a few agents of the Hudson's Bay Company occupied themselves with buying up pelts from Indian tribes, with the passage of some 10-15 years, have been transformed into the liveliest of trade centres. Today the extent of trade going through Pacific Ocean ports is estimated at 15,000,000 tons annually. Like Victoria, so Vancouver participates actively in the catch of the sea and annually they fit out a substantial number of vessels which go whaling, fishing and sealing in the Pacific Ocean. Additionally, Vancouver is a main centre of the lumber trade.

The population, both of the towns and the interior of the regions of British Columbia, consists predominantly of Englishmen and Indians, who live nomadically and fish and hunt. The latter, according to the official statistics of 1896, are no more than 25,000 in the whole province. Of 59 Indian tribes scattered today throughout all of North America, there are only six within the borders of British Columbia. In addition to these peoples, there is a large number of Chinese and Japanese here, having flooded the country over many years, until their migration was limited by a special law designed to protect the local population from the pressure of falling wages.

My general impression after visiting British Columbia comes down to this, that this province is the a most varied and very rich region, only beginning to come to life. Along with untouched mineral wealth, it has limitless valuable forests and significant expanses of land good for agriculture and fruit-bearing trees. Under the influence of the warm Japanese Current, the southern portion of the Pacific Ocean coast knows absolutely no winter; the climate and vegetation reminds one of the southern countries of Europe. I saw fruit orchards in southern Vancouver Island, planted but four years ago, and already bearing significant fruit.

This is a region which doubtless has a great future and which, for us Russians, has many analogies with certain areas of our expansive motherland, and thus constitutes a truly special interest.

In concluding this present brief sketch description of certain regions of Canada, it would not be superfluous to say a few words about her trade.

The preferential tariff for goods imported into Canada from Great Britain and her colonies could not, and will probably not be able in future to give Britain products an exclusive domination to the detriment of imports from the United States of America. To the contrary, one sees in Canada a constantly increasing tendency toward closed trade relations with the trans-Atlantic republic, a tendency which, one might suggest, has forced the present government of Canada to make an effort to turn to the metropolis [with a request] for increased protectionism. The preference for imports from the United States doubtlessly stems from the similarity of tastes and needs of the Canadian and American populations on the one hand, and with the ability of American producers to accommodate themselves to the particularities of the needs of their northern neighbours on the other.

In Canada, truth to say, everything reminds one more of the United States than England, beginning with the railroads and ending with the periodical press. Construction, the interiors of homes, farm management and all sorts of [business] transactions are immeasurably closer to the American type. Canada inexorably is moving ahead along the road of progress; but its course is drawing ever more closer to the great road defined by North American culture, and no artificial measures can either stop or delay, it seems, this natural movement.

During 1899-1900 (the accounting year ends on 30 June), goods subject to tariffs exported from the United States of North America into Canada were valued at 44,000,000 dollars; at the same time British imports into the colony were valued at a sum of only 28,500,000 dollars.

The percentage of import into Canada from the United States and Great Britain and her colonies relative to the whole import into the country can be as follows, [starting] with the year 1890:

Year	United States of North America	Great Britain
1890	46.37	38.48
1891	47.36	37.10
1892	45.42	35.35
1893	47.84	35.45
1894	46.89	34.23
1895	51.91	29.58
1896	52.91	29.58
1897	55.39	26.43
1898	60.22	24.86
1899	60.37	24.05

The dollar value of overall imports into Canada for the preceding decade of 1890-1899 can be construed as follows:

Year	Value in Dollars
1890	112,765,584
1891	113,345,124
1892	116,978,943
1893	121,705,030
1894	113,093,983
1895	105,252,511
1896	110,587,480
1897	111,294,021
1989	130,698,006
1899	154,051,593

Great Britain exports to Canada largely consist of cotton, carpets, woolen goods, styles and haberdashery goods, plates and dishes, and spirits.

Imports from the United States of North America, grouped by most important category and value in dollars, can be seen as follows below for the last three years:

Name of Goods	Value in Dollars		
	1898	1899	1900
Steel Rails	1,555,405	1,720,503	2,882,667
Paper Products	2,465,630	2,759,164	2,668,906
Agricultural Implements	781,415	1,521,054	2,006,943
Books and Publications	722,049	844,410	1,012,986
Lighting Oils	737,389	762, 624	1,012,986
Skins	878,054	821, 530	952,846
Steel Products	719,326	906,047	818,917
Carriages	183,233	582,094	544,465
Watches	349,498	410,237	433, 635
Foot Ware	285,054	427,023	413,487
Furniture	523,424	439,536	394,328
Bicycles	614,003	582,500	387,767
Turpentine	207,600	230,758	332,069
Measuring Instruments	305,016	492,734	276,777
Copper Ware	155,515	146,635	226,356
Sewing Machines	141,172	163,095	193,920
Fertilizers	93,470	131,587	155,230
Rubber and Tar	111,482	132,190	141,637
Vegetable Oils	115,648	111,517	126,010
Tobacco	62,139	82,84	117,280

F. Emiliia Kirillovna Pimenova, *The Land of Grain Growers (Canada)* (1917)[1]

The English colony Canada lies to the north of the great transatlantic republic, the United States of America, and borders upon it. It is the only remaining European possession in North America, but in essence it is almost an independent state governed by its own laws. Canada is a democratic republic and a fully self-governing union or federation of individual provinces settled mainly by the descendants of French and English colonists. Therefore Canada is divided between the French and English. French Canadians live mainly in the province of Quebec and the maritime regions. They are all Catholics.

The Peoples of Canada
English Canada is inhabited by the English, Scots, Irish and also quite a few Germans, but the dominant language in this province is English. Russians who belonged to the sect of Doukhobors settled in Canada in 1898. They founded Russian villages. Besides the newcomers, descendants of European colonists, who form their own Canadian nation, there remain the original inhabitants, different Indian tribes. Eskimos live in the North and North-West. However, all of these peoples live in harmony with each other and, in Canada, it appears that the difficult problem of peaceful co-existence of varied groups has been solved.

Peasant Kingdom
Canada may justly be called "the kingdom of farmers," because the farmers or peasants, petty owners, are the class which enjoys the greatest influence in the country. There is neither an hereditary aristocracy nor any special ruling classes in Canada; nor is there in the neighbouring republic — the United States of America, which is

---

[1]   Pimenova, *Strana khleborobov. (Kanada)* (Kniga: Petrograd, 1917). Translated by Yana Kuzmin. This little book sold for 20 kopeks. The list of 71 Kniga titles carried on the inside of its covers concluded with the following statement: "The book depot 'Kniga' has set for itself the task to sell all editions with a marxist inclination, and also all the literature issued by other socialist parties on worker and peasant questions." Bold as in original. Among Kniga's authors were Anatolii Lunacharskii, later Bolshevik minister of education, and Leon Trotskii.

The book is as interesting for its many historical errors as it is for the particular tone it sets out for its youthful audience.

astonishing by its colossal industrial development. But in Canada the predominance of power lies not with those who control millions in trade companies, but with petty peasant-owners who till the land themselves. That is why Canada, as an agricultural country, must be of special interest for Russian citizens.

The State System

In area Canada is a little smaller than the United States and its climate is reminiscent of Siberia. At present Canada is one of the most free and prosperous countries, although not so long ago it was a poor and almost uninhibited country. The first colonists to conquer the country (the French) did not do Canada much good. The English, having conquered and taken it away from the French, showed far greater understanding of their own interests. To be sure, this understanding did not come at once; but only after a rebellion of Canadian colonists known as the "American Revolution". The English had to grant the Canadians the right to self-determination, liberty and independence. When several Canadian provinces decided to form a union or federation for the common good and convenience they discussed the draft of the federative system and informed the British Government about it. The government had only to ratify this agreement. It was done without either the direct or indirect participation of the English Parliament in the discussion of this project.

At present a Governor-General appointed by the English government is at the head of the government of the Canadian Federation. But his authority in fact is only formal, and the country is governed by the responsible minister [prime minister] and a federal parliament consisting of two houses: The Senate and House of Commons, that is, an assembly of people's representatives. The senators are appointed by the Governor-General. These appointments must be approved by the prime minister, who depends on the confidence of the House of Commons. Consequently, senatorial appointments can take place only with the consent and the advice of people's representatives.

The members of the federal parliament or House of Commons are elected for five years by the entire adult population, but men only, of Canada. Meanwhile, in England universal suffrage has still not been introduced. In this respect Canada is ahead of England. Both languages in Canada, French and English, enjoy equal rights. Individual provinces of Canada, nine in number, are governed completely independently. Although at the head of each there is a governor appointed by the Canadian Governor-General (this appointment must be confirmed by the signature of the prime minister), each province has its own parliament and council of ministers answerable to this parliament.

Thus, Canada is a democratic federal republic made up of several separate democratic republics, which enjoy wide self-government in all local matters. The ties between Canada and England are purely formal. Though the relations of Canada with foreign countries are conducted through English government and English ambassadors, it has direct relations with the United States. In military matters Canada declared itself formally independent of England as early as in 1910, that is, having the right in case of war between England and some country to take or not to take part in this war subject to its own decision.

Over the last twenty years the local self-government of Canada, both in town and in the country, made great progress and it may in all fairness now be called the most democratic in the world.

For the people engaged in independent agricultural work the Canadian federation has many attractive features. The climate and soil in Canada are favourable for agriculture. There is still enough vacant land available. Cattle-breeding is thriving. One of our compatriots [Kriukov, ed.], who visited Canada, says: "If you could go up and look at Canada from above this country would present a very original picture; there are towns in some places and between them all the habitable space is taken by farms. Plots of land adjoining the farms are fenced around. These fences stretch in all directions and cover the country like a continuous net. The Canadian farm is what we call a *khutor* [family farm], where the owner works himself with the help of his family and very seldom with the help of hired workers."

Canadian farmers do all kinds of agricultural work and therefore can be compared with Russian peasants in the work they perform. But their way of life is significantly different, as most of them live at the level of our middle level landowner.[2] Moreover agricultural machines are widely used in Canada. Naturally it makes agricultural work much more productive than in Russia.

The Land Question
It is extremely easy to acquire land plots in Canada. This helps increase the number of peasant-owners or farmers, as they are called there. Here, for example, are the conditions for purchasing land in French Canada, in the province of Quebec: for a desyatina of state

---

2 Pimenova used the term "pomeshchiki," which would be at the level of landed gentry.

land suitable for agricultural crops, the government set a price of from one to three rubles, and the buyer is required to provide only twenty percent of the sum at the time of purchase. The rest can be paid by instalments over four years. However, the following condition was laid down: the farmer has to settle on his plot within two years after the purchase and build a house which must be no less than sixteen feet in width and twenty feet in length. The owner of the plot had also to clear every year and prepare for agriculture no less than one tenth of his land. No more than seventy four desyatinas were sold to one person.

After meeting these conditions and, in any case, no earlier two years after the transaction, the land becomes the property of the buyer and he receives free of charge the appropriate document for ownership of the land. In fact, the government gives the land away almost free of charge, as the money received from the buyer barely covers the cost of setting out the boundaries of the plot and laying out the roads.

In this same province, special protection is extended to the large families of farmers. Those who have twelve and more children receive thirty seven desyatinas of vacant government land free of charge. A family with many children must merely submit a certificate from a Justice of Peace after which it is entered in the lists of the department of agriculture and is allotted a plot of land as has been mentioned above. It must be noted that Canadian families are known for a great number of children. In 1897 in Quebec two and a half thousand families were entered in the lists of those who had twelve children.

In Quebec's neighbouring Canadian province, Ontario, there are even more favourable conditions for acquiring land. There every head of the family, man or woman — all equally, if only he or she has children under eighteen, has the right to receive free of charge 74 desyatinas of vacant land owned by the provincial government. Anyone who has no children may receive half the amount but everyone who receives such an uncultivated plot must live on it no less than six months a year, i.e. as long as necessary for agricultural work. Some provinces even established awards — premiums of around hundred rubles to those landowners who cleared new plots for agricultural work and organized their agriculture in the best way possible, built better houses and other buildings and made improvements in their work.

It is evident from all this that the democratic government of the Canadian federation takes special care to create a more numerous class of peasant-owners-petty landowners who work up their plots with their own labour. For them agriculture is the main or the only source of existence and therefore they are trying to improve it. Canadian farmers or peasants-owners are very interested in all kinds of improvements in agriculture. In every Canadian province there are agricultural unions and societies which arrange agricultural exhibitions and meetings, where reports are made and various innovations are discussed. There are up to 100 such societies in the province of Ontario alone. Thanks to this, stagnation in agriculture is impossible. Agriculture is developing all the time and Canada recently began to compete with Russia in the export of agricultural products to other countries. It exports mostly timber and agricultural products to England and, both from there and the United States, gets manufactured goods and hardware in return.

Education

There are many schools in Canada and especially agricultural, horticultural and dairy schools. They are organized in such a way that not only children but also grown up peasants may attend if they want to supplement their knowledge on a certain branch of agriculture. Tuition in these schools is mostly free. A great number of subscribers to agricultural magazines is an indication of the high level of development of Canadian peasants.

Without A Permanent Army

Every young peasant in Canada even if he has little money may become a landowner, because the government of the federation does everything possible to facilitate the purchase of plots of land and in more remote places it distributes small plots almost free of charge.

Young Canadians are not forced to lose their best years in military service, as in other countries. In Canada there is no compulsory military service and not even a permanent army. Very often young peasants who have no money to start their own farms get jobs at other farms to save the money to buy a plot of land. At an age when our peasants must serve in the army young Canadians, sons of farmers, become workers at farms and later become landowners.

Enjoying full rights in a free state, as a result of their numbers Canadian peasants play a leading role in the political life of the country. This explains the fact that the Canadian federal government pays special attention to all needs of agriculture. As a result, the economic position of Canadian peasants is very good and the death rate among them is twice as low as that of the Russian peasant population, which is always half-starving. Since each Canadian province is fully self-governed, the federal government does not interfere in local matters.

Therefore the organization of schools, the setting of curricula, and the appointment of teachers do not depend on the federal government. Every Canadian province sets itself the task to take care of education and in this respect it is by no means behind but, rather, is even ahead of some European countries.

This is how the population of Canada, the greater part of which is made up of peasants-grain producers, arranged its life.

Russian peasants should get much better acquainted with the life of their overseas brothers who so warmly received our Doukhobors, who have fled to Canada from tsarist oppression.

Much may be learned and a good deal may be modelled on the order established by the people of the "peasant kingdom."

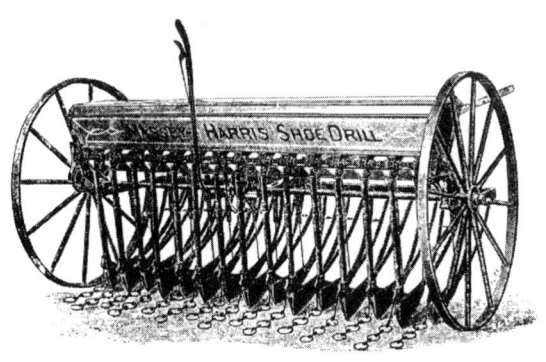

Index of Names

Numbers in italics refer to material in footnotes

Adams, John Quincy, 63f
Alexander I, Tsar, 15-16, 28-29, 63ff, 77, 112
Alexander II, Tsar, 18, 19, 35, 36, 42, 44, 78, 111
Alexander III, Tsar, 16, 18, 92, *105*
Aleksandr, Empress, 23
Alekseev, Admiral, *104*
Aleksei Mikhailovich, Grand Duke, 42
Arakcheev, A.A., 16
Bakunin, M.A., 21
Beethoven, 40
Bell, J. Mackintosh, 123
Bentkovskii, A.K., 92, 93, 94, 129, 146
Berberova, Nina, 22
Bering, Vitus J., 17, 27
Bismarck, Otto von, 91
Bodisco, A.A., 69ff, 73ff, 80, 81
Bogaraz, Vladimir, *59*
Bonch-Bruevich, V., 47, 48
Borden, Robert L., 133, 148, 149, *156*
Braithwaite, A.D., 153
Bratford, Mr., 222
Brien, J.-B.-H., *96-97*
Brown, George, 72
Brown, John, 51
Brunnov, F.I., 78, 79, 80
Bulgarin, F., 39
Bury, George, 122
Butlerov, Yu.R., 155
By, Colonel, 191
Cabot, John, 164
Cabot, Sebastian, 164, 176
Calhoun, John C., 65
Cartier, Jacques, 172, 176
Cassini, A.P., 93
Catherine the Great, *144*
Chaadaev, P., 33
Champlain, Samuel de, 168, 176, 183, 205
Chateaubriand, François de, 35, 37, 205, 206

Chernyshevskii, N.G., 21, 39
Chertkov, Vladimir, 108, 110
Chikhachev, N.M., 87
Clay, Henry, 65
Colborne, John, 73, 56, 98
Cooper, James Fenimore, 34, 35
Czartoryski, A.J., 77
Custine, Marquis de, 17, 23
Dallas, George Mifflin, 70f, 74, 75, 77, 78
Dashkov, A.Ya., 65ff
Dawson, G.M., 229
Demens, P.A. (Tverskii), 47-48, 60, 129, 130, 146
Dennis, mr., 128
Dennis, Col. J.S., 153
Dickens, Charles, 43
Disraeli, Benjamin, 86
Dobrolyubov, N.A., 39, 40
Dostoevsky, F.M., 21
Douglas, James, 84
Dumont, Gabriel, 44
Durham, Lord, 33, 34, 52, 77, 79f
Edward VII, King, 149
Elkington, Joseph, 224
Engels, Friedrich, 107, 116, 147
Epanchin, N.A., 127, 142
Epanchin, N.N., 127-128, *142*, 146, 148
Fox, Henry, *101*
Gilbert, Sir Humphrey, 164
Gilpen, H.D., 75
Gladstone, W.E., 48, 121
Gogol, N.V., 19
Goldstein, I.M., 133, *144*
Golitsyn, G.S., 126
Goncharov, I.A., 19
Goremykin, I.L., 23, 152
Haxthausen, August von, 17-18
Hays, Charles Melville, 112
Hennepin, Louis, 204, 205, 206
Hespeler, William, 111, 110
Hindenlang, Charles, *99-100*

Howe, Joseph, 84
Hughes, Otis Capt., 90
Imshenik-Kontradovich, A.I., 116-117
Ivin, Ivan, 110
Izmailov, A.E., 30
Izvolskii, A.P., 119
Johnson, William, 34, *56*, 74
Just, C.F., 152, *157*
Karamzin, N.M., 28-30, 31-32, 37, 38,
    40, 41, 51, 52, 53, 63, 71, 126, 127,
    154, 159-162
Karintsev, N.A., *61*
Khilkov, Prince Dmitrii, 47, 110
Kielchen, P.A., 73-75, 76
Kipling, Rudyard, 91
Kon, Louis, 115, *138*, 153
Konstantin, Grand Prince, 42
Korff, S.A., 48, 52
Kovaloff, Col., 152
Kozlov, N.Ya., 65f
Kravchinskii, S.M., 21
Krehmer, E.I., 69-75
Kriukov, N.A., 48, 49, 50, 61, 95, 108,
    118, 123-126, 127, 131, 133, 134, *142*,
    143, 146, 148, 212-218, 219
Kropotkin, Piotr, 95, 107-110, 118, 126,
    128, 129
Krugilov, N.S., 116-117
Kruzenshtern, I.F., 31, 82, *101*
Lakier, A.B., 36-40, 41, 42, 45, 46, 49,
    51, 52, 85, 108, 127, 131, 167-211
Lamsdorff, V.N., 90, *104*
Laurier, Wilfrid, 148, 225
Leibnitz, Gottfried, 27
Lieven, Kh.A., 67
Likhachev, S.A., 113, 135, 150-151, *157*
Likhachev, Admiral I., 87, 89
Lisianskii, Yu.F., 31
Lvov, Prince G.E., 130
Macdonald, John A., 86
Macdonald, G.W., 123
Macdonald, R.O., 131
Mackenzie, W.L., 69ff, 72, 73, 75-76, *96*
Maissonneuve, Sieur de, 177
Makhortov, P., 110
Maksutov, Prince, *104*
Maltitz, F.P. De, 67, 68

Manners, R.C., *98*
Mathers, Henry, 94, 134, 145
Maynard, Sir John, 21
Mavor, James, 108, 109-110, 129, *141*,
    150
McLeod, Alexander, 82-83
Menshikov, A.S., 70
Middleton, F.D., 44
Mikhail Pavlovich, Grand Duke, 71
Miliukov, Paul, 48-51, 130
Mizhuev, P.G., 48ff, 108, 131
Montcalm, Gen. Louis de, 184
Montgomery, Gen. Richard, 163
Morse, Frank W., 112, *137*
Murav'ev, M.N., 93-94, 124
Napoleon Bonaparte, 15, 63, 64, 65, 66
Napoleon III, 41, 169
Nechaev, S.G., 21
Nelson, Dr. Robert, 68f, 70, 72, 75, 76-77
Nesselrode, K.M., 66, 67, 69, 71-72, 73,
    76ff, 79, 81
Nicholas I, Tsar, 16, 17, 20, 22, 31, 33,
    35, 36, 39, 67, 68ff, 86
Nicholas II, Tsar, 16, 19, 23, 94, 146,
    149, 152
Ogden, C.N., 73, 75
Oliver, Frank, 112, 129
Orlov, A., 75
O'Sullivan, John L., 75
Owen, Ross, 153
Palmerston, Lord, 75, 77, 79, 80
Papineau, Louis, 71, 75-76, 79
Paskievich, I.F., 69, 70, 72, 78, 79
Passek, N., 113, 133-134, 135, *143*, 145,
    150
Paul I, Tsar, 15, 27, 28, *54*
Peter I, The Great, 17, 18, 27, 67, *155*
Peters, Klaas, 220, 227
Pimenova, E.K., 48, 51-52, 150, 154,
    234-39
Pobedonostsev, K.P., 16, 21, 23, 44, 47,
    48, 146
Pokotilov, D.D., 118
Polevoi, N., *55*
Pozzo di Borgo, C.A., 69ff, 71, 73, 78
Pushkin, A.S., 33, *57*
Preston, T.R., 68, 73

Rezanov, N.P., 64
Riel, Louis, 43-44, 51, 87, 108, 111, 121
Roberts, Charles D., 53, 150
Robinson, G.T., 21
Robyk, K., *155*
Romanov, D., 41-42
Rousseau, J.-J., 28
Rozen, I.B., 126
Rumiantsev, N.P., 63, 64, 65ff
Salisbury, Lord, 121
Salktykov, Fedor, 27
Sanders, William, 109
Sazonov, S.D., 152
Senkovskii, Osip, 31-32
Seraphin, *155*
Seward, William H., 83
Shelekhov, G.I., 64
Shestakov, I.A., 42-43, 85-86
Sifton, Clifford, 110, 124
Simpson, George, 81
Sorge, F.A., 108
Speranskii, M.M., 16
Staahl, Ye.Ye., 93
Stark, Vice-Admiral, *104*
Stepniak, Sergeius (Kravchinskii), 110
Stolypin, P.A., 16, 111-112, 113, 116,
    123, 127, 130, 147
Strathcona, Lord (D.A. Smith), 124
Stroganov (Family), 35
Studitskii, F., 40-41, 53
Struve, Nikolai B., 94-95, 112, 113, 114,
    116, 129, 134, *142*, 145-146, 149, 218-
    233
Suchkov, S.N., 148
Sulerzhitskii, L., 129
Suvorov, Alexander, 15
Svinin, Pavel, 30-31, 55, 163-166
Sydenham, Lord, (C.O. Thomson), 82
Tikhon, 147
Thompson-Seton, Ernest, 53
Timlin, M.F., 110
Tizengausen, A.E., 87
Tocqueville, Alexis de, 37
Tolstoy, Lev (Leo), 47, 108, 109, 110,
    111, 128, 129, 130, 131
Tolstoy, Sergei, 111
Tyrtov, P.P., 90

Turgenev, A.I., 34-5, *57*
Ustinov, M.M., 113, 128, 145
Uvarov, S.S., 16
Van Buren, President Martin, 68, 74
Van Horne, William, 117, 121
Vasiliev, A.V., 117
Velichkova, Vera M., 47
Verigin, Anastasia V., 224
Verigin, Peter, 112, 129, 130, 147
Viazemskii, P.A., 37
Vilenkin, Ya.A. (James Wilenkin), 152
Voloshinov, N.A., 116, 118, 120, 121
Walton-Johns, Dr. W.H., *105*
Whyte, William, 122, *140*
Wilenkin, James (See Vilenkin)
Wilgress, Dana, 153
Wilhelm II, Kaiser, 92
William IV, King of England, 79
Witte, S.Yu., 16, 19-20, 22, 93, 94, 119,
    120, 122, 127
Wolf, Gen. James, 184
Wrangel, F., 81, 82
Yadrinstev, N.M., 46
Yelena (Helene) of Württemberg,
    Grand Duchess, 71
Zavalishin, D.I., 46, 107, 108

Краснокожій обитатель Канады.

"Redskin Dwellers of Canada"

Index of Subjects and Places

Some of the locations listed below appear throughout (e.g., St. Petersburg) but are included here only where they are part of the story.

Afghanistan, 19, 26, 46, 89, 122, 123, 151

Agriculture (Canadian & Russian), 18, 24, 39, 47, 50ff, 110ff, 125, 133-135, 148, 155, 161f, 182, 184, 192ff, 214-219, 220, 224ff, 233f, 236ff

Alaska, 29, 69, 83, 85, 86

Alberta, 130

Aleutians, 29, 85

Americans/ America, Nature of, 13, 30, 31, 33, 38-42, 43, 45, 52-53, 87-88, 171, 184, 199-200, 201-202

American-British Relations, 66ff, Chapter 2, *passim*

Anglo-Russian Treaty (1825), 69

Annie Moore, 94

Anti-Semitism, 24-25, 116, 127, 136, 215

Ariel, 93

Armenians, 24

Austria-Hungary, 17, 19, 66, 81, 112, 117-118, 152, 153

Australia, 90, 127, 215

Autocracy, 18, 20, 21, 25, 31

Aylmer, 194

Azerbaijan, 66

Barshchina, 18

Bering Sea, 47

Biblioteka dlia Chteniia, 33

Black Sea, 71-72, 74, 81, 86, 88

BNA Act, 50, 54, 85 (see also Confederation)

Bolsheviks, 49, 155, 156

Brandon, 223f

British Columbia, 47, 84, 86, 87, 88, 92, 135, *145*, 229f (see also Vancouver, Victoria, Esquimalt)

Calgary, 228

California, 50, 66, 148, 226

Canada, Armed Forces, 88-89, 90, 152, 240-241

Canada, Dept of External Affairs, 86

Canada, Economics, 52, 150 (see Translations, *passim*)

Canada, Industry, 52 (Translations, *passim*)

Canadian-American Relations, 31, 36, 39-40, 42, 43, 48, 51, 52, Chapter 2, *passim*, 110, 149-150, 167, 171ff, 174f, 199, 200, 232ff, 237

Canadian Association of Wagon and Metal Factories, 154

Canadian Bank of Commerce, 151, *158*

Canadian-British Relations, 34ff, 45, Chapter 2, *passim*, 149-150 (see also Rebellions)

Canadian Copper Company, 115

Canadian Expeditionary Force, 152

Canadian Locomotive Company, 154

Canadian Manufacturing Association, 153

Canadian Pacific Railroad (see also Railroads), 44, 52, 89f, 94, 96, *105*, 110, 111, 114ff, 117-125, 126, 129, 130, 151, 155, 216f, 221

Canadians/ Canada, Nature of, 13, 30, 31, 38-42, 45, 52-53, 93-94, 112, 117, 127-128, 162, 171, 184, 203f, 216-219

Cape Breton, 94

Carmolita, 92

Caroline, 84

Caspian Sea, 19

Caucasus, 19, 26, 66, 71-72, 74

Central Asia, 26

Censorship, 13, 17, 20, 34-35, 37, 46, 47, 153

Census, Russian (1897), 20-21, 24

Champlain, Lake (see Lake Champlain)

China, 19, 85, 90, 118, 124

Confederation, Canadian (1867), 54, 84, 85 (see also BNA Act)

Constitutional Monarchy, 25, 31, 51, 55

Constitutions, 20, 31, 39, 42

Cossacks, 21, 37

Consulate(s), Russian in Canada, 12-14, 94ff, 107, 124, 134-135, 136, 147-155, *156*. Others, 147f
Convention, Anglo-American (1824), 69, 76
Crimean War, 20, 37, 38, 40, 86-87, 88, 128, 181
Cuba, 38, 42
Decembrists, 22, 35, 37, 48
Doukhobors, 11, 12, 48-49, 53-54, 61, *63*, 110, 111, 112-114, 116, 130-133, *145*, 148-149, 221, 223-227, 229, 236
  Stundists, 226
Eastern Wagon Works, 154
Edmonton, 228f
Education, 20, 24, 31, 35, 39, 46, 51, 52, 54, 177ff, 187f, 204-205, 223, 240
Egypt, 79, 81, 130
England (see Great Britain)
Emigration (see Immigration)
Esquimalt, 86, 87, 89, 90, 94, *105*
Experimental Farm System, 111
Finland, 66, 114
  Finlanders, 24, 115, 152, *158*
Fishing Industry, 44, 91ff, 126, 165-168, 231-232 (see also Fur Seals)
Forestry, 126, 161ff, 176, 192, 193f, 195-198, 228f
France, 17, 21, 34, 65ff, 78, 81, 95, 123, 147
French Canadians, 38, 42, 43, 46, 52, *60*, 82, 169-174, 178f, 188-189
French-English Relations, Canada, 38, 39, 40, 42, 43, 51f, 54, 77-78, 110, 167-126 *passim*, 236f
Frost & Wood Company (Smith Falls), 133, 134
Fur Trade, 33, 37, 43, 84, 85, 182, 230, 232
  Fur Seals, 47, 83, 85, 91-94, 151-152 (see also Hudson's Bay Co.)
Georgia (Circassia), 19, 66, 70, 71, 74-75
Germany/ Germans, 18, 27, 94-95, 123, 127, 135, 147, 148, 150, 153, 155, 215, 222-223
Ghent, Treaty of, 68
Governments (Structure) of,

Britain, 51f, 174ff
  Canada, 52, 53-54, 132, 237-238
  France, 51, 54
  Lower Canada, 204
  Russia, Intro, *passim*, 113-114, 126, 129, 136ff
  Upper Canada, 161-162, 204
Great Britain, 17, 18, 19, 26, 31, 34, 31, 34, 35, 51, 65ff, 214f
Great Reforms, 20, 21, 88
Guelph, 224
Halifax, 33, 43, 69, 94, 96, 117, 136
Hall, 92
Hudson's Bay Company, 12, 30, 37, 69f, 83, 84, 85-86, 111, 126, 182, 191, 195, 221, 232
Icebreakers (Cdn), 153
Immigration/ Emigration, 50, 52, 110, 112ff, 123ff, 133f, 135-137, 152, 154, *158*, 190f, 222ff
  Irish, 188, 190
  Russian, 48ff, 112, 112-115, 116-117, Chapter 3, *passim*, 158
  Scots, 197-199
  Ukrainian, 112, 115, 117, 152, *158*, 228f
Imperial Munitions Board, 153-154
India, 29, 70, 89, 90, 123, 130, 215
Italy, 147
Japan, 19, 26, 29, 85, 87, 90, 91, 93, 122, 124, 147
Jewish Colonization Society, 115-116
Jews, 24-25, 115ff, 127, 136, 215
Judicial System,
  Canada, 39, 40, 177, 186-187, 200f, 204
  Russia, 20, 187
Kamchatka, 29, 33, 87
Kanada, 153
Kingston, 43, 171, 200f
Kommandorskii Islands, 91
Koreans, 124
Kreiser, 90
Kuril Islands, 85
Lachine, 182, 184, 192
Lake Champlain, 38, 43, 170-171
Land Act, 119

Local Government, Canada, 40, 51, 52-53, 176ff

Lower Canada, 38, 52, 66ff, 82, 161f, 163f, 176ff, 191ff (see also Quebec)

Mackenzie's Gazette, 36, 70ff

Manitoba, 46, 109, 156

Marxism, 23

Massey-Harris Co., 52, 127, 133-134, *143*, 148, 151, 154, 217, 220

Marie, 92

Mennonites, 12, 88, 110, 111f, 116, 128, 132, 139, 221-222

Meshchane, 21, 26

Métis, 45-46

Mining Industry, Canada, 126, 150, *157*, 229, 230-231

Monroe Doctrine, 69, 87

Montmorency Falls, 188-189

Montreal (Ville Marie), 43, 87, 116, i, 163, 179ff, 203

Moskovskiia vedomosti, 34, 35

Murmansk, 155

Native Peoples, Canada, 30, 32, 33, 37, 40, 43, 45, 51, 53, *57*, 86, 163-164, 170, 175, 182-183, 189-190, 193f, 195, 197, 198

Navy, Russian, 29, 33, 44f, 84, 85, 89ff, *104*, 150f, 153
  Canadian, 150-151
  British, 33, 87, 150-151

New Brunswick, 76, 82

Newfoundland, 33, 44, 82, 153, 165-168

New York, 154

Niagara Falls, 32, 40, *60*, 162, 189, 205-213

Niagara River, 45, 45, 162, 205f

North Pacific, 26, 33, 47, 83, 85, 87, 96, 151

North West Company, 37, 221

Nova Scotia, 38, 47, 82, 92, 152

October Manifesto, 1905, 21

Ogdensburg, 199-200

Okhrana, 20, 46

Omsk, 155

Ontario (see Upper Canada)

Orthodox Church (see Religion)

Otechestvennye zapiski, 41, 42

Ottawa (Bytown), 38, 116, 193ff, 199

Ottawa, River, 188f, 192, 197-198

Pacific Ocean, 19, 26, 30, 79, 83, 88, 229f, 232 (see also North Pacific)

The Peasant Kingdom, 12, 50ff

Peasantry, 23f, 51f, 114, 129, 132

Persia, 19, 199f

Poland, 19, 24, 66, 72, 74, 79, 94, 116, *146*

Prescott, 199f

Pribylov Islands, 91f

Prussia, 19, 81

Quebec, 40, 54, 149, 203, 238-240 (see also Lower Canada)

Quebec City, 43, 110, 183ff, 186-187

Queenston, 161

Railroads, Russian,21, 39, 40, 43-44, 48, 111, 119, 124ff, 154, 155 (see also Trans-Sibirian)

Railroads, Canadian, 39-40, 43-44, 46, 48, 110f, 114, Chapter 3, *passim*, 173f, 191f, 199, 216f (see also CPR)

Rebellions, Canada of 1837-38: 12, 34-36, 40, 42, 52, 53, 70-83, *101-102*, of 1855: 45-46, 89, 123
  Greece, 73, 74
  Poland, 72, 73ff, 79, *101*

Regina, 227, 229

Religion, 43, 187f, 193, 204f, 218f
  Catholicism, 54, 171f, 177ff, 191ff
  Protestantism, 193f
  Russian Orthodox, 21, 24, 85, 130, 149, 152, *157* (See also Jews, Doukhobors, Mennonites)

Revolution/ Revolutionaries, 20, 22-23, 31, 32, 46; of 1905: 21, 26, 50, 53, 112, 122, 129; of 1917: 124, 125, 129, 132

Riel Rebellion (see Rebellions, 1885)

Romania, 66

Rosie Olsen, 92, 93

Ross, Fort, 69

Russian-American Commercial Treaty (1832), 74

Russian American Company, 12, 29-30, 34, 37, 66, 69f, 83-84, 85-86

Russian-American Relations, Chapter 2, *passim*
Russian-American Steamship Line, 117, 136, *146*
Russian-British Relations, Chapter 2, *passim*, 124, 151
Russian Eastern-Asiatic Steamship Line, 136-137, *146*
Russian-French Relations, 65ff, 81, 94ff
Russification, 24, 74
Russo-Canadian Trading Syndicate, 135
Russo-Japan War (1905-05), 95, *106*, 124, 128, 151
Ruthenians, 152-153
Saint John, 48, *61, 98*
Sakhalin Islands, 87
Saskatchewan, 113, 131
Sault Ste. Marie, 150, *158*
St. Lawrence River, 38, 43-44, 48, 150, 161f, 171-213, *passim*
Sankt-Petersburgskie vedomosti, 34
Secret Police, 20, 37, 41, 46, 112, 114
Serfdom, 17, 18, 20, 32, 38, 39, 42
Severnaia pchela, 34, 41, 58
Siberia, 19, 37, 47-48, 51f, 83f, 94, 110ff, 113-114, 119ff, 126f, 155, 224
Sitka, 33, 83
Slavery, 31, 32, 39, 41-42
Sovremennik, 36, 41
Spain, 67
Straits Convention (1841), *81*
Suez Canal, 96, *105*
Svet, 47
Syn Otechestva, 34, 35, 49, 58
Sweden, 19, 66
Telegraph, Atlantic, 45, 210
Tilsit, Treaty of, 65
Toronto (York), 116, 161f, 201, 202f, 220
Trade, 52, 133ff, 148, 153, 214f, 220f, 233-234
   Canadian-Russian, 45, 95f, 125, 134-135, 150, 151, 152-154, 214-219, 220-235
   Canadian-American, 68, 149, 233-234
   Russian-British, 65ff, 79-80, 95, 153, 214f

Russian-American, 66f, 68-72, 83, 134
Trans-Siberian Railroad, 89, 92, 96, 113, 115, 118-125, 129, 133 (see also Railroads)
Travel Agents, 115, 116, 136-137
Treaty of London (1840), 81
Treaty of Paris (1856), 38
Treaty of San Stefano (1877), 88
Tupper, 92
Turkey, 17, 18-19, 26, 32, 66, 71ff, 79, 81, 88, 123
Ukraine, 24
United States, 19, 30, 32, 34, 35, 38ff, 52-53; Chapter 2, *passim*, 147, 171ff, 199-200, 203f, 211, 233-234
Unofficial Committee, 17, 79
Upper Canada, 30, 38, 52, 67ff, 82, 161-162, 176f, 191ff, 203ff (see also Ontario)
Vancouver, 90, *105*, 136, 154, 232
Vancouver Belle, 92
Vestnik Evropy, 30, 32, 56
Victoria, BC, 92, *105*
Vixen, 72f, 75, 79
Vladivostok, 89, 93, 122, 123, 136, 153, 154, 155
War of 1812, 12, 52, 67ff
Welland Canal, 45
Whitehall, NY, 38, 43
Willie MacGowan, 93
Winnipeg, 116, 131, 148, 221
Workers, Russia, 18, 22-23, 128-129
World War I, 25, 135, 152
York (see Toronto)
Yorkton, 131, 148, 225
Zemstvos, 20

Скалистыя горы и Канадская железная дорога (къ стр. 49).

"Skalist Mountains and the CPR"

Канадскій охотникъ (трапперъ) XVIII столѣтія на лыжахъ. (Снимокъ съ гравюры XVIII столѣтія).

"Canadian Trapper/Hunter in the 18th Century, on Snow Shoes"